新词,流行词,常用词翻译

总编译 梁为祥　肖　辉　陶长安
主　编 魏新俊　李轶楠
副主编（以姓笔画为序）
　　　　　王玉明　冯晓英　徐　英
　　　　　邴照宇　黄媛媛　陶驷腾

东南大学出版社
SOUTHEAST UNIVERSITY PRESS
·南京·

图书在版编目(CIP)数据

新词,流行词,常用词翻译/魏新俊,李轶楠主编.
—南京:东南大学出版社,2014.10
ISBN 978-7-5641-5291-8

Ⅰ.①新… Ⅱ.①魏…②李… Ⅲ.①英语—新词语
—翻译 Ⅳ.①H315.9

中国版本图书馆 CIP 数据核字(2014)第 250458 号

新词,流行词,常用词翻译

出版发行	东南大学出版社
出 版 人	江建中
社　　址	南京市四牌楼 2 号(邮编 210096)
印　　刷	南京京新印刷厂
经　　销	全国各地新华书店
开　　本	700 mm×1000 mm　1/16
印　　张	13.50
字　　数	265 千字
版　　次	2014 年 10 月第 1 版　2014 年 10 月第 1 次印刷
书　　号	ISBN 978-7-5641-5291-8
定　　价	28.00 元

* 东大版图书若有印装质量问题,请直接与营销部调换。电话:025-83791830。

Preface 前言

社会的发展和进步迎来了信息化时代。在这样一个时代里,大量的新词、流行词和常用词在各个方面不断地涌现出来。为了满足广大学习者的学习和使用的需求,我们编译了《新词,流行词,常用词翻译》一书,期待此书能起到指导、参考和辅导作用。

本书内容涵盖社会生活、政治、经济、贸易、商业、投资、房地产业、企业及企业管理、金融货币、证券、保险、文明和谐、教育与人才、文化及思想教育、旅游业、工业、农林牧业、电视及电脑网络、媒体、信息技术、外交、法律、环保、医疗卫生、餐饮业等。本书具有鲜明特点:第一,具有时代性、实用性、可读性和多样性;第二,编译的词语具有广泛性,且编译简练,内容安排合理易查;第三,每一项内容做到近义归类,方便读者获得信息。

编译者相信,此书能够帮助有关学科领域里的学习者学习参考,是一本开卷有益、使用简便的综合性案头工具书。尤其是对大专院校学生、翻译工作者以及英语学习者来说,无疑是一本良师益友的工具书。

本书在词语广泛性和编译准确性等方面,可能还存在着一些不完善或不够到位的地方,恳请广大读者提出宝贵意见。

在编译过程中,参考了近年来出版的《中国翻译》、《英语学习宝典》、《政府工作报告》以及和本书内容相关的教材、词典等,在此向这些原作者表示谢意。在编译过程中得到东南大学出版社史建农编辑的大力支持,在此表示感谢。

有关高校的专家参加了本书编写工作,本书由东南大学外国语学院梁为祥教授以及肖辉教授、陶长安教授担任总编译。

编译者
2014.6

Contents 目录

一、流行词，新词和常用词翻译（Translation on Vogue Words, New Words and Everyday Expressions）/ 001
  1. 社会生活，政治及民生（Social Life, Politics & People's Livelihood）/ 001
  2. 服务业（Business and Service）/ 011
  3. 时政及政策（Politics and Policy）/ 013
  4. 构建和谐社会（Build Harmonious Society）/ 031

二、外交（Diplomacy）/ 036
  1. 外交机构（Diplomatic Establishment）/ 036
  2. 外交职衔（Diplomatic Ranks）/ 037
  3. 外交团体（Diplomatic Groups）/ 038
  4. 外事活动和方针（Diplomatic Activities and Policy）/ 039
  5. 外交常用语（Diplomatic Expressions）/ 042

三、贸易，商业，房地产，经济（Trade, Business, Real Estate and Economy）/ 045
  1. 贸易类（Trade）/ 045
  2. 商业类（Business）/ 050
  3. 房地产（Real Estate）/ 057
  4. 经济类（Economy）/ 059

四、金融，融资，货币（Finance, Financing and Currency）/ 070
  1. 金融（Finance）/ 070
  2. 融资（Financing）/ 077
  3. 货币（Currency）/ 077

五、企业及管理（Enterprise and Management）/ 083
  1. 企业（Enterprise）/ 083
  2. 企业管理（Enterprise Management）/ 083
  3. 科技管理用语（Common Terms of Management in Science and Technology）/ 085

4. 资金管理（Fund Management）/ 087

六、信息技术术语（Terms of Information Technology）/ 089

七、证券，保险（Securities and Insurance）/ 091
    1. 证券 (Securities) / 091
    2. 保险（Insurance）/ 094
    3. 其他（Others）/ 096

八、旅游（Tourism）/ 098
    1. 旅游机构 (Tourism Agency) / 098
    2. 旅游地（Tourist Destination）/ 098
    3. 中国著名旅游景点（China's Famous Tourist Attractions）/ 098
    4. 名胜古迹（Scenic Spots and Historical Sites）/ 109
    5. 著名自然风光（Famous Natural Scenery）/ 110
    6. 国外著名旅游景点（The Famous Tourist Attractions of Foreign Countries）/ 110
    7. 旅游方式（Tourist Ways）/ 112
    8. 其他旅游词语（Other Tourist Terms）/ 113

九、产业经济（Industrial Economy）/ 115

十、电脑，网络语言（Computer and Network Language）/ 118

十一、文化和思想教育（Culture and Education in Thought）/ 122
    1. 思想教育 (Education in Thought) / 122
    2. 文化（Culture）/ 122
    3. 节日文化（Festivals and Culture）/ 124
    4. 常用文化术语（Useful Cultural Terms）/ 124
    5. 文化团体与机构（Culture Group and Organization）/ 125
    6. 文化多样性（Cultural Diversity）/ 126
    7. 音乐人（Musician）/ 127
    8. 文化娱乐场所（Culture and Entertainment Place）/ 127
    9. 乐器（Musical Instrument）/ 127
    10. 美术类（Fine Arts）/ 128
    11. 奖项（Prize）/ 129

十二、文明（Civilization）/ 130

十三、教育及人才（Education & Talents）/ 132
    1. 教育（Education）/ 132
    2. 人才（Talents）/ 140
    3. 出国留学（Overseas Study）/ 141

十四、医疗卫生（Medical Treatment and Health）/ 143
    1. 医疗机构（Medical Establishment）/ 143
    2. 医院科室（Departments in Hospital）/ 143
    3. 医务人员称呼（Names for Medical and Nursing Staff）/ 145
    4. 常见病（Common Diseases）/ 146
    5. 医疗常用词语（Common Terms in Medical Treatment）/ 148
    6. 医疗器械和器具名称（Names of Medical Machinery & Instruments）/ 154
    7. 诊断术语（Diagnosis Terms）/ 156

十五、媒体（Media）/ 158
    1. 电台，电视台（Broadcasting / Radio Station，TV. Station）/ 158
    2. 广播电视人（Personnel）/ 159
    3. 栏目，节目（Column, Programme）/ 160
    4. 电视制作（TV Production）/ 162
    5. 广播电台节目（Broadcasting Program）/ 163
    6. 其他类（Others）/ 163

十六、环境与环保（Environment and Environmental Protection）/ 165
    1. 保护环境（Protection of Environment）/ 165
    2. 污染现象及处理（Polluted Phenomenon and Disposal）/ 166

十七、中国法律（China's Laws）/ 170
    1. 法律（Law）/ 170
    2. 民事法（Civil Law）/ 172
    3. 刑事案件（Criminal Cases）/ 174
    4. 法律术语（Law Terms）/ 175

十八、食品蔬菜类（Foods and Vegetables）/ 176
    1. 蔬菜（Vegetable）/ 176
    2. 豆制品（Bean Products）/ 177
    3. 肉类（Meat）/ 177
    4. 鱼类（Fish）/ 177
    5. 中餐类菜谱（Menu in Chinese Food）/ 178
    6. 西餐（Western Food）/ 189
    7. 中国菜系（Families of Chinese Cuisine）/ 191
    8. 与菜关联的词语（Words Related to Dishes）/ 192

十九、工业与农林牧业（Industry, Agriculture, Forestry and Animal Husbandry）/ 193
    1. 工业（工业，钢铁，化工，煤炭，石油，矿物，机械，纺织，电子和无线电）（Industry—Mine, Steel and Iron, Chemical, Coal, Machinery, Textile, Electronics and Radio）/ 193
    2. 农林业（Agriculture & Forestry）/ 198

1 流行词，新词和常用词翻译
Translation on Vogue Words, New Words and Everyday Expressions

1. 社会生活，政治及民生（Social Life, Politics & People's Livelihood）

工薪族	the wage-earners		stable job seekers
求职族	the job-seekers	代排族	the hired queuer
刷卡族	the card-users	隐婚族	the pseudo-singles
追星族	the star-chasers	装嫩族	the youngster's look-alike / kidult
单身族	the singles	洋漂族	the job-hopping foreigners
丁克族	the Dink—double income no kids	网络晒衣族	the Internet clothing shaker
		单身寄生族	the parasite singles
无孩族	the childless	桌边神游族	the desk potato
蚁族	the city ants / ant tribe graduates	网络闲逛族	the cyber flaneur
刷卡族（划卡族）	the credit card sliding	虐童	child abuse
慢活族	the slow living race	低保	the basic subsistence allowance
陪拼族	the shopping follower	打工	to do work for others
捧车族	the idle-car owner	钟点工	part-time employees
试药族	the trying medicine race / the new-medicine testees	积分卡	loyalty card
		迷卡	mini card
急婚族	the wedding rusher	公休	public holiday
啃椅族	the chair sticker	冷遇	cold reception
合吃族	the joint eaters	名嘴	chatterati / pundit / the popular TV presenter
乐活族	the happy living race / lifestyles of health and sustainability		
		"吗咪"	Facebook
赖校族	the sticky graduates	"风衣"	trend coat
飞鱼族	the flying fish	"软技能"	soft skills
吊瓶族	the bottle group	晒（摆）	to show off / bask
奔奔族	the rushing clan	骨性	moral fortitude / moral fortitude and personal character
零帕族	the stress-free type		
考碗族	the gold-rice-bowl seekers / the	谷歌	google

001

博客	blog		competition
微博	Microblog	吐槽	to disclose one's secret
粉丝	fans	卖萌	to act cute
嘉年华	carnival	淡定	to be calm / unruffled
桑拿	suana(源自芬兰语)	形婚	marriage of convenience
脱口秀	talk show	腹黑	scheming
在线	on line	范儿	the style
搞定	to work it out	萝莉	Lolita
裸奔	streaking	秒杀	seckill / speed skill
裸婚	simplistic marriage / bare-handed marriage / naked marriage	禁电	prohibition of electric
		路菜	travel-ready dishes
裸考	non-extra-mark examination	蜗居	to snail dwelling / dwelling narrowness
裸替	body double / nude stand-in / naked body double	海选	auditions
		海归	the returned talents after studying abroad / overseas returnee
笔替	ghostwriter / to substitute calligrapher		
		跳槽	job-hopping / seek a better job
文替	to substitute writing and reading	下海	to start a business / go into commercial business
饭替	eating substitute		
忽悠	here and there / fabricate	大腕	the man of importance / big shot / top notch
嘚瑟	to show out		
吉祥物	mascot	大款	the wealthy individual / fat cat / money bags / tycoon
三陪	women who provide illegal sexual services(especially prostitutes or escort services)		
		小清新	like(好似)a breath of fresh air
紧俏	to sell well / in short supply		
臭美	to show off one's looks / talents	穿越剧	the time-travel TV drama
		微睡眠	to microsleep
山寨	fake / or counterfeit / copycat	打酱油	to see no evil / hear no evil / none of my business
宅男	Otaku("homebody" in English)/ geek		
		炒鱿鱼	to give sb. the sack / sack or to disemploy sb. / to fire sb.
被雷(倒)	in shock		
纠结	to be ambivalent		
忐忑	to be anxious	点钞费	coin-counting fee
悲催	a tear-inducing misery	流浪儿童	street children / street kids
坑爹	reverse of one's expectation	留守儿童	left-behind children
拼爹	daddy-is-the-key / parents privilege	恼人乘客	harassenger(harass &

流行词，新词和常用词翻译
Translation on Vogue Words, New Words and Everyday Expressions

刷单/刷信誉	click farming
两会博客	blogs for NPC & CPPCC
信息网络	information network
微博控	twuilt（来自于 twitter 和 guilt 两个字，表示不发微博心里就内疚）
睡眠博客	sleeping blog
李娅空翻	Liya's somersault
丁克家庭	Dink family
老公椅	husband chair
宠物保姆	pet sitter
折翼天使	an angel with broken wings
神龙见首不见尾	office ghost
魔幻现实主义	magical realism
红楼选秀	Red Mansion's casting competition
门槛者	thresholder
红衫军	red coat army
灰色技能	grey skill
会议大使	a convention ambassador
羡慕嫉妒恨	to be envious, jealous and hateful
恶性骚扰	malicious harassment
发烧友	fancier
好人综合征	nice guy syndrome
超级生活记录	hyper-documentation
赶趟式生活	just-in-time lifestyle
第一世界问题	the first-world problem
打招呼列表	hello list
网络游民	Internet hobo
网络羞涩	web shy
美丽垃圾	beautiful rubbish
哥只是传说	Brother is only a legend.
伤不起	to be vulnerable / be prone to getting hurt
年龄歧视	ageism
富二代	second-generation rich / silver-spoon kids
独二代	sub-mono-children
时髦人物	flavor of the month / the stylish character
领军人物	personages
新领阶层	new collar
监控门	monitoring gate
潜规则	unspoken rule
橡皮人	jaded / indifferent to the world
吹风会	cascade / briefing
林来疯	Linsanity
凡客体	Vanclize / Vancl Style
桌游	board role-playing games
奖骚扰	award harassment
交强险	motor vehicle accident liability compulsory insurance / compulsory traffic accident liability insurance
搏出位	to be a famewhore / to seek attention
博斗	blog tussle
博文	articles in the blog
博客话剧	blog drama
自主招生	university autonomous enrollment
解说门	explaining gate
犀利哥	Brother Sharp
菜鸟/新手	green hand
傍大款	to find a sugar daddy
个体户	self-employed labor
下岗工人	laid-off workers
持证上岗	to go about one's duties with

003

	one's certificate
赚钱糊口	to earn one's bread
铁饭碗	lifelong job / the job-for-life system
年夜饭	dining together on the lunar New Year's Eve
远程工作	telework
人肉搜索	human flesh search engine / cyber manhunt
神马都是浮云	It is all fleeting cloud. / Everything is nothing.
最重要是开心	Happiness is the way. / Happiness is the most important thing.
不管你信不信,反正我是信了。	Whether you believe it or not, I am convinced.
目标责任书	letter of responsibility
一次性补偿	the one-off compensation
恪守承诺	to honor the commitments
饭气攻心	food coma
公车表情	bus look
肥胖谈话	fat talk
超级工作者	supertasker
短信期待	text pectation
暖巢管家	house keeper for the old
诺亚规则	Noah Rules
明星枪手	star promoter
群策群力	to pool one's wisdom and efforts
出手要快	to act fast
出拳要重	to be forceful
措施要准	to take targeted measures
正能量	positive energy
工作要实	to stress implementation
抓好改革	to press ahead with reform
科技开发	scientific and technological R&D
经济活力	more vigorous economy
改革试点	pilot reform / reform experimentation
把握大局	to grasp the overall situation
调整结构	to adjust the structure
上经济水平	to raise the level of economic development
振兴之路	ways to rejuvenate
择校税	tax on school-choosing fee
创业板	ChiNext stock market
升级版	upgrading edition
银色产业	silver industry
弹性就业	flexible employment
自谋职业	to look for jobs on one's own
自主创业	to become self-employed
隐形就业	stealth re-employment / the hidden employment
重视民生	to give top priority to ensuring people's well-bing
家电下乡	to bring home appliances to the countryside
农机下乡	to bring agricultural machinery to the countryside
汽车下乡	to bring automobiles to the countryside
摩托下乡	to bring motorbikes to the countryside
分手代理	breaking up agent
科研包头士	labour contractor of scientific research
工作午餐	business lunches
人质午餐	hostage lunch

个人隐私	individual privacy	更高质量就业	higher quality employment
公款吃喝	wining and dining by billing the organization / the wining and dining on public funds	零就业家庭	zero-employment family
		更多就业岗位	more jobs
		生活水平和质量	living standard and quality of life
大锅饭	egalitarian practice of everyone taking food from the same big pot	群众基本生活	Everyone has access to basic necessities.
村务公开	to make village affairs public	特困户群众	extremely vulnerable groups
三高农业	"three highs" agriculture (including: yield, quality, efficiency)	基本养老保险	basic old-age insurance
		职工养老保险	old-age insurance for working people
大病统筹	to composite package medical service for major sick cases	食肉主义者	meatarian
		生活半径	life radius
看病难,看病贵	inadequate and overly expensive medical services	民生之基	foundation of people's wellbeing
		民生之本	basis of people's wellbeing
城乡低保水平	subsistence allowances to urban and rural residents	民生之源	source of people's wellbeing
		收入分配	income distribution
就业和社会保障	employment and social security system	职业年金	occupational annuities
		首次贷款	loan of the first home / the first loan of purchasing house
城镇登记失业率	registered urban unemployment rate	创业板(二板)	second board
职工安置和就业	reemployment to workers laid off	半拉子工程	a never-to-be finished project
城镇新增就业	to create urban jobs	豆腐渣工程	jerry-built projects
就业优先战略	strategy of giving top priority to employment	物流店/幕后店	the dark store
		移动商标	mobile brand
就业创业环境	employment and business startup environment	让票区	ticket-transfer zone
		温饱问题	problems in finding enough food and clothing
以创新引领创业	to foster business startup in an innovative way	单亲家庭	single-parent family
		单身母亲	single mother
创业家综合征	entrepreneur's syndrome	挂钥匙妻子	to latch key wife
就业创业服务	employment and business startup services	入户育婴师	a special family nurse
		巫毒娃娃	voodoo doll
就业创业比例	rate of employment and business startup		

弱势群体	disadvantaged groups
草根网民	grassroots netizen
数码痴呆症	digital dementia
电视购物	to be informercial / TV shopping
团购	group purchasing
作秀	to showcase / to make a show
小康	a relatively comfortable living
炫富	showing off / display of wealth
泡吧	to kill time in a bar
虚报	to make a false report
瞒报	to make a concealed report
伪报	fraudulent report
漏报	incomplete report
出让（土地使用权）	to grant (right to use land)
划拨（土地使用权）	allocation (right to use land)
转让（土地使用权）	to transfer (right to use land)
内耗	in-fighting
医闹	medical dispute / hospital violator
医诉	medical treatment lawsuit
帅呆	cute guy
恶搞	parody joke
雷人	shocking / weird / wacky
给力	to be gelivable / thrilling / cool
伪娘	drag queen
盗板党	pirate party
倒扁	anti-Chen
穷人跑	cheap sports car
拍拖	to go out with / go steady with / see sb. / date sb.
决选名单（最终候选人名单）	short list
内环高架	inner ring flyover
外环高架	outer ring flyover
知情权	the right to know
能上能下	to get sb. prepared for both promotion and demotion
最佳途径	the best way
炒作 / 恶炒	hype / publicity
一次性筷子	throw away chopsticks / disposable chopiticks
摇钱树 / 金库	cash cow
饭桌金融	table banking
白色收入	a legal income
黑色收入	an illegal income
灰色收入	a semi-overt income / off-the-book income
绩效工资	performance-based salary
凯特效应	Kate effect
社会救助	a social assistance
性骚扰	a sexual harassment
二人世界	the world of two / the life of two
流行字眼	vogue words
追发邮件	to remail
马路新闻	hearsay gossip
八卦焦点	gossip magnet
午夜弥撒	midnight Mass
比基尼	bikini
三点式泳衣	three-point bathing suit / bikini
摆花架子	to show off oneself
搞花架子	to do something superficial
咨询关怀	to care and consultation
重点地区	priority region
地沟油	gutter oil / illegal cooking oil
走私贩毒	smuggling and drug trafficking
卖淫嫖娼	prostitution
茶话会	tea party
茶点	tea / tea and pastries / refreshment

流行词,新词和常用词翻译
Translation on Vogue Words, New Words and Everyday Expressions

小菜一碟	a piece of cake
粗茶淡饭	bread and cheese / simple diet
转基因食品	genetically modified food
抢走别人的饭碗	to take the bread out of someone's mouth
核心家庭 / 小家庭	nuclear family
良性互动	harmonious interactions
你懂的	You understand what I mean.
攀高枝	to put oneself under the patronage of a higher-up
同一个起跑线	a level playing field
性别平等	gender equality
家庭暴力	domestic violence
家庭软暴力	soft domestic violence
拼图家庭	Jigsaw family
世界家庭峰会	the World Family Summit
玛丽苏情节	Mary Sue complex
少生快富	to have fewer children and quicker prosperity
扫黄打非	to fight against pornographic and illegal publications
白领犯罪	white-collar crime
拜金主义	money worship
大环境	an overall situation (the social, political and economic environment)
大换血	an overall renewal of the membership of an organization
冗余人员分流	a reposition of redundant personnel
舌尖上的中国	a bite of China
保障民生	to ensure people's wellbeing
国民待遇	a national treatment
优惠待遇	a favored treatment
工薪阶层	salary persons
留职停薪	to retain the job with salary suspended
停薪留职	to retain one's position with one's salary suspended
三公消费	funds spending on official reception, vehicles and overseas trips
三公经费	expenditures spending on official overseas visits, official vehicles, and official hositality
剩男剩女	leftover men and women
陪购男友	shopping boyfriend
育婴假	parental leave
病假	sick leave
事假	casual leave
产假	maternity leave
陪产假	paternity leave
恋童癖	pedophile
恶意威胁电话	hoax call
笑点,泪点,痛点	bursting point
支持率	favorability rating
拉选票	to seek a vote
民调持平	too-close-to-call polls
强迫购物	forced shopping
完美疲劳	perfection fatigue
捂盘惜售	to insist on a conservative way in selling a real estate
养老金入市	pension funds into the country's capital market
退休金双轨制	dual pension scheme
津贴增长机制	a mechanism for increasing allowances
申报个人财产	to declare personal assets
个税起征点	individual income tax threshold

返券黄牛	shopping coupon scalper
人际泡沫	social bubble
文化低保	non-material allowance for the inferior
办公桌心里	desk psychology
办公室怒气	office rage
暗箱操作	black case work
咖啡脸	coffee face
手机脸	smart phone face
手机手	cell-phone-worn hand
点钞机	currency-counting machine
手机幻听症	cellphone auditory hallucinations
钟点爸爸	hourly dad / hired dad
蜜月保姆	honeymoon sitter
网络钟点工	virtual troubleshooter
临时工	temporary personnel
临时工介绍所	temporary-personnel agencies
新明星学者	new star-scholar
一线明星	A-list celebrity
末流明星	Z-list celebrity
愚人节狂想	April Fools paranoia
牙膏之吻	colgate kiss
高富帅	high-rich-cute (or handsome) man
标签女	tag hag
女汉子	tough girl / cowgirl
假小子	tomboy
学术超男	superman-scholar
学业预警	school precaution
员工福利	employee benefits
退休金	retirement pension
软福利	soft benefit
收入差距	imcome gap
居民收入	personal income
城乡居民收入	both urban and rural incomes
可支配收入	disposable income
人均纯收入	per capita net income
减员增效	to cut payroll to improve efficiency
需求下滑	falling demand
地方债务	local debts
影子银行	shadow banking
和谐社会	a harmonious society
M型社会	M-typed society
城市化率	urbanization rate
城市化进程	process of urbanization
世界城市化	urbanization in the world
发展方式转变	transformation of growth model
爬坡过坎	to come one challenge after another
城市群	city clusters
搞笑	to amuse / to provoke laughter
微笑圈	a smile ring
微笑北京	to smile in Beijing
中国学	Chinese studies
同心结	knot of one heart
中国结	Chinese folk knot
中国梦	China's dream / Chinese dream
舞动的北京	a dancing Beijing
农民工	rural migrant workers
邻避效应	not in my back yard
白大褂效应	white coat effect
第一夫人效应	the first lady effect
予以通报	The matter shall be made known in an official circular.
打出王牌	to pay one's trump card

举报电话	a reporting hotline	求婚新三件	three new prerequisites for marriage-proposal
公务用车	official vehicle		
解困来电	escape call	自拍	selfie
性别歧视	gender discrimination	自拍轰炸	selfie bombing
随迁配偶	drifting spouse	自拍瘾	selfie addict
到期约会	an expiration dating	腿部自拍	legsie
黄昏恋	to love in the sunset of one's life	头发自拍	helfie
婚外恋	an extramarital affair	锻炼自拍	welfie
异地恋	a long-distance relationship (LDR)	喝酒自拍	drefie
离婚预约	a divorce appointment	久坐症	sitting disease
离婚协议	a divorce agreement	度假恋	vacationship
起步婚姻/新手婚姻	starter marriage	抱抱团	free hugs
快餐式婚姻	fast-food marriage	抱抱装	baobao clothing / dress
婚嫁大年	wedding year	平底鞋	flat shoes
半糖夫妻	weekend couple	重启一代	to reset generation
青春损失费	dally money	爱时髦	to clotheshorse
午餐研讨会	a brown bag session	7时代	7 times
数字世界原住民	digital native	急时代	the age of fast pace
数字世界移民	digital immigrants	五月病	May disease
国际高考移民	immigrants for NCEE	推手民调	to push poll
成考移民	immigrants for NMT	粉丝圈	fandom
生态移民	eco-migrations	宝贝时差	baby lag
城市依赖症	urban-dependence disease / city addiction	错时上下班	staggered office hours
		二时歇业令	two out of order
完美主义瘫痪症	a perfectionist paralysis	三位一体	trinity
		哥儿们时间	girls time / guy time
复古学堂	back-to-the-ancients school	江南风	Gangnan Style
新中间阶层	a new intermediate stratum	擒人节	to grab people's day
熊猫烧香病毒	panda burning incense virus / worm.whboy.cw	轻熟女	sexy child woman
		二奶专家	pseudo-scholar
不雅视频	a sex video	游戏手	game hands
影像亲近症	videophilia	男士感冒	man flu.
过劳肥	obesity from overwork	作弊克	cheating grams / exam-cheating killer
情景式亲密	situational intimacy		
不插电婚礼	unplugged wedding	掘客卡神	digger cardman

辣妹催眠	hotness hypnosis	印客	self-publishing people / Inker
电话门	a calciopoli scandal	游贿	tourism bribery
电子环保亭	an electronic environment pavilion / electronic junk center	吊丝	plebeian / the folk
		人球	the kick-out
脚环鸡	ring-tagged chicken	土豪	local tyrant
白银书	silver book	纳米	nanometer
痛快吧	happy bar	职粉	vocational fans
图书漂移	book crossing / book drifting	砸票	desperate voting
福利腐败	a corruption in the execution of welfare policy	饭票	meal ticket
		彩票	lottery
彩票头奖	a jackpot	终统	to stop the national unification committee
土腐败	a soil corruption		
洋腐败	a corruption happening in multinational company	废统	to stop the national unification programme
感恩红包	a red envelope to teachers (or to somebody)	众包	crowd sourcing
		压洲	pressure delta
高薪跳蚤	high-salary job hopper	跑酷	parkour (French: parcourir)
死猫洞	dead-cat hole	派活	to assign work
转型跳槽	career shifting	拼卡	card partaking
座椅旅游	armchair tourism	拼客	partaker / pinker
换草运动	to swap date	晒客	Internet sharer
两餐半人	meal skipper	换客	exchanging fans
饼干谈话	cookie talk	房奴	mortgage slave / mortgage burden / a slave to one's mortgage
单手食物	one-handed food		
白色食物	white food / whole grains	墓奴	slave of grave
访谈	to interview	垄奴	monopoly slave
情结	a complex	节奴	festival slave
打黑	to crack down on evil forces	证奴	slave of certificate
把关	to guard a pass	白奴	white slave
暗恋	unrequited love	车奴	car slave
走光	wardrobe malfunction	二手病	secondary disease
放猫	herding cats	熟年	a year of good harvest
跳城	the city hopping	断背	brokeback
盐爹	salt daddy	世宗(韩国地名)	Sejong (Yongzheng Emperor)
威客	witkeyer		

冻容　youth freezing
法商　Law Quotient
沸腾可乐　boiling cola
世情　global conditions
国情　national conditions
党情　the Party conditions
民情　people's conditions
AA制　Dutch treatment / go Dutch

2. 服务业（Business and Service）

第一桶金　the first pot of gold
服务业增加值　value-added of the service sector
服务贸易协议　agreements concerning trade in services
科技服务平台　science and technology service platforms
基本公共服务　basic public services
优质高效服务　high-quality and efficient services
物流配送　logistics and delivery
服务业市场　service industry market
后座购物者　backseat buyers
清仓义卖会　to rummage sale
简化服务　pared-down services
服务消费　consumption of services
消费热点　new areas of consumption
消费政策　consumption policies
服务贸易　service trade
星级饭店　starred hotel
桑拿浴室　sauna
按摩室　massage parlour
美容店（室）　beauty salon / beauty shop
健身房　gym / body-building club
避暑山庄　summer resort
度假村　holiday resort / vacational village
民俗村　folk customs park
五天工作制　five-day week
带薪休假　paid vocations
室内温泉游泳池　indoor hot-spring swimming pool
音乐茶座　music cafe
恢复营业　to resume operation
职业介绍所　a job center
公关小姐　public relations Misses
以人为本　human oriented / connecting the people
软性销售　a soft sell
大包干　all-round responsibility system
假钞辨别仪　a currency detector
假钞　counterfeit money
假酒　adulterated wine
假新闻　a pseudo-event
菜篮子工程　non-staple food project
抢手货　hot buy
扩大内需　to expand domestic demand
礼品券　gift voucher（token）
免费样品　free sample
大包装　economy size
以旧换新　to trade in
票房欺诈　box-office fraud
传销活动　a pyramid selling
地沟油　hogwash oil / recycled cooking oil
垃圾综合处理　integrated garbage treatment
生产绿色食品　to produce green food
舌尖上的安全　Every bite of food we eat is safe.

食品药品安全	safety for food and drugs
横向合并	horizontal integration
纵向联合	vertical integration
品牌形象	brand image
企业标识	corporate identity
企业形象	corporate image
拓展业务	to branch out
投资兴业	to invest and do business
二级市场	secondary market
买方市场	buyer's market
市场份额	market share
市场化	marketization
标识	logo
按揭	payment by instalment
外卖	to take away meals / the take-out
赠品	free gift / free offer
餐饮业	catering business (industry / trade)
服务业	service industry
休闲服务业	leisure industry
团购优惠券	group-buying / group coupon
专门招待费	entertainment allowance (expenses)
再就业服务中心	re-employment service center
投资消费关系不协调	investment being not in keeping with consumers' demand
明星广告	an advertisement by star
差异性和互补性	differences and complementarity
增加有效供给	to increase effective supply
监控录像	security camera
条形码	bar code
售货亭	kiosk
饮食一条街	a food court
上门推销员	door-to-door salesman
皮包公司	a paper company / a bubble company
专卖店	a special outlet
足量广告	saturation compaign / testimonial advertising
广告时段	advertising slot
商品标识	commodity logo
黄金时段	prime slot
恶意营销	smear campaign
绿色促销	green marketing
消费期望	consumer expectation
即期消费	immediate consumption
消费物价指数	the CPI
物价调控	to keep prices under control
意大利面碗效应	the Spaghetti Bowl effect
快餐观点	fast food opinions
快餐店	fast-food restaurant / the snack bar
强迫购物	forced shopping
优惠券	cash voucher
名牌产品	famous-brand products
技术孵化	technology incubation
创新驱动	innovative capability
务实合作	pragmatic cooperation
国际化	internationalization
市场化	market-oriented
工业化	industrialization
城镇化	urbanization
信息化	informatization

3. 时政及政策 (Politics and Policy)

服务型政府	service-typed government / the government for serving people
创新政府	an innovative government
法治政府	a law-based government
廉洁政府	a clean government
依法治国	law-based governance
廉洁奉公	to perform one's duties honestly
勤勉尽责	to perform one's duties diligently and faithfully
依法严惩	to penalize offenders
决不姑息	without mercy
政务公开	to make one's operations
服务型政府	service-typed government / the government for serving people
创新政府	an innovative government
法治政府	a law-based government
廉洁政府	a clean government
依法治国	law-based governance
廉洁奉公	to perform one's duties honestly
勤勉尽责	to perform one's duties diligently and faithfully
依法严惩	to penalize offenders
决不姑息	without mercy
政务公开	to make one's operations more open
村务公开	village affairs transparent
居务公开	community affairs transparent
举行公投	to hold a referendum
民主管理	democratic management
民为邦本	the people being the foundation of a nation
本固邦宁	A nation can enjoy peace only when its foundation is strong.
补短板	to improve weak links
兜底线	to help those in need of subsistence assistance
局势风云变幻	a volatile environment
霸权主义	hegemonism
强权政治	power politics
基本文化权益	basic cultural rights and interests
知情权	rights to be informed
参与权	rights to participate
表达权	rights to oversee
政治体制改革	reform of the political structure
国家长治久安	China's long-term stability
国家治理体系	country's governance system
行政执法体系	a system of government law enforcement
公务员素质	competence of public (civil) servants
中国社会阶层	China's social stratum
保证社会公共需要	to guarantee social needs
保障性安居工程	a government-subsidized housing
激励创新的政策体系	a policy mechanism to encourage innovation

伟大复兴的中国梦	Chinese Dream of the great rejuvenation
创新能力的各类人才	personnel with innovative potential in various fields
农民工职业技能提升	vocational skills training to rural migrant workers
城镇社会保障体系	urban social security system
城镇住房制度改革	a reform of the urban housing system
最低生活保障	a basic living allowances
基层民主	community-level democracy
保障和改善民生	to ensure the well-being of the people and improve their lives
生产安全事故	work accident / accident at work
职工医疗保障	medical insurance for workers
新生代农民工	new generation of migrant workers
农村转移人口	rural people in urban areas
实行总体战略	to follow a master strategy
科教兴国战略	the strategy of developing the country by depending on science and education
处理城乡关系	to handle the relationship between urban and rural areas
国有企业改革	a reform of state-owned enterprises
粗放发展方式	a model of inefficient and blind development
统筹国内发展	to well coordinate the domestic development
坚持科学发展	to pursue scientific development
坚持和谐发展	to pursue harmonious development
坚持和平发展	to pursue peaceful development
走和平发展道路	to carry out the path of peaceful development
增强国际竞争力	to sharpen our international competitiveness
解放思想,实事求是	to emancipate the mind, to seek truth from facts
自强不息,顽强奋进	heroic efforts
两个毫不动摇	to develop both the public and non-public sectors of economy
全心全意为人民服务	to serve people wholeheartedly
四项基本原则	the Four Cardinal Principles
党管媒体的原则	the principle that the Party supervises the work of the mass media
坚持社会主义道路	to keep to the socialist road
封闭僵化的老路	the old and rigid closed-door policy
改旗易帜的邪路	to abandon socialism and take an errorneous path
生动的新局面	a dynamic new

	environment
人民主体地位	principal position of the people
党风廉政建设	to build a fine Party culture and keep its organization clean
最严格的监管	the strictest supervision
最严格的处罚	the strictest possible punishment
党的创造力	Party's creativity
党的凝聚力	Party's cohesion
党的战斗力	Party's competence
党的立党之本	foundation for building the Party
提高党员素质	to improve the quality of Party membership
党的创新理论	Party's innovative theory
党的先进性	Party's vanguard nature
走在时代前列	being always in the forefront of the times
立党为公	Party working for the public
执政为民	to assume power for the people
血肉联系	flesh-and-blood contacts
吃苦在前	first to bear hardships
享乐在后	last to enjoy themselves
执政之基	the cornerstone for Party's exercise of state power
力量之源	a source of Party's strength
基层民主	democracy at village and community level
公平正义	fairness and justice
行政问责制	an administrative accountability system
舆论监督	correct orientation should be maintained in public opinion
组织群众	to mobilize the people
宣传群众	to inform the people
教育群众	to educate the people
服务群众	to serve the people
坚持人民民主专政	to uphold the people's democratic dictatorship
共产党的领导	leadership by the Communist Party of China
党的创造力	Party's creativity
生机和活力	vigor and vitality
执政能力	governing capacity
党管人才	Party organization should take charge of human resources
为人民执政	to exercise power for the benefit of the people
靠人民执政	to exercise power with the people
安居乐业	to live and work in contentment
社会安定有序	society being stable and orderly
国家长治久安	country enjoying enduring peace and stability
马克思列宁主义	Marxism—Leninism
毛泽东思想	MaoZedong Thought
高度负责	a strong sense of responsibility
改革开放	reform and opening-up
机构改革	reform of the governmental agencies
压缩开支	to put down expenses
政府职能的转变	to change the functions of the government agencies perform
外交和内政	external and domestic

	dimensions		in the Western Regions
远近兼顾	to balance between long-term and immediate interests	四化同步	to integrate the development of industrialization, IT application, urbanization and agricultural modernization
松紧适度	appropriateness between the speed and dimension		
内需和外需	domestic demand and international demand	中部地区崛起	the rise of the Central Regions
两个大局	overall interests both internal and external situations	社会主义规律	a socialist law
		社会主义基本制度	a basic system of socialism
科学发展观	scientific outlook on devlopment	社会主义初级阶段	primary stage of socialism
落实科学发展	to perseveringly promote the scientific development	东部地区率先发展	coastal areas to be the banner-bearer in economic development
城乡协调	coordination between the urban and rural areas		
东西互动	interaction between the eastern and western regions	中西部地区城市群	city clusters and towns in the central and western regions
内政外交	to exchange between China and the outside world	城乡发展一体化	to integrate rural and urban development
上下结合	integration between the central and local initiatives	新型城镇化	a new type of urbanization
		棚户区改造	rebuilding of rundown urban areas
推进改革开放	to spur the reform and opening-up to the outside world	城乡二元结构	to integrate the urban and rural structures
		稳妥推进企业（政策性破产工作） to prudently proceed with work related to policy-mandated bankrupt of enterprises	
不搞重复建设	to prohibit redundant projects		
煤炭行业落后产能	backward production facilities in the coal industry	政治体制改革	a reform of political institutions
		减政放权	to streamline administration and delegate more power/ to lower level governments
生产能力过剩行业	industries with excess production capacity		
老工业基础	the outmoded industrial bases	进入深水区	to enter a deep water zone
西部大开发	Grand Development Drive	进入攻坚期	to enter a critical stage

政绩考核	to evaluate officials' performance
评估体系	an evaluating system
民族区域自治	autonomy of ethnic regions
深化企业改革	to further carry out the reform of enterprises
企业公平竞争	fair competition between all various business entities
市场中介组织	the commercial intermediaries
市场准入制度	the market access rules
引进来,走出去	bring-in and go-globe strategies
行业协会	industry associations
创新型国家	an innovative country
城市主干路	city avenue
城市快速路	city expressway
公共客运系统	public passenger transport system
园林景观道路	landscape roads
杜绝劣质工程	to prohibit inferior projects
艰苦奋斗	hard work and plain living
勤俭建国	building up the country through thrift
城乡二元结构	dual structure of urban and rural areas
农民种田缴税	farmers paying taxes for tilling their land
农村扶贫标准	rural poverty line
优质高产农业	high-quality and high-yields agriculture
金融体制改革	a reform of the financial system
农村经济改革	rural economic reform
农业结构改革	restructuring reform in agriculture
农业特产税改革	a reform of tax on agricultural specialty products
农业制度改革	agricultural system reforms
深化农村税费改革	to deepen the tax-for-fees reform
粮食购销体制改革	a reform of grain purchase and sales
农民补贴方式改革	a reform of subsidies to farmers
农村医疗制度改革	a reform of the rural medical and health services
政策性农业保险	policy-supported agricultural insurance
新的支农资金渠道	alternative funding sources for the agricultural development
农村综合试点改革	trials of comprehensive rural reform
农村信用社体制改革	a reform in the system of rural credit cooperatives
农村最低生活保障	a subsistence allowance system for rural residents
城市最低生活保障	a basic cost of living allowances for urban residents

维护农村社会稳定	to maintain the social stability in the rural areas
农业综合生产能力	total agricultural production capacity
农业基础设施建设	agricultural infrastructure construction
农民的生产生活条件	living and working conditions of the farmers
农村社会化服务体系	commercial agricultural services
农村经济社会全面发展	overall development of the rural economy and community
高效,生态,安全农业	cost-effective, eco-frienldly and safe agriculture
稳产高产基本农田	to make primary farmland capable of producing stable, high fields
加大对农业贷款支持	to increase credit support to agriculture
整合扶贫资源	to merge resources of alleviating poverty
农村灾害防御能力	the disaster preparaedness in rural areas
农业投入稳定增长	to ensure a steady increasing input into agriculture
农村面貌有明显变化	remarkable changes in rural areas
"万村千乡"市场工程	the project of developing rural retail network
新型高效农业机械	new types of efficient agricultural machinery
新型农业经营主体	the new types of agricultural businesses
农村集体建设用地	use of collective land for construction
农业综合生产能力	overall agricultural production capacity
土地承包经营权	rights to contracted use of land
尊重农民意愿	to respect farmers' wishes
农民合法权益	farmers' legitimate rights and interests
集体林权	right of collective forests
政府自身建设	government self-improvement
支农,惠农政策	policies of supporting agriculture and benefiting farmers
强农惠农政策	policies to aid agriculture and benefit farmers
敞开粮食的政策	a policy of purchasing grain without limitation
农村粮食政策性补贴	rural policy-related grain subsidies
"米袋子","菜篮子"	to ensure food supply
出口退税历史欠账	long-standing arrears in export tax rebates
规范收入分配秩序	to standardize

	pattern in income distribution
按劳分配制度	system of distribution according to work
粮食流通体制改革	reform of the grain distribution system
发展农村教育	to develop the rural educational programs
发展农村卫生	to develop rural sanitation services
农村文化事业	cultural activities in the rural areas
农村剩余劳动力	the surplus rural workers
第一责任人	the person of chief responsibility
农村贫困地区	rural poverty-stricken area
到地方挂职	to take up provisional post in a locality
定向培训	to train for specific posts
产业结构调整	industrial restructuring
产业优化升级	industrial upgrading
高新科技产业群	hi-tech industrial clusters
产业结构升级	to upgrade industrial structure
综合生产能力	overall production capacity
专业合作组织	specialized cooperatives
农民就业创业	rural residents find jobs or start their own businesses
农业产业化经营	industrialization of agriculture
农业基础地位	the position of agriculture as the foundation of the economy
农业科技进步	advances in agriculture-related science and technology
农村经济改革	a reform of the rural economy
农村综合改革	a comprehensive reform in rural areas
取消农业税	to rescind agricultural tax
取消牧业税	to rescind livestock tax
取消特产税	to rescind tax on special agricultural products
支农惠农政策	policies to support and benefit agriculture
土地承包经营权	land contract and management rights
减轻农业特产税	to repeal all taxes on special agricultural products
行政事业性收费	administrative charges
减轻农民负担	to alleviate / relieve farmer's heavy load
多种农业经营	diversified economy in agriculture
扶贫开发	to alleviate poverty through development
爱心工程	a loving care project
安家费	setting-in allowance
农业合作组织	agricultural cooperatives
农机具补贴	the subsidies for agricultural machinery and tools
兴修水利	to launch water-conservancy projects
农村电网改造工程	projects to upgrade rural power grids
农村适龄儿童	rural school-age children

农村绿带运动	rural green belt movement
农村留守儿童	stay-at-home children in the countryside
农村良种补贴	rural subsidies for growing superior grain cultivators
集体林权制度	collective forest rights system
转移农民就业	to create more jobs for rural supplus labor force
农村民生工程	projects related to the well-being of rural residents
衣食住行条件	daily necessities such as clothing, food, housing
三农	rural economy, rural development and rural demography
三高农业	high-yield, cost-efficient and high-tech farming
主产区	major agricultural areas
对三农的支持力度	to increase support for the "three rurals"
农村基本经营制度	a basic rural management system
复杂而艰巨的斗争	a complicated and arduous battle
长期共存,互相监督	long-term coexistence, mutual supervision
肝胆相照	to be sincere with each other
荣辱与共	sharing of weal or woe
成就举世瞩目	to achieve great success
重大历史关头	a critical historical juncture
城市化进程	urbanization course
粮食流通体制	a grain distribution system
国家粮食安全	China's food security
谷物基本自给	basic self-sufficiency of cereal grains
最低收购价格	minimum purchase prices
农产品目标价格	the guaranteed basic prices for agricultural products
临时收储政策	the policy on purchasing and stockpiling
解放生产力	to empancipate the productive forces
发展生产力	to develop the productive forces
重点领域改革	a reform in important fields
关键环节改革	a reform in crucial links
行业垄断	industrial monopolies
部门分割	sectoral fragmentation
大基地,大企业	major industrial bases and large enterprises
大项目,大品牌	major projects and well-established brands
基础设施建设	construction of infrastructural facilities
产学研战略联盟	the strategic alliances between industry, academic and research community
有计划按比例发展	to develop proportionately
合理区间	within proper range
保持定立	to maintain confidence
加强征管	to tighten collection and management
基层监管	grass-roots supervision
开发性承包	a development contract

流行词，新词和常用词翻译
Translation on Vogue Words, New Words and Everyday Expressions

堵塞漏洞	to plug up loopholes
守住稳增长	to maintain steady growth
用好增量	to make good use of additional monetary
制度不健全	institutional deficiencies
基本公共服务	basic public services
管理不到位	the poor oversight
解放思想	to free our minds
与时俱进	to keep up with the times
求真务实	to be realistic and pragmatic
凝聚力量	to pool our strength
攻坚克难	to overcome all difficulties
原始创新	to make original innovation
集成创新	to make integrated innovation
再创新能力	a capacity for making further innovation
标本兼治	to address both the symptoms and root cause
引进消化吸收	to import and absorb advanced technology
不搞一刀切	don't impose a single solution
开放搞活	to open up and enliven the economy
责任追究制度	the system of accountability
科技决策制度	a scientific policy-making system
加强廉政建设	to strengthen efforts to ensure clean government
加强国防建设	to strengthen national defense
加强制度创新	to intensify institutional innovation
知识创新工程	an innovation project in knowledge
自主创新能力	capacity for independent innovation
科技创新体系	an innovation system for science and technology
取得阶段性成果	to obtain the phased objectives
国家重点科研项目	the national key scientific research
重点领域投资	investment in the key areas
国防科研和国防工业	national defense-related scientific research and national defense industry
国家重大科学工程	major state science projects
国家级实验室	national laboratories
国家级工程研究中心	national engineering centers
加大宏观调控力度	to tighten macrocontrol
人均国内生产总值	per-capita gross domestic product (GDP)
加大处罚力度	to severely punish those who violate the laws and disciplines
有识才的慧眼	to have the insight to spot capable people
关心群众疾苦	to show concern for the sufferings of the people
乡财县管乡用	county management of township budget
用才的气魄	the resolve to use the capable people

爱才的感情	the heart to cherish the capable people
聚才的方法	the ways to attract the capable people
广纳群才	to gather large numbers of talented people
胸怀理想	to remain true to our ideal
坚定信念	to never act recklessly
不动摇	to never vacillate in our efforts
不懈怠	to never relax in our efforts
不折腾	to never act recklessly
顽强奋斗	to forge ahead with tenacity
知人善任	to know how to bring out the best in one's subordinates
人尽其才	to put talented people to the best use
能上能下	to get sb. prepared for both promotion and demotion
不辱使命	to live up to the mission assigned to sb.
不负重托	to live up to the full trust placed on sb.
政府主导	government leadership
廉政政府	an honest government
勤政政府	a diligent government
务实政府	a pragmatic government
高效政府	an efficient government
社会参与	mass participation
第一要务	top priority
政企分开	to separate administrative functions from enterprises management / to separate administration from management
多部门合作	multi-sector cooperation
全社会参与	public participation
发展为人民	development for the people
发展靠人民	development by the people
强国之路	the path to a strong China
兴国之要	the vitality to invigorating our country
生产发展	the expanded production
改革红利	reform benefits
生活富裕	a better life
生态良好	a sound ecological and environmental conditions
兴旺发达	robust growth
长治久安	lasting stability
明确目标	to make clear one's goals
落实责任	to define job responsibility
省直管县	direct provincial supervision of county finance
突发事件	salient events
廉租房制度	the low-rent housing program
最低工资制度	minimum wage syastem
房屋拆迁	housing demolition and relocation
实名购票制	the ID-based ticket booking system
棚户区改造	to rebuild shanty areas
多领域	multi-field
多层次	multi-level
多渠道	multi-channel
一个确保	one goal to attain
三个到位	three tasks to accomplish
五项改革	five areas to undergo reform
一个中心,两个基本点	one center, two basic points
工作基本思路	a basic approach for the work

一个窗口办事　one-window services
一站式审批　one-stop review and approval model
自身改革建设　self-reform and improvement
重要战略机遇期　current important strategic opportunities
实现好人民的根本利益　to realize the fundamental interests of the people
维护好人民的根本利益　to uphold the fundamental interests of the people
发展好人民的根本利益　to expand the fundamental interests of the people
人民享受发展成果　people sharing the developmental fruits
勇于变革，勇于创新　to make bold changes and innovations
发展为第一要务　to make development as our top priority
一要吃饭，二要建设　subsistence first and development second
聚精会神搞建设　to concentrate on construction
一心一意谋发展　to develop wholeheartedly
又好又快地发展　sound and fast development
搞好宏观调控　to exercise macro-control
统筹兼顾　to balance the stakes of all aspects
注重改革创新　to pay attention to reform and innovation
科教兴国战略　the strategy of rejuvenating the country through science and education
人才强国战略　the strategy of strengthening the nation by developing talents
可持续发展战略　the strategy of sustainable development
对外宣传工作　to conduct public diplomacy program
霸权主义　hegemony policy
强权政治　power politics
重返亚太　Asia pivot（U.S.A. takes Asia-Pacific regions as its pivot）
再平衡　rebalancing
讲信修睦　honoring promises
协和万邦　to live in harmony with all others far and near
南南合作　the South-South cooperation
文明多样性　diversity of the civilizations
世界多样性　the world diversity
世界多极化　multi-polarity in the world
公仆意识　public servant consciousness
权为民所用
The government departments must function by mandate of the people.
情为民所系
The government departments must sympathize with the feelings of the people.
利为民所谋
The government departments must work for the well-being of the people.
五个要求　"five balances" requirement
角色错位　role reversal

社会底层	low social stratue
优势互补	complement each other's advantages
反腐败	to fight against corruption
乱罚款	an unreasonable / unproper fines
乱收费	an unreasonable / unproper charges
财务负担	financial burden
主流社会	predominate society
时代的主旋率	main theme of the times
热评	critically acclaimed
退耕还林	to restore the reclaimed land to forest
扶贫	to help the poor / to help the poor get rid of their poverty
特困地区	the destitute areas
摸着石头过河	to wade across the stream by feeling the way
大锅饭	the food prepared in a large canteen cauldron
三包	3-R guarantees
三公	the principle of equal opportunity, fair treatment and open competition
两个开放	an open policy in two aspects, namely to open up both externally and internally
三个面向	three faces
面向现代化	to face the modernization program
面向世界	to face the global perspective
面向未来	to face our nation's future goals
四大目标	four goals (build a port of large size, foster an industry of large scope and develop an economy of large scale and achieve prosperity of large magnitude)
四自原则	four-self principle (self-supporting in finding partners, self-reliance in raising capital, self-decision in management and self-responsibility for losses and gains)
劳动力流动	labor mobility
裁员	to cut down the number of persons / to reduce the staff
预警机制	a contingency planning mechanism
自律机制	a self-restraining system
遵纪守法	to observe the relevant code of conduct and law / to observe discipline and law
廉洁奉公	to honestly perform one's official duties
高层互访	an exchange of visits by the two leaderships
扩大共识	to deepen the mutual understanding
欧盟一体化	E U. Integration
翻两番	quadruple / multiply by four times
劳动力密集的	to be labor-intensive
生产能力过剩	over-capacity in production
透明度	transparency
基本国策	basic state policy
锐意进取	to forge ahead with determination
全力以赴	to need mind's endeavour / go to all lengths
顽强拼搏	to strive to / to indomitably struggle hard

振兴中华	revitalization of the Chinese nation
综合国力	comprehensive national power
现代生活型	modern-life consumption pattern
扩大内需	to boost the domestic demand
科学发展观	the scientific strategies of development
互利共赢	mutual benefit and win-win outcome
一国两制	one country with two systems
三讲	three stresses: study, political awareness and integrity
三讲教育	"three emphasis" education
三个代表	three representatives (represent the development requirements of China's advanced productive forces, the orientation of the nation's advanced culture and the fundamental interests of the great majority of the Chinese people)
两岸关系	the relationship between the two sides of the Taiwan Straits / relation across the Taiwan Straits
"九二共识"	the 1992 consensus
"两岸一家亲"	We people on both sides of the Straits are one family.
八七扶贫攻坚计划	Aid the Poor Programme Aimed at Lifting 80 Million People out of Poverty in Seven Years / the Poverty Alleviation Plan to Assist 80 Million people in Having Sufficient Food and Clothing within Seven Years
富强,民主,文明的现代化强国	a prosperous, strong, democratic and culturally advanced modern country
社会主义核心价值体系	a system of core socialist values
建设创新型国家	to make China an innovative nation
前沿技术研究	research in frontier technology
社会公益性技术研究	the research in technology for public welfare
科技成果市场化	to gear scientific and technological achievements to the market
科技成果产业化	to gear scientific and technological achievements to the production
改革开放符合党心民心	Reform and opening up accord with the aspirations of the Party membership and the people.
顺应时代潮流	to keep up with the trends of the times
对外开放广度和深度	to open up in scope and depth
改革开放取得重大突破	The major breakthroughs were made in reform and opening-up.
全面提高开放水平	to improve opening-

全面建设小康社会	to build a moderately properous society in all respects
全面协调可持续发展	comprehensive, balanced and sustainable development
党的三代中央领导集体	three generations of central collective leadership of the CCP
中国特色社会主义	socialism with Chinese characteristics
发展和稳定的关系	relation between development and stability
行动纲领和大政方针	strategic outlines and policies
群众路线教育实践活动	campaign to highten awarenesss and implement the mass line
高昂的精神状态恪尽职守	to carry out our duties with great drive
贯彻落实科学发展观	to apply "Scientific Outlook on Development"
各方面体制改革创新	institutional reform and innovation in various sectors
决策科学化,民主化	a scientific and democratic decision-making process
保障和改善民主	to ensure and improve people's democracy
兜住民生底线	to keep people's basic living needs
城乡低保标准	subsistence allowances for urban and rural residents
政治建设,文化建设	political and cultural development
农村基层政权建设	government function at township level
政府工作的基本思路	basic approach for the work of government
政府性债务	governmemt debt
修正行政法规	to revise administrative regulations
调解联动工作	to mediate disputes
积极盘活存量	to make good use of existing monetary
释放潜在需求	to unleash potential demands
中央八项规定	the CPC Central Committee's eight-point decisions
反对"四风"	to oppose formalism, bureaucracy, hedonism and extravagance
约法三章	three point decisions
完善社会保障体系	to improve the social security system
优惠意识和塑造意识	a sense of urgency and willingness to shape things
牢记执政为民的宗旨	to keep in mind our obligation to govern for the people

人民生活更加殷实	The people will enjoy a more comfortable life.
政府职能转变滞后	The government functions are behind schedule.
加快社会事业发展	to quicken the development of social welfare projects
法治政府建设	to enhance law-based government administration
党内事务透明度	the transparency in Party affairs
两个文明建设	development of both material and culture
国家公务员考试	national civil servant examination
党要管党	The Party supervises its own conduct.
从严治党	The Party strictly enforces its discipline.
党群关系	the Party-mass relationship
完善信访	to handle people's complaints expressed in letters or visits
各级党组织	the Party organizations at all levels
基层党组织	the grass-roots Party organization
基层社区管理机构	the grass-roots community management organization
办事机构	administrative organization
党的建设	the Party building
基本生活型	a consumption pattern of low-income groups
党政机关	Party and government organizations
电子政务	e-government
互相推诿	to shuffle between each other
棘手问题	the thorny issue
发展潜力	a potential for development
发展势头	a momentum for development
行政审批	administrative approval
户籍制度	a household registration system
绿色通道	green channel
党务公开	an open management of Party affairs
财产申报	to report assets
公开财产	to disclose assets
差额选举	a competitive election
等额选举	a single-candidate election
全体会议	plenum
对人民高度负责	to maintain a high sense of responsibility
反对官僚主义	to oppose bureaucratism
反对形式主义	to oppose formalism
公务接待费	hospitality spending
坚持反腐败	to adhere to cracking down on corruption
政治体制改革	a political structure reform
反对铺张浪费	to combat extravagance and waste
反对奢侈浪费	to oppose luxury and waste
政府机构改革	a reform of government institutions
事业单位改革	to reform public institutions
公立医院改革	a public hospital reform
改善民主制度	to improve institutions

	for democracy
年报公示制度	annual reporting to incentivize market actors
民主更加健全	a more democratic system
国家政通人和	state's stability and harmony
国家兴旺发达	prosperity across the land
兴边富民	to boost development of border regions and improve the lives of people
和平发展	peaceful development
法制教育	education in rules and laws
矛盾凸显期	a period of major challenges
自主创业	to become self-employed
开拓进取	pioneering spirit
合作应对	to work together
共度难关	to tide over the difficulties
多难兴邦	A country will emerge stronger from adversities.
学有所教	the young educated
病有所医	the sick treated
老有所养	the old cared for
赢得主动	to take the initiative / master the situation
后发优势	a late-comer advantages
滥用职权	an abuse of power / power abuse
徇私枉法	to bend the law for selfish ends
不作为（履职不利）	a dereliction of duty
行政审批	an administrative approval procedures
国际惯例	an international practice
良性循环轨道	a sound track
履行义务	to fulfull one's obligations
城市化进程	the process of urbanization
新型城镇化	a new type of urbanization
创新驱动发展	innovation-driven development
人力资源	human resources
互利合作	to conduct mutually beneficial co-operation
冷战思维	the cold-war mentality
单边主义	unilateralism
多边主义	multilateralism
区域合作	a regional cooperation
公务员	civil servants
迎合潮流	trend-right
法人资格	a legal entity
正在崛起	to be on the rise / to be rising
"三步走"战略	three-step strategy
抓大放小	to manage large enterprises well while easing control over small ones
申报个人财产	to declare personal assets
反映社会民意	to reflect social conditions and public opinions
维护群众利益	to safeguard the interests of the people
促进社会公平	to advocate the social fairness
人民各尽其能	all people doing their best
人民各得其所	all people being content with their lives / each being in their proper place
发展老年事业	to develop the programs for the old age (the aged)
理顺分配关系	to develop a better program for income redistribution

社会服务体系	commercialized services
社会保障支出	an expenditure for social security
社会保障基金	the social funds for security
社会组织形式	an organized way of the society
社会利益格局	the pattern of social interests
社会大结构	a major structure of society
粮食风险基金	the risk funds of grain
特大自然灾害	a large-scale natural disasters
防灾减灾能力	the ability to guard against disasters and mitigate their damages
重大疾病保险	a critical illness insurance
基本医疗体系	a basic healthcare insurance system
农村合作医疗	cooperative medical care in rural areas
战略机遇期	a period of strategic opportunity
战略的眼光	strategic foresight
改革攻坚	a further reform in difficult areas
深化改革	to deepen its commitment to reform
减政放权	to streamline government and delegate powers
技术创新体系	a system for technological innovation
企业为主体系	a system being led by enterprises
市场为导向体系	a system being led by the market
产学研相结合	to integrate the efforts of enterprises, universities and research institutes
转变政府职能	to transform the functions of the government
人力资源开发	human resources development
西电东送	a transmission of electricity from the west to the east
西气东送	the pipelines for transmitting natural gas from the west to the east
灾后重建	the post-disaster reconstruction
重建家园	to rebuild one's homes
圆桌会议	a roundtable meeting
综合国力	overall (or comprehensive) national strength
重要宗旨	an important purpose
难得机遇	a precious opportunity
世界多极化	a multi-polar world
解决国际争端	to settle international disputes
二十国集团领导人峰会	G20 leaders Summit
21世纪海上丝绸之路	a 21st century maritime Silk Road
亚太经合组织领导人非正式会议	The APEC Economic Leaders Meeting
金砖国家领导人会晤	The BRICS Leaders Meeting
东亚领导人系列会议	The East Asian Leaders Meeting
上海合作组织峰会	The Shanghai Cooperation Organization Summit

《南海各方行为宣言》 Declaration on the Conduct of Parties in the South China Sea
两岸关系和平发展 peaceful growth of cross-straits relations
国际关系民主化 democracy in international relations
国际恐怖势力 international terrorists
民族分裂势力 the ethnic separatists
极端宗教势力 the religious extremists
国际和地区事务 international and regional issues
国家领土主权完整 China's sovereignty, territorial integrity
国家海洋权益 China's maritime rights and interests
枪支管控 gun control
跨国犯罪 transnational crimes
黄岩岛僵局 Huangyan Island impasse / Huangyan Island standoff
巴厘路线图 the Bali roadmap
政治风波 the political turbulences
内忧外患 both internal and external troubles
妄自菲薄 to belittle oneself
老年化问题 problem of population aging
时代主旋律 main theme of the times
敢为天下先 to do what has never been done before
发展创新 innovative development
增长联动 interconnected growth
营改增 to replace business tax with valuew-added tax（VAT）
利益融合 converging interests

大胆探索 to be bold enough to explore
勇于开拓 to be bold enough to make advances
敢于啃硬骨头 to have the courage to crack the "hard nuts"
不廉不勤 perform one's duties without integrity and diligence
敢于涉险滩 to navigate the uncharted waters
严重挑战 formidable challenges
深刻变革 a profuond transformation
国家创新体系 a state innovation system
过渡时期内阁 a caretaker cabinet
粮食分配体系 a grain system of the distribution
宏观调控体系 a system of macro-regulation
公共服务体系 a system for the basic public services
分配制度改革 reform of income distribution system
生产要素价格 factor price
推进资源节约 to set up the resources conservation
安全隐患 a hidden danger
领海基线 a territorial sea baseline
劳保条例 labor insurance regulations
能耗转移 a transfer of energy consumption
劳动力流动 labor mobility
保就业下限 The employment does not fall below the prescribed minimum level.
劳务派遣工 contractor
红包协议 hongbao stipulation /anti-

	bribery agreement	敢于担当	to be eager to take on challenges
金税工程	Golden Tax Project	毫不懈怠	to work tirelessly
围湖造田	to wrest / reclaim farmlands from lakes	忧患意识	sense of vigilance against potential dangers
退耕还湖	to convert marginal farmland back to the lake-plots	过度政府	an interim government
		赢得连任	to win re-election
形象工程	the projects designed to build images of local affairs	战略性	strategic vision
		宏观性	broad perspectives
看守政府	a caretaker government	政策性	policy considerations

4. 构建和谐社会（Build Harmonious Society）

思想道德建设	moral education		seek gains at the expense of others
社会公平正义	the social equity and justice	以诚实守信为荣	honor to those who are trustworthy
八荣八耻	eight-honour and eight-shame	以见利忘义为耻	shame on those who trade integrity for profits
以热爱祖国为荣	honor to those who love our motherland		
以危害祖国为耻	shame on those who harm our motherland	以遵纪守法为荣	honor to those who abide by laws and disciplines
以服务人民为荣	honor to those who serve the people	以违法乱纪为耻	shame on those who break laws and disciplines
以背离人民为耻	shame on those who betray the people		
以崇尚科学为荣	honor to those who quest for science	以艰苦奋斗为荣	honor to those who uphold plain living and hard struggle
以愚昧无知为耻	shame on those who refuse to be educated	以骄奢淫逸为耻	shame on those who wallow in extravagance and pleasures
以辛勤劳动为荣	honor to those who are hardworking		
以好逸恶劳为耻	shame on those who indulge in comfort and hate work	建设一个和谐世界	to build a harmonious world
		增强社会守法意识	to strengthen social abiding awareness
以团结互助为荣	honor to those who help each other	以高尚的精神塑造人	to shape one's outlook with noble ideas
以损人利己为耻	shame on those who		

增强公德意识	to strengthen social ethics awareness	和谐劳动关系	harmonious labor relations
体育道德精神	to be in the true spirit of sportsmanship	向往和谐生活	to look forward to a harmonious life
和谐凝聚力量	The harmony rallys strength.	家和万事兴	a family of harminy prospers / a harmonious family prospers
秉持开放包容	to uphold the approach of openness and inclusiveness	具有亲和力	to be more friendly
心心相印	to share mutual affinity	甜柠檬心理	sweet lemon psychology
和睦相处	to live in harmony	自重，自省	to maintain self-discipline, self-examination
息事宁人	to patch up a quarrel and reconcile the parties concerned	自警，自励	to maintain self-caution, self-motivation
守望相助	to help each other	忧患意识	adversity consciousness
民族和睦	national concord	反三俗	to fight against three forms of vulgarity
家庭和睦	family harmony		
和平相处	peaceful coexistence	公民道德	civic morality
和平主义	pacifism	政务诚信	government integrity
说话和气	to speak politely / gently	商务诚信	business integrity
和和气气	to be polite and amiable	社会诚信	public integrity
和气生财	amiability begets riches	学术诚信	academic integrity
相处和洽	to live in harmony	向往和谐	to yearn for harmony
态度和善	kind and gentle attitude	和则两利	Peace benefits both.
和谐气氛	a harmonious atmosphere / a benign countenance	和和美美	perfect harmony
和颜悦色	to have a kind face	和蔼可亲	to be amiable
化解社会矛盾	to defuse social conflicts	和风细雨	to be in the manner of " a gentle breeze and a mild rain"
增进人民福祉	to increase people's happiness	和和睦睦	to live in amity
国家公祭日	national memorial day	和善者	a kind and gentle man
友好和睦关系	friendly and harmonious relations	和为贵	Peace is to be cherished.
		和则生谐	Reconciliation leads to harmony.
宗教关系和谐	harmonious relations among religions	和实生物	Harmony generates vitality.
和谐医患关系	harmonious relations among doctors and patients	同则不继	Sameness stifles vitality.
		和而不同	harmony in diversity

以和为贵	Harmony is most precious.
天人合一	the unity of human and nature
和谐共赢	all-win harmony
和谐发展	a harmonious growth
和衷共济	to work together with one accord (in time of difficulty)
从善如流	to do good naturally and happily
骨肉情谊	one's kindred friendship
和谐成就伟业	Harmony leads to great successes.
就业与社会保障	employment and social security
各民族平等,团结,互助	equality, unity, and mutual assistance among all ethnic groups in our country
海纳百川,有容乃大	One should be as tolerant as the vast ocean which admits hundreds of rivers.
顺民意,和民情	to tally with the popular will and sentiments
凝聚同胞心力	to work together with our compatriots
讲公道话,办公道事	to be fair in words and deeds
维护社会公平,正义	to safeguard social fairness and justice
保证人民的知情权	to ensure people's right to know
保证人民的参与权	to ensure people's right to participate
保证人民的监督权	to ensure people's right to supervise
保证人民的表达权	to ensure people's right to express
政务信息透明度	the administrative transparency
实现文明对话	to facilitate dialogue among civilizations
实现共同安全	to achieve common security
实现协调合作	to enhance coordination and cooperation
实现共同发展	to advance common development
坚持包容开放	to stay open and tolerant
吸纳百家优长	to draw on other's strengths
坚持民主平等	to uphold democracy and equality
推进教育公平	to make education more equitable
放宽落户条件	to relax restrictions on granting permanent residency
科学民主决策	to make decisions scientifically and democratically
坚持和睦互信	to ensure harmony and mutual trust
坚持公正互利	to uphold / adhere to justice and mutual benefits
民主的世界	the democratic world
法制的国家	the country of laws
安全专项整治	to carry out more special programs to address safe problems
纠正有法不依	to resolve the problems of laws not being abided by

纠正执法不严	to resolve the problems of laws not being fully enforced
纠正违法不究	to resolve the problems of lawbreakers not being prosecuted
纠正粗暴执法	to resolve the problems of abusing in law enforcement
反对暴力恐怖犯罪	to oppose violent crimes of terrorism
反对涉医犯罪行为	to oppose crimes involving medical disputes
纠正渎职失职	to resolve the problems of dereliction and neglecting of duty in law enforcement
纠正执法腐败	to resolve the problems of corruption practices in law enforcement
稳定的国家	the country of stability / the stable country
公正和包容的世界	the world of justice and tolerance
和平和繁荣的国家	the country of peace and prosperity
把各项政策落到实处	to truly put all policies into effect
促进大学生就业	to promote employment of university graduates
城镇就业困难人员	urban residents having difficulties in finding jobs
五讲四美	five stresses and four points of beauty (stress on decorum, manners, hygiene, discipline and morals; beauty of the mind, language, behavior and the environment)
城镇登记失业率	the registered unemployment rate in cities and towns
城镇社会保障体系	urban social security system
城镇住房制度改革	reform of the urban housing system
城镇职工医疗保险制度改革	reform of the medical insurance for urban workers
增加中低收入者的收入	to increase the income of people in the low and middle brackets
深入了解群众疾苦	to better understand the problems troubling the people
着力解决民生问题	Every effort will be made to improve the people's well-being.
注重民生	to care for people's well-being
政府自身建设	Government efforts to enhance performance.
社会更加和谐	a more harmonious society
酒后代驾	the designated driver (DD)
婴幼儿奶粉质量	milk powder quality

	of infant formula
重大安全事故	major workplace accidents
食品药品监管	food and drug supervision
食品药品安全	food and drug safety
市场监管	market supervision
社会治安	public order
安全级别	security level
安静地铁	low-noise subway
安慰奖	consolation prize
安全检查	security overhaul
安全隐患	potential risk

2 外交
Diplomacy

1. 外交机构（Diplomatic Establishment）

外交部	ministry of foreign affairs / foreign ministry
外交机关	diplomatic establishments
外交部办公厅	general office of foreign ministry
外交部机关党委	Party committee of foreign ministry
外交部国外工作局	bureau for Chinese diplomatic missions abroad
外交部档案馆	bureau of archieves
外交部干部司	department of personnel of foreign ministry
中国驻外机构	China's institutions in foreign countries
外国驻华机构	foreign institutions in China
中国驻外使领馆	Chinese embassies and consulates in foreign countries
离退休干部司	bureau for retired personnel
北美大洋洲司	department of North American and Oceania affairs
边界与海洋事务司	department of boundary and ocean affairs
涉外安全事务司	department of external security affairs
拉丁美洲和加勒比司	department of Latin-American and Caribbean affairs
外交部海内外服务中心	the ministry of foreign affairs service center at home and abroad
外事管理司	department of foreign affairs management
西亚北非司	department of west Asian and north African affairs
政策规划司	department of policy planning
条约法律司	department of treaty and law
境内机构	domestic entity
境外机构	foreign entity
外事局	bureau of foreign affairs
国际司	department of international organizations and conferences
亚洲司	department of Asian affairs
欧洲司	department of European affairs
非洲司	department of African affairs

欧亚司	department of European-central Asian affairs
行政司	administrative department
新闻司	information department
礼宾司	protocol department
领事司	department of consular affairs
财务司	department of finance
翻译司	department of translation and interpretation
军控司	department of arms control
监察司	department of supervision
港澳台司	department of Hong Kong, Macau and Taiwan affairs
领事团	consular corps
领事处	consular section
总领事馆	consulate general
公使馆	legation

2. 外交职衔（Diplomatic Ranks）

外交部长	minister of foreign affairs
外交使节	diplomatic envoy
外交大使	ambassador of foreign affairs
外交大臣	foreign secretary
外交官	diplomatist
外交特命大使	ambassador extraordinary of foreign affairs
外交特命全权大使	ambassador extraordinary and plenipotentiary of foreign affairs
外交特命全权公使	envoy extraordinary and minister plenipotentiary of foreign affairs
外交行政技术人员	members of the administrative and technical staff for foreign affairs
外交总领事	consul-general of foreign affairs
外交巡回大使	roving ambassador of foreign affairs
外交使团团长	dean (doyen) of the diplomatic corps
外交友好使者	friendly envoy of foreign affairs
外交文化参赞	cultural secretary of foreign affairs
外交政治参赞	political counselor of foreign affairs
外交文化专员	cultural attaché for foreign affairs
外交新闻文化参赞	press and cultural counselor of foreign affairs
外交商务参赞	commercial counselor of foreign affairs
外交商务专员	commercial attaché of foreign affairs
外交名誉领事	honorary consul of foreign affairs
外交高级特派员	high commissioner
外交和平使者	peace envoy for foreign affairs
外交光荣使者	honourable envoy for foreign affairs
外交领事团	consular corps for foreign affairs
公使衔外交代表	minister resident
非常驻大使	non-resident ambassador

公使衔参赞	counselor with the rank of minister		affairs
职业外交家	professional diplomatist	外务大臣	minister of foreign affairs
外交联络主任	chief coordinator for foreign affairs	外交随员	attaché of foreign affairs
		外交武官	military attaché of foreign affairs
外交教廷公使	internuncio for foreign affairs	外交信使	diplomatic courier
外交常驻使节	resident envoy for foreign affairs	外交专员	attaché for foreign affairs
		外交代表	diplomatic representative
		常驻代表	permanent representative
外交首席使节	doyen of the diplomatic corps	外交密使	secret envoy (emissary) of foreign affairs
外交一等秘书	first secretary of foreign affairs	外交女大使	ambassadress of foreign affairs
外交二等秘书	second secretary of foreign affairs	外交发言人	spokesman of foreign affairs
		文化使节	cultural ambassador
外交三等秘书	third secretary of foreign affairs	驻外公使	minister resident
		驻外武官	military attaché resident
外交档案秘书	secretary-archievist	公使衔参赞	minister-counsellor
外交特派员	commissioner for foreign	领事	diplomacy consul

3. 外交团体 (Diplomatic Groups)

参观团	visiting group	政府代表团	governmental mission
代表团	delegation	政党代表团	the Party mission
观光团	visiting group / sightseeing party	政协代表团	delegation of political consultative conference
领事团	consular corps		
官方代表团	official mission	人大代表团	delegation of the National People's Congress
国事访问团	state visiting corps		
和平代表团	peace team	宗教代表团	religion delegation
高级代表团	top delegation	民间代表团	folk delegation
军事代表团	military delegate group	教育代表团	educational delegation
体育代表团	sports delegation	艺术代表团	art delegation
文化代表团	cultural delegation	谈判代表团	delegation for negotiation
新闻代表团	press delegation	联合国代表团	delegation of the United Nations
友好访问团	good-will mission		
正式访问团	official visiting group	民主党派代表团	delegation of the

| | democratic Party | 检阅仪仗队 | to review the guard of honour |
| 社交性访问团 | social visiting group | | |

4. 外事活动和方针（Diplomatic Activities and Policy）

友好外交	friendly diplomacy	诚挚的会谈	sincere talk
国民外交	national diplomacy	友好谈判	friendly negotiation
公开外交	open diplomacy	延长谈判	prolong negotiation
穿梭外交	shuttle diplomacy	全面谈判	all-round negotiation
和平外交	peace diplomacy	秘密谈判	secret negotiation
预防外交	preventive diplomacy	双边会谈	bilateral negotiation
集团外交	collective diplomacy	举行会谈	to hold talks
秘密外交	secret diplomacy	停战谈判	cease-fire negotiation
民间外交	people-to-people diplomacy	正式会谈	formal talk
乒乓外交	ping-pong diplomacy	和平谈判	peace negotiation
强权外交	power diplomacy	边界谈判	boundary negotiation
人民外交	people's diplomacy	双方会谈	talk of the two parties
经济外交	economic diplomacy	正式拜会	official call
微笑外交	smiling diplomacy	正式接见	official interview
周边外交	neighbourhood diplomacy	正式约见	to make a formal appointment with sb.
尿布外交	diaper diplomacy		
武力外交	armed diplomacy	正式会见	formally meet with sb.
等距离外交	equidistant diplomacy	国际交往	international intercourse
仪仗队	Honor Guard / Ceremonial Guard	国事访问	state visit
友好访问	friendly visit	设国宴	to give a state banquet
正式访问	formal visit	国宾宴会	state guest banquet
非正式访问	informal visit	告别宴会	farewell banquet
官方访问	official visit	答谢宴会	reciprocal banquet
非官方访问	non-official visit	欢迎宴会	welcoming banquet
试探性谈判	exploratory negotiation	盛大宴会	elaborate banquet
最高级别会谈	top-level talk	举行晚宴	to hold dinner party
马拉松式会谈	marathon talk	设宴招待贵宾	to give a banquet in honour of the distinguished visitors
富有成果的会谈	fruitful negotiation		
预备性会谈	preliminary negotiation		
非正式会谈	informal negotiation	设午宴	to give a midday banquet
大使级会谈	ambassadorial talk	设晚宴	to give an evening banquet

鸡尾酒会	cocktail party		Ministry
午餐会	mid-day banquet / luncheon party	外交谈判	diplomatic negotiation
欢送会	farewell meeting	外交磋商	diplomatic consultation
欢迎辞	welcoming speech	外交回访	to pay a return visit of foreign affairs
即席讲话	to make an impromptu speech		
夹道欢迎	lining the streets to give guests a welcome	外交互访	exchange visit of foreign affairs
盛大欢迎	red-carpet reception	外交承认	diplomatic recognition
盛情接待	cordial hospitality	外交斗争	diplomatic struggle
工作午餐	working luncheon	外交攻势	diplomatic offensive
秘密会晤	secret interview	外交活动	diplomatic activities
民间往来	folk contact	外交手腕	diplomatic technique
私人访问	private visit	外交场合	diplomatic occasion
私人拜会	personal call	外交语言	diplomatic languages
普通照会	verbal note	外交法	diplomatic law
通知照会	circular	外交家	diplomat
正式照会	formal note	外交界	diplomatic circles
外交照会	diplomatic note	出访他国	to visit other nations
相同照会	identical note	召见大使	to summon ambassador
官方声明	official statement	政治对话	political dialogue
政府声明	government statement	强烈抗议	strong protest
私下会晤	private talk	书面抗议	written protest
来访求见	to come to call and ask for an interview	提出抗议	to lodge a protest
		提出警告	to give a warning
礼节性拜会	courtesy call	口头交涉	verbal representation
礼节性访问	complimentary visit	口头抗议	verbal protest
对外工作	external work	拜见	to pay a formal visit
举行招待会	to give a reception	参见	to pay one's respects to sb.
鸣礼炮	fire a gun salute	答词	to answer speech / thank-you speech
祝酒辞	toast		
遭冷遇	to suffer cold reception	答谢	to express appreciation
双边合作	bilateral cooperations	赴宴	to attend a banquet
双边渠道	bilateral channels	发展友好合作关系	to develop the relations of friendship and cooperation
书面声明	written statement		
外交部声明	statement of Foreign		

外交 Diplomacy

单方面中断外交关系	the one-sided suspension of diplomatic relations
建立大使级外交关系	to establish diplomatic relations at ambassadorial level
建立战略协作伙伴关系	to establish strategic partnership of coordination
确立正确的对外方针	to establish correct foreign policy
外交工作开创新局面	to make new ground in conducting China's diplomacy
建立战略伙伴关系	to establish a strategic partnership
建立外交关系	to establish diplomatic relations
建立领事关系	to establish consular relations
恢复外交关系	to resume the diplomatic relations
维持外交关系	to maintain diplomatic relations
断绝外交关系	to break off / sever diplomatic relations
经济外交	economic diplomacy
外交引渡	diplomatic extradition
外交关系升格	to upgrade the diplomatic relations
外交豁免权	diplomatic immunity
恢复行使主权	to resume the exercise of sovereignty over…
缓和国际形势	to ease the international situation
缓和紧张局势	to ease the tension
履行国际义务	to fulfill the international obligations
良好周边环境	a favorable climate in areas around
高级别对话	high-level dialogue
南北对话	south-north dialogue
南南合作	south-south cooperation
高层对话	high-level dialogue
全方位合作	all-round cooperation
全面禁止核武器	to completely prohibit nuclear weapon
彻底销毁核武器	to thoroughly destruct nuclear weapon
全面接触	comprehensive engagement
全方位对话	all-directional dialogue
彼此交换意见	to exchange notes with each other
产生积极影响	to produce positive impact
采取积极防御	to take active defense
两国关系基石	cornerstone of relations between two nations
领事协定	consular agreement
框架协议	framework agreement
礼尚往来	reciprocal (mutual) courtesy
解决分歧	to resolve differences
结交新友	to establish new contacts
互谅互让	mutual understanding and mutual accommodation
互派大使	to exchange ambassadors
互通有无	exchange of needed goods
互相承认	mutual recognition
合法权益	legitimate rights and interests
审时度势	to size up the situation

5. 外交常用语 (Diplomatic Expressions)

外办	office of foreign affairs
外邦	foreign country
外币	foreign currency
外宾	foreign guests (visitors)
外钞	foreign bank note
外汇	foreign exchange
外敌	foreign enemy
外籍	foreign nationality
外教	foreign teacher
外电	dispatches from foreign news agencies
邦交	diplomatic relations
避难	asylum
领空	territorial air
领海	territorial sea
领事证书	exequatur
领事条例	consular act
领事委任书	certificate of appointment of consul / consular commission
领土管辖权	territorial jurisdiction
领土毗连	territorial contiguity
领土争端	border (territorial) disputes
领海范围	limits of territorial sea
边界地区	border region
边界现状	present situation of the boundary
流血冲突	bloody conflict
外汇储备	foreign exchange reserve
外汇管理	foreign exchange control
外汇交易	foreign exchange transaction
外汇行情	foreign exchange quotations
外汇兑换券	foreign exchange certificate
外籍工作人员	foreign personnel
外交备忘录	diplomatic memorandum
全方位外交	all-directional diplomacy
外交准则	diplomatic norms
外交程序	diplomatic procedure
外交辞令	diplomatic language
外交护照	diplomatic passport
外交惯例	diplomatic practice / diplomatic usage
外交礼节	diplomatic protocol
外交签证	diplomatic visa
外交特权	diplomatic privilege
外交邮件	diplomatic mail
外交文书	diplomatic papers
外交政策	foreign policy
外交制裁	diplomatic sanction
外交摩擦	friction of foreign affairs
外交僵局	diplomatic stalemate
外交途径	diplomatic channel
外交休兵	diplomatic truce
外交使命	diplomatic missions
外交语言	diplomatic languages
外交豁免权	diplomatic immunity
外交斡旋	diplomatic offices
外汇率	foreign exchange rate
外国语	foreign language
外国人	foreigner / alien
外国租界	foreign settlement / foreign concession
外国货	imported goods / foreign goods
外国人居留证	residence permit for foreigners
外国驻华机构	foreign institutions in China

外交 Diplomacy

公认的国际法准则	generally-accepted principles of international laws
外国驻华使领馆	foreign diplomatic and consular missions in China
不附加任何条件	never to attach any conditions
人民之间的交流	people-to-people exchanges
采取惩罚行动	to take punitive actions
采取协调行动	to take concerted steps
推翻一国政权	to topple a regime
唯一合法政府	sole legal government
新殖民主义	neo-colonialism
维护国家利益	to assert state interests
专属经济区	exclusive economic zone
各国利益	interests of all countries
万国公法	nations' laws
人道主义者	humanitarian
建立盟国关系	to establish the relations of allies
不结盟国家	non-aligned country
关系正常化	normalization of relations
对外方针	foreign policy
国际权利和义务	international rights and interests
国际关系准则	principles of international relations
战略协作伙伴关系	strategic partnership of coordination
国与国之间关系	relations between state and state
新的世界形态	a new world pattern
必要的妥协	necessary compromise
必要的让步	necessary concessions
边界谈判	boundary negotiation
裁军谈判	disarmament negotiation
中东局势	the situation of Middle East
道义上支持	moral support
种族隔离	racial segregation
种族灭绝	racial genocide
种族歧视	racial discrimination
种族矛盾	racial tensions
主权国家	sovereign country
宗主国	metropolitan states
中立国家	neutralized state
发达国家	developed country
发展中国家	developing country
最不发达国家	least-developed country
边界紧张局势	tension along the borders
处理突发事件	to provide escort and handle emergencies
环太平洋国家	around Pacific Rim countries
环太平洋地区	around Pacific Rim
发表声明	to issue a statement
常驻代表	permanent representative
海外侨胞	overseas compatriots
海外资源	maritime resources / overseas resources
政治框架	political framework
沉着应对	to cope with the situation steadily
反恐维稳	countering terrorism, maintaining stability
侵犯他国	to encroach on other nations
居留权	right of residence
侨居国	nations of one's residence
双重国籍	dual nationality

国际惯例	international common practice	共同协作	common coordination
第三世界	the third world	携手合作	hand-in-hand cooperation
国际水域	international waters	文化交流	cultural exchange
国际形势	international situation	国家利益	state interests
国家元首	head of state	世界形态	the world pattern
政府首脑	head of government	发布唁电	to declare message of condolences
同等尊严	equal dignity		
完全平等	complete (all) equality	一贯政策	consistent policy
维持现状	to maintain the current state	意识形态差异	ideological differences
合作关系	cooperative relationship	中外人文交流	people-people and cultural exchanges between China and foreign countries
和睦关系	harmoniuous relationship		
协调关系	to harmonize the relation		
签订协议	to sign an agreement		

3 贸易, 商业, 房地产, 经济
Trade, Business, Real Estate and Economy

1. 贸易类 (Trade)

欧盟单一货币　European Union's Single Currency
对外贸易仲裁委员会　Foreign Trade Arbitration Commission
加勒比自由贸易联盟　Caribbean Free Trade Association
商贸联委会　Joint Commission on Commerce and Trade
拉丁美洲自由贸易联盟　Latin American Free Trade Association
欧洲货币兑换机制　European currency exchange mechanism
国际贸易基本准则　international trade norms
发展, 平等, 互利　development, equality, and mutual benefit
北美自由贸易协定　North American Free Trade Agreement
法国对外贸易中心　French National Centre of Foreign Trade
欧洲自由贸易区　European Free Trade Area
中美洲共同市场　Central American Common Market
互惠贸易政策　reciprocal trade policy
中国贸易中心　China Foreign Trade Center
外贸公司　Foreign Trade Company
市外贸公司　municipal foreign trade corporation
省外贸公司　provincial foreign trade corporation
国际贸易公司　international trade corporation
欧洲共同市场　European Common Market
外贸机构　foreign trade organizations
进出口公司　Import & Export Corporation
ABC 进口公司　ABC Imports
对外贸易中心　foreign trade centre
外贸局　foreign trade bureau
跨国公司　multi-national enterprises
国内贸易　domestic trade
对外贸易　foreign trade
贸易大国　trading power
贸易伙伴　trading partner
出口贸易　export trade
进口贸易　import trade
转口贸易　transit trade / entrecote trade
外贸顺差　foreign trade surplus
外贸逆差　foreign trade deficit

自由贸易市场	free markets and fairs
自由贸易区	free trade zone
贸易差额	trade shortfall
双边贸易	bilateral trade
多边贸易	multilateral trade
互惠贸易	reciprocal trade
边境贸易	border trade
记账贸易	escrow barter
中介贸易	intermediary trade
保护性贸易	protective trade
过境贸易	transit trade
补偿贸易	compensation trade
出口配额	export quotas
出口升级	to upgrade exports
国际贸易仲裁	international commercial arbitration
中国国际贸易促进会	China Council for the Promotion of International Trade
中国国际经济贸易仲裁委员会	China International Economic and Trade Arbitration Commission (CIETAC)
关税及贸易总协定	General Agreement on Tariffs and Trade
世贸组织	World Trade Organization (WTO)
多边贸易体系	multilateral trading system
贸易和投资	trade and investment
乌拉圭回合	Uruguay Round
博鳌亚洲论坛	Boao Forum for Asia
(财富)全球论坛	(Fortune) global forum
东盟自由贸易区	ASEAN Free Area
欧洲自由贸易联盟	European Free Trade Association
中欧经济贸易	China-EU economic trade
促进双边经贸关系	to promote bilateral trade and economic relations
最大贸易伙伴	the largest trading partner
第一大贸易伙伴	the first largest trading partner
第二大贸易伙伴	the second largest trading partner
最大出口市场	the largest export market
外商投资企业	foreign invested business
主要投资来源地	a major source of investment
第四大外资来源	the fourth largest source of foreign investment
欧盟的投资增长	EU investment growth
贸易界的业内人士	trade experts
防止一场贸易战	to avert a trade war
自由贸易协定	free trade agreement
转口贸易货物	goods in transit trade
纺织品贸易问题	issue on textile trading
解决贸易争端	to solve trade disputes
求大同存小异	to seek consensus on major issues and reserve differences on minor ones
避免经贸问题政治化	to avoid making economic and trade issues politicized
稳定的国际贸易环境	a sound international trade environment
货物实际进出境口岸	the port of the actual entry and exit of the

贸易，商业，房地产，经济
Trade, Business, Real Estate and Economy

出口大幅波动　exports fluctuate drastically
增强市场信息信心　to enhance public confidence in the market
美中贸易逆差　US trade deficit with China
不扩大赤字　don't increase the deficit
不超发货币　don't issue excessive currency
双边结汇易货　straight barter sales
许可证贸易　trade under licence
贸易集团　trading bloc
贸易条例　trade regulations
贸易条约　trade treaty
贸易政策　trade policy
直接贸易　direct trade
转口贸易　transit trade
自由贸易　free trade
海上贸易　maritime trade
保护贸易措施　protectionist policies（or measures）
世界贸易模式　world trade model
亚太自由贸易区　a free trade area of the Asia Pacific
双边经贸协调机制　coordinating mechanisms in our bilateral trade and economic relations
加工贸易进口货物　goods imported under processing trade
商队及海上贸易　caravan and maritime commerce
文化搭台，经贸唱戏　Cultural events set the stage and trade activities play the star role. / Cultural events set up the stage to pay the way for economy and trade.
三来一补　three plus one trading mix
合作主办方　co-sponsor
贸易国　trading nations
正常贸易关系　normal trade relations
互利共赢　mutual benefit and win-win outcomes
凝聚共识　to coagulate the common wisdom
抓住机遇　to seize the opportunity
务实合作　to work together in a down-earth manner
资金融通　financing
贸易伙伴　trading partner
技术转让　technology transfer
乡村贸易市场　village fair and rural market
贸易渠道　trade channel
集市贸易　village fairs
活禽贸易　live poultry trading
服务贸易　trade in service
欧中贸协　Europe-China Business Association
亚太价值链　an Asia Pacific value chain
地区内贸易　regional trade
正常贸易关系　normal trade relations
国际转口贸易　international enter pot trade
放开外贸经营权　to lift controls over access to foreign trade
贸易与投资壁垒　trade and investment barriers

贸易和竞争政策	trade and competition policy
优惠贸易待遇	preferential trade treatment
进口寄售货物	import consignment
进出口许可证	import and export licence
放宽市场准入	to expand market access
外国来华投资	foreign investment in China
贸易自由化	trade liberalization
贸易便利化	trade facilitation
贸易保护主义	trade protectionism
经贸合作伙伴	partners in trade and economic cooperation
贸易投资便利化	facilitation of trade and investment
外汇储备多元化	diversification of foreign exchange reserve
双边贸易协定	bilateral trade agreement
最惠国待遇	most-favoured nation treatment
永久正常贸易关系	permanent normal trade status
多边的贸易体制度	multilateral trading system
改进外贸增长方式	to change the way which China's foreign trade grows/increases
转变外贸增长方式	evolution of the growth pattern of China's foreign trade
利用外资质量	to optimize the use overseas investment
经济体的贸易额	trade volume of economic entities
进出口贸易总额	total import and export trade volume
进口环节增值税	import value added tax
进口环节消费税	import consumption tax
放宽市场准入制度	system of relaxing control over market entry
地区贸易投资环境	region's trade and investment environment
区域贸易和投资自由化	regional trade and investment liberalization
摆脱亚洲金融危机影响	to shake off the impact of the financial crisis
跨境贸易人民币结算	settling cross-border trade accounts in RMB
深化经贸合作	to forge closer cooperative ties in economy and trade
经贸合作平稳发展	stable development of the cooperation of trade and economy
反对贸易保护主义	to combat trade protectionism
贸易关系新亮点	a new highlight of the trade relations
恢复贸易平衡	to restore the balance of trade
欧洲联盟条约	treaty on European Union
贸易代表团	trade mission
投资贸易研讨会	investment and trade forum (or symposium)

贸易,商业,房地产,经济
Trade, Business, Real Estate and Economy

对外贸易值	value of foreign trade
国际贸易值	value of international trade
进口配额制	import quotas
增值服务	value-added services
文化贸易	cultural trade
等价贸易	trade of equal value
贸易顺差	trade surplus
促进贸易	to step up trade
补偿贸易	to compensate trade
抵偿贸易	compensatory trade
往返贸易	to counter trade
购货合同	purchasing contract
贸易减让	trade concession
贸易平衡发展	balanced growth of trade
单方贸易制裁	unilateral trade sanctions
累计实现顺差	to accumulatively realize trade surplus
对外贸易类型	varieties of international trade
加工贸易转型升级	transformation and upgrading of processing trade
备忘录贸易	memorandum trade
竞价投标	competitive bidding
平等协商	consultations on equal terms
标准固定汇率	standard fixed rate
贸易摩擦	trade frictions
贸易壁垒	trade barriers
贸易争端	trade dispute
进口壁垒	import barrier
进口补贴	import subsidy
进口检疫	import quarantine
进境检测	goods entered for testing
维修货物	maintaining goods
增值税	value-added tax
进口税	import duties
进口限额	import quota
进口配额	an import quota
出口配额	an export quota
国际采购	international purchase
国际分销	international allocation
国际配送	international distribution
国际中转	international transit
双边贸易总额	bilateral trade volume
进口环节税	import linkage tax
调整出口退税	adjustment in the level of export tax rebates
海关监管货物	goods under Customs supervision
地区外贸公司	regional foreign trade corporation
星球电子公司	Star Electronics
中国电子进出口公司	China Electronics Import and Export Corporation
中国工艺品进出口公司	China National Arts and Crafts Import and Export Corporation
中国粮油进出口公司	China National Cereals Oils and Foodstuffs Import-export Corporation
中国机械进出口公司	China National Machinery Import and Export Corporation
中国五金矿产进出口公司	China National Metals and Minerals Import and Export Corporation
中国土产畜产进出口公司	China National Native Production and Animal Byproducts Import and Export

Corporation
中国纺织品进出口公司
China National Textiles Import and Export Corporation
中国茶叶进出口公司
China Tea Import and Export Corporation
中国出口商品交易会
China Export Commodities Fair
贸易和投资保护主义
trade and investment protectionism
自由贸易区战略　FTA strategy
中国上海自由贸易试验区
China（Shanghai）Pilot Free Trade Zone

2. 商业类（Business）

商业部	Mininistry of Commerce
商检局	bureau of commodity inspection
商业区	business quarter
商务处	trade representative's office
商业网	commercial network
电子商务	e-commerce
商品贸易	merchandise trade
商务参赞	commercial counselor
商务代表	commercial representative
商务秘书	commercial secretary
商务专员	commercial attaché
商用卫星	commercial satellite
商品检验局	the commodity inspection bureau
商业局	business bureau
商业销售	business sales
商品倾销	commodity dumping
商品进口	commodity import
商品出口	commodity export
商品价格	commodity price
商品交换	goods exchange
商品流通	commodity circulation
商品质量	commodity quality
商业网络	business network
商品港口税	port duties of commodity
商品印花税	stamp duty of commodity
国际市场价格	international market price
国内市场价格	domestic market price
商品期货价格	forward price of goods
商品现货价格	spot price of goods
商品现行价格	current price of goods
商品进口许可证	import licence of commodity
商品出口许可证	export licence of commodity
成本加运费价	cost & freightcost
商品含佣价	commodity price including commission
商品到岸价	cost, insurance and freight of commodity
商品批发价	wholesale price of commodity
商品零售价	retail price of commodity
商品净价	net price of commodity
商品离岸价	commodity free on board（FOB）
商品码头价	wharfage of commpdity
商品运输费	goods freight
商品折扣费	discount of commodity
商品报关税	customs duty of goods
商品报关	clerarance of goods
商品交货	delivery of goods

贸易，商业，房地产，经济
Trade, Business, Real Estate and Economy

交货时间	time of delivery	批发商	distributor
商品收货人	consignee of goods	进口商	importer
商品目录	goods catalogue	出口商	exporter
商品封样	sealed sample of commodity	招商	to invite outside investment
商品复样	duplicate sample of commodity	商标	trademark
商品规格	goods specification	商埠	commercial port
商品标准	standard type of commodity	商场	bazaar
商品样品	commodity sample	商船	merchant ship
商品商检	commodity inspection	商队	trade caravan
对等样品	counter sample	商兑	to consult and consider / discuss and deliberate
参考样品	reference sample		
花色搭配	color assortment	商法	commercial law
商业索赔	business claim	商贩	small retailer
商品争端	dispute for commodity	商港	commercial port
商品仲裁	arbitration for commodity	商贸	business and trade
商品净重	net weight of goods	商界	business circles
商品毛重	gross weight of goods	商检	commodity inspection
商品订单	goods order	商会	chamber of commerce
商品订购	commodity booking	商洽	to arrange with sb.
购货合同	purchasing contract	商情	market conditions
销售合同	sales contract	商人	businessman / merchant / trader
商务洽谈	business discussion	商亭	stall / kiosk
交易磋商	business negotiation	商务	commercial affairs
商品条码	bar code	商号	shop / store
市场调节价	market regulating price	商行	trading company / commercial firm
指示性价格	indicative price	商栈	caravansary / inn
原样商品	original sample of commodity	商誉	goodwill
代表性样品	representative sample	商务交易法	law of commercial transactions
大路货商品	fair average quality of goods		
产地证明书	certificate of origin	商业信贷	commercial credit
订货确任书	purchasing confirmation	商业周期	business cycle
销售确任书	sales confirmation	商业银行	commercial bank
市场化手段	market policies	商业中心	commercial centre
市场业绩	market value	商业资本	commercial capital
代理商	agent	商品交易会	trade fair

商品经济	commodity economy	名优产品	famous-brand high-quality products
商品流通	commodity circulation		
商品生产	commodity production	无形产品	intangible commodities
商标注册	trademark registration	拳头产品	core products / blockbuster
商品住宅	commercial residential building	次货商品	substandard goods
		存货商品	stock goods
商业计划书	report of business plan	畅销商品	best-selling goods
商业在线服务	commercial online service	在线商品	goods online
营商环境	conditions of doing business	呆滞商品	slow-selling goods
商业软件	commercial software	处理商品	shopworn goods
商标法	trademark law	代用商品	substituted goods
商标权	trademark rights	高档商品	high-priced goods
商品房	commercial housing	在家购物	home shopping
商品化	commercialization	在线顾客	customer online
商品粮	commodity grain	在线服务	online service
投机商	profiteer	特价	special price
盲目投资	haphazard investment	报价	quotation
服务营销	services and marketing	比价	comparative price
营销经理	marketing executives	差价	price gap
营销部门	marketing departments	出价	to bid price
营业周期	business period	单价	unit price
高层管理	top management	底价	upset price
公私合营	joint state-private ownership	调价	to readjust price
市场份额	market share	跌价	to fall in price
城镇市场	town markets	标价	to price
马路市场	roadside stand	官价	official price
叫卖商贩	peddlers	还价	counter-offer / counter-bid
新产品发布	to release new products	基价	basic price
联营商店 / 连销商店	chain stores	加价	to hike
商品销售市场	outlet for goods	开价	to price
适销对路产品	marketable products	降价	to reduce price
季节性商品	seasonal commodity	净价	net price
进口商品	imported goods	毛价	gross price
出口商品	exported goods	牌价	to list price
非卖商品	commodity not for sale	要价	to charge

贸易, 商业, 房地产, 经济
Trade, Business, Real Estate and Economy

议价	to negotiate price	地区差价	price difference of regions
原价	the original price	二道贩子	middleman
涨价	to increase/ raise price	便宜无好货	cheap buyer takes bad meat
折价	to evaluate in terms of money	现代物流	current logistics
折扣	to discount	物流中心	logistics center
促销	sales promotion	促销活动	promotional campaigns
外卖	take-out	独家代理	exclusive (or sole) agency
最低价	bottom price	独家经营	sole management
优惠价	preferential price	专营权	exclusive right
批发价	wholesale price	独立承包商	independent contractors
黑市价	black market price	无线电子商务	wireless electronic commerce
出厂价	factory price		
零售价	retailing price	在线商品价格	goods' price online
附加价格	additional price	在线售后服务	online after-sales service
垄断价格	to monopoly price	在线销售渠道	sale place online
可行价格	workable price	电子商务网站	EC website
内定价格	administrative price	厂家特价直销	deal direct with manufacturer
现货价格	spot price		
现行价格	current price	稳定消费预期	to ensure consumer confidence
浮动价格	to slide scale price / the floating price		
		扩大即期消费	to expand immediate consumption
价格波动	price fluctuation		
价格标签	price tag	市场需求不旺	a feeble demand at the market
价格管理	price control		
价格目录	price card	不少支出增长	many increases in expenditure
价格平衡	price equilibrium		
价格体系	price system	人民币汇率	RMB exchange
价格条款	price term	平均价格	average price
价格紊乱	price confusion	平抑物价	to stabilize commodity price
价格稳定	price steadiness	期货物价	forward price
价格政策	price policy	起步价	flag fall
价格制定	price setting	市场价	market price
统一价格	uniform price	市价表	current price
国家定价	fixed price by government	讨价还价	to bargain
国家指导价	directive price by government	八折优惠	20% off

今日特价	daily special	连锁店	chain stores
市场调研	marketing research	零售店	retail stores
市场共享	market pooling	赊买	to buy on credit
市场繁荣	The markek is brisk (or prosperous).	到岸价	Cost, Insurance and Freight (CIF)
市场行情	market quotation	离岸价	Free on Board (FOB)
市场业务	market functions	信用证	Letter of Credit (L/C)
市场机制	market mechanism	提单	Bill of Lading (B/L)
市场定位	market positioning	付款交单	Documents against Payment (D/P)
市场准入	market access		
市场竟争	market competition	凭单付款	Cash against Documents
市场占有率	market share	中等品	Fair Average Quality (FAQ)
市场营销	marketing	普惠制	Generalized System of Preference (GSP)
市场营销业	marketing profession		
公平交易	arm's-length transaction	预抵期	estimated time of arrival (ETA)
质量三包	3-R guarantee in quality	销售合同	sales contract (S/C)
中间商	middlemen	销售确认书	sales confirmation (S/C)
销售预测	sales projections	增值税	value-added tax (V.A.T./VAT)
直销/人员销售	personnel selling	无商业价值	no commercial value (N.C.V.)
补偿供货商	to reimburse the providers		
贷方传票	a credit slip	杂货	general cargo (G.C)
服务收费	a service charge	货代	freight forwarder
商业中间人	commercial middlemen	货方	credit (CR)
个体工商户	private industrial and commercial household / provitely-owned industrial and commercial household	附件	enclosure (ENC)
		保险费	premium (PREM)
		交易	transaction
		承兑	accept (ACPT)
营业机构	business organization	收讫	receive (RCVD)
猎头公司	head hunter	取样	sampling (SMPLG)
商品代码	commodity code	短缺额	shortage (SHTG)
品牌创立	innovative development of highly competitive products	商品/货物	merchandise (MDSE)
		利率	rate of interest
分销渠道	distribution channel	互利共赢	mutual benefits and win-win outcomes
交叉销售	cross sale		
收银台	check-out	极大的互补性	highly complementary

	nature	期货	forward
消费水平	consumption levels	海运保险单	marine insurance policy
热点消费	consumption in areas of high consumer interest	净利润	net profit
		预约保险单	open policy
劳动力成本低	low labor costs	货主负担风险	owner's risk
市场广阔	a huge market	风险投资者	venture capitalist
资金短缺	lack capital funding	核心竞争力	core competitiveness
资本充足	abundant capital fund	打造自主品牌	to create Chinese brands
产权过户/转让	transfer of ownership	仓储市超市	warehouse store
平等协商	consultation on equal terms	紧俏商品	commodities in short supply
资产重组	assets organization	市场营销活动	market sales campaign
楼上公司	upstairs firms	直接交易市场	over-the-counter market
皮包公司	bogus company	治理商业贿赂	to combat business bribery
佣金代理	commission agent	反倾销措施	anti-dumping measures
当时报价	prevailing quotations	综合运营成本	comprehensive operating costs
付款方式	terms of payment		
发货付款	cash on shipment	服务提供商	service provider
货币政策	monetary policy	多语言服务提供商	multi-language vendor
差别价政策	policy of differential pricing		
打通关政策	national project to facilitate customs clearance	单语言服务提供商	single language vendor
		制售假冒伪劣商品	to manufacture and sell the counterfeit or shoddy goods
货币	currency（CUR）		
汇票	draft		
汇款单	money order		
订货付款	cash with order	销售点信息系统	information system at sale point
支票汇款	remittance by check		
汇票汇款	remittance by draft	消费者之间的交易	deal between C to C
电报汇款	remittance by cable (or telegraph)	以市场为导向	to follow the guidance of the market
交货前付款	cash before delivery	咨询服务业	consulting service industry
交货付款	cash on delivery	服务方项目	vendor project
预付现金	cash in advance	服务方联系人	vendor contact
交货期	delivery date	客户方项目	client project
交货单	delivery order	客户方联系人	client contact
运费单	freight bill	提供商	provider

服务方	vendor
展览业	convention and exhibition industry
快餐业	fast food industry
采购商	buyer
供采机制	supply and purchase system
议定书/备忘录	protocol
大额交易	block trades
采购全球化	globalization of procurement
现货供应	supply from stock
检验费	inspection fee
一般条款	general terms and conditions
基本条款	basic terms and conditions
展览馆	exhibition center
参展商	exhibitor
新品发布会	conference on release of new products
产品战略	product strategy
限价商品房	commercial housing with price ceilings
试点展会	pilot trade fairs
海峡展	exhibition relating the theme of "Taiwan Strait"
撤展	to dismantle the stand
布展	to set up the stand
展位	stand
广交会	Conton Fair
车展	auto show
招标	invitation for bids
投标	to submit a tender / enter a bid
成交	to conclude business
交货期	delivery date
采购	procurement
订购	to place an order for
让利	to surrender part of the profits
南南合作	South-South partnership
种种风险	all kinds of risks
可支配收入	disposable incomes
百强IT公司排行榜	a list of the top 100 IT companies worldwide
金光大道会展中心	Costal Strip Exhibition and Conference Center
全球消费趋势	global consumption trend
市场潜力巨大	vast market potential
个人所得税起征点	the threshold for personal income tax
刺激消费者需求	to work up consumers demand
扩大投资支出	to boost investment spending
嘉年华	carnival
规范市场秩序	to maintain market order
大陆市场	mainland market
售后服务	after-sale service / after service
民间投资	private investment
民间财富	wealth in the private sector
民间力量	private capacity
资本外逃	capital flight
追求利润	go after profit
牟取暴利	to make exorbitant profits
平等互利	equality and mutual benefits
信贷价值	credit-worthiness
经纪人	broker
佣金	commission
消费品	consumer products
便利品	convenience goods

保健食品	health food	互动营销	interactive marketing
营业税	turnover tax	电子商务	electronic business
商品倾销	the goods dumping	电子商城	virtual electronic commerce city
企业经营	business venture	电子零售	B to C
恢复营业	to resume operation	电子钱包	E-wallet
赢得市场	to gain a larger share of the market	电子分销	E-distribution
最大客户	largest customer	电子货币	electronic money
用户界面	user interface	电子现金	E-cash
用户帮助	user assistance	电子消费者	E-consumer
服务角色	role of service	电子出版商	E-publishing merchant
服务要素	element of service	电子收款机	electronic cash register
服务流程	process of service	电子资金转账	electronic fund transfer
服务种类	types of service	电子商务网站促销	promotion by E-commerce website
现场服务	onsite service	跨境电子商务	cross-border e-commerce
记账服务	to account services	电子交易市场	E-marketplace
互通有无	to buy and exchange each other' goods and services	电子购物中心	electronic mall
采购协定	an agreement concerning procurement	电子订货系统	electronic ordering system
销售战略	merchandising strategies	电子公告栏	bulletin board system
客户服务端	client server	电子操纵系统	electronic operating system
个性化营销	personalized marketing		

3. 房地产（Real Estate）

房地产公司	real estate company	筒子楼	the tube-shaped apartment
房产中介	real estate agent	公租房	public-rental housing
闲置地产	vacant property	廉租房	low-cost rental housing
商业地产	commercial property	保障房	government-subsidized housing
住宅地产	residential property	囤房捂盘	the price maintenance in real estate
增值地价	added-value fees	首套房贷款	loans for first time homebuyers
购房契税	property deed tax	集资房	houses built with the funds collected from the buyers
便利设施	amenities		
按揭购房	to buy a house on mortgage		
按揭贷款	mortgage loan		

民心工程	the project in the public interest / pro-people project	楼市调控措施	measures to rein in property prices
房地产市场	real estate market	楼层建筑面积	floor space
房地产经纪人	estate agent / house agent / realtor	房地产开发区	real estate zones for development
房地产泡沫	real estate bubble	主体功能区	priority development zones
住房公积金	housing provident funds		
共有产权住房	joint-ownership housing units	地段等级	location classification
		棚户区改造	to rebuild shanty areas
中小套型商品房	small and medium-sized commercial housing	旧区改造	reconstruction of old areas
		农村危房	rural houses that are ready to collapse / unsafe houses
房屋市场指数	housing index	商品房	commercial residential building / commercial housing
住房空置率	housing vacancy rate		
住房保障制度	housing security system	绿色产房	green delivery room
违法征地拆迁	illegal land expropriations and housing demolitions	经济公寓	tenement
		房屋拆迁	housing demolition and relocation
新建住房价格	price for new residential properties	稳住房价	to stabilize housing price stability
保障性住房房源	resources of affordable housing	中小套型商品房	small and medium-sized commodity housing
保障性住房管理	management of affordable housing		
		两房一厅	two bedrooms and one living-room
房地产市场过热	overheated property sector	公共租赁住房	public rental housing
房地产市场平稳	a stable and healthy real estate market	第二套住房	to buy or to have the second-home
居民住房支付能力	housing payment capacity of local residents	购买自住房	to purchase home
		政策性住房	policy-related house
转让住房营业税	property transaction taxes	改善性住房	to make home improvement
		商住综合楼	commercial & residential complex
房地产开发项目	residential property projects	经济适用房	affordable housing
住房信贷政策	housing credit policies	普通购房者	private home buyer

保障性住房	low-income housing	群租房	group-rented house
自主性住房	owner-occupied houses	学区房	school nearby house
小产权房	house / apartment with limited property rights	过渡房	starter home
住房限购	home purchase restriction	限价房	price-capped housing
住房用地供给	residential land supply	棚改房	housing in run-down areas that will undergo renovation
土地有效供应	effective land supply	三限房	three-restricts' housing
胶囊公寓	capsule apartment	村证房	village-certificated house
土地使用证	certificate for land use	二手房	second-hand house
观望态度	wait-and-watch attitude	房魔	the housing devil
房产交易	property transactions	房产	house property
分期付款	payment by installment	房主	house-owner
维修费	allowances for repairs and maintains	房租	rent (for a house or a room or flat)
售后回租	leaseback	期房	forward delivery housing
土地增值税	land value-added tax	首付	down payment
印花税	property stamp duty	房价	housing price
折旧税	depreciation allowances	囤地	land reserves
物业税	property tax	房基	foundations of a building (or a house)
钉子户	nail households	板楼	slab-type apartment building
炒房者	real estate speculator	塔楼	tower building
房产证	property ownership certificate	现房	complete apartment
停车位	parking space	地王	land king
宅地基	foundation of a house / the site of a house	房东	owner and lessor of a house
		房荒	housing shortage

4. 经济类 (Economy)

严峻的国际经济环境
a grim economic environment worldwide
新兴经济体　emerging economies
开放型经济　an open economy
综合经济实力　comprehensive economic strength
联合国千年发展目标
United Nations' Millennium Goal of Development
中国经济与国际接轨
to bring China's economy more in line with international practice
巴俄印中南经济体　BRICS economic system
保持经济适度快速增长
to maintain an appropriate rapid economic

growth

充满活力的社会主义市场经济
robust socialist market economy

推进社会主义经济建设
to promote socialist economic development

抢占经济科技制高点
to capture the economic, scientific and technological high ground

推动经济进入创新驱动
to put economic development onto the track of endogenous growth driven by innovation

经济社会发展的后劲
to sustain economic and social development

经济增长由偏快转为过热
rapid ecohomic growth becoming overheated

两国经济具有极大的互补性
highly complementary nature of the two economies

中国经济可能硬着陆
China's economy would have a "hard landing"

国内外经济发展的相互关系
mutual interconnectedness of domestic and international economic development

实行积极的财政政策
to implement the proactive fiscal policy

省级经济开发区
provincial-level economic and technological development zones

新型的高科技开发区
new high-tech development zones

切实转入科学发展轨道
to truly put development on a scientific track

实实在在的经济利益
to produce tangible economic benefits

周边地区经济繁荣
economic well-being of their surrounding areas

东部地区经济实力
economic strength in the eastern region

经济体良性互动　a sound interaction of economies

经济稳中向好　to sustain steady economic growth

跌宕的经济形势　economic fluctuations

经济合理区间　economy within proper range

经济持续下行　economic growth rate continued to decline

防膨胀的下限　Inflation does not the above projected level.

世界经济增长　globle economic growth

经济发展模式　economic development model

经济一体化　economic integration

新的经济格局　a new pattern of economy

海洋经济　marine economy

经济核算　economic accounting

经济实体　economic entity

经济命脉　economic lifeline / economic arteries

专属经济区　exclusive economic zone

参与全球经济　to enter the global economy

墓产经济　funeral-related economy

润滑经济　lubricating economy

她经济　she-economy

大肚子经济	pregnancy-oriented economy
经济联合体	economic association
两大经济实体	two hugely important economies
网络经济学家	web-economist
计划体系	planned system
经济杠杆	economic lever
高科技经济的转型	transition to a high-tech economy
激发经济内在活力	to stimulate the internal vitality of the economy
涉外经济体制	regulatory mechanism governing external economic relations
经济技术转让	economy-technology transfer
优化经济结构	to optimize the economic structure
新的经济增长点	new growth areas in the economy
经济资源的分配	allocation of financial resources
扩大经济范围	expansion of operations
港澳经济发展	economic growth of Hong Kong and Macao
增长经济后劲	to sustain China's economic development
经济相互依从	economic interdependence
经济互利合作	mutually beneficial economic cooperation
经济开放区	open economic region
经济环境	economic environment
经济特区	special economic zones
国民经济	national economy
国家收支	balance of state payments
太空经济	aerospace economy
网络经济	network economy
特色经济	economic activities with local characteristics
知识经济	knowledge-based economy
恢复经济	to achieve economic recovery
经济强省	economically strong province
循环经济	circular economy
经济运行	be in the operation of the economy
经济推动力	economic growth engine
经济互补	economically complementary
经济量大	a large economic size
资本充足	abundant capital funds
规模经济	economies of scale
稀缺经济	scarcity economy
经济扩张	economic expansion
经济整合	economic integration
经济危机	economic crisis
经济恐慌	economic crisis
经济萧条	economic depression
经济杂交	commercial crossbreeding
经济制裁	economic sanctions
经济秩序	economic order
经济主义	economism
经济法规	laws and regulations pertaining to the economy / economic statutes
经济复苏	economic resurgence
经济制度	economic system
经济效益	economic performance (or economic effectiveness / benefits)
外向型经济	outward-looking economy

开放型经济水平	open economy level
多种产业经济	multi-industrial economy
多种农业经营	diversified economy in agriculture
发展集体经济	to develop collective economy
繁荣市场经济	to flourish the market economy
非公有制经济	non-public sector of the economy
文化经济政策	policies pertaining to the cultural economy
高度集中的计划经济	highly centralized planned economy
经济增长的环境资源	environmental resources of the economic growth
促进经济可持续发展	to promote sustainable economic development
抵抗全球经济衰退	to combat the global economic slump
调控宏观经济运行	to regulate operation of the maroeconomy
理顺和规范经济关系	to rationalize and regulate various economic relations
完善经济法律体系	optimize the economic legal system
投资结构和经济结构	investment and economy structures
个体经济,私营经济	self-employed and private business
各地区经济发展的客观需要	need of the economic development of different regions
国民经济可以承受的范围之内	within the limits of the national economic strength
复杂多变的国内外经济环境	complicated and volatile economic environment at home and abroad
坚持经济持续较快增长	to maintain a sustainable and comparatively rapid development
确保经济平稳快速发展	to ensure a steady and relatively fast growth of the economy
控制固定资产投资规模	to rein the excessive investment in fixed assets
对经济增长的拉动作用	to enhance the stimulative impact on the growth of the economy
经济结构的战略性调整	strategic economic restructuring
壮大县域经济	to expand county economies
宏观经济预期目标	macroeconomic targets
加快经济结构调整	to accelerate economic restructuring
经济欠发达地区	economically underdeveloped areas
拉动经济增长	to stimulate economic growth
提高经济效益	to improve economic returns
保持循环经济	to keep an eco-efficient economy

循环经济促进法	circular economy promotion law
循环经济试点法	pilot projects on circular economy
以经济建设为中心	to make economic development into our central task
深化经济体制改革	to deepen economic structural reform
中国新的经济增长点	new growth point of China's economy
世界经济衰退	the world economic downturn
CPI 的增长幅度	rise of the CPI
外部经济风险	external economic risks
经济回升向好	economic upturn
国内经济运行	domestic economic growth
世界经济复苏	global economic recovery
经济发展模式	economic development model
防止经济过热	to prevent an overheated economy
防止泡沫经济	to avoid a bubble economy / too many bubbles in economy
过渡型经济体	transition economies
经济实力大幅提升	economic strength increased substantially
保持经济平稳发展	to maintain steady economic development
保持经济较快发展	to maintain rapid economic development
做大经济"蛋糕"	to make the economic pie bigger
实实在在的经济利益	tangible economic benefits
私人非盈利活动	private non-profit activities
团体非盈利活动	group non-profit activities
调控的预见性	more proactive of macro control
调控的针对性	targeted macro control
调控的有效性	effective macro control
出口大幅度减少	exports substantially decreased
扩大内需	to expand the domestic market
保持增长	to sustain economic growth
控制物价	control price
资产负债表	balance sheet
量化货币宽松政策	quantitative easing monetary policy
损益表	statement of income and expenses
所得税负债	income tax liabilities
国家预算	state budget
国家收入	national income
国有资产	state-owned assets
流动资产	current assets
固定资产	fixed assets
宏观调控	macro control
易变现资产	liquid assets
产业核心竞争力	core competitiveness of industries
产业升级	to upgrade industries
统筹	package
存货	inventories / stock
应收款项	receivables
假币	counterfeit money
折旧	depreciation

抵押　mortgage
净值　net worth
账面价值　book value
额外费　surcharge
交货　delivery
附加税　surtax
超市　supermarket
成本加运费　cost and freight
现金折扣　cash discount
成本加保险费　cost and insurance
国民生产总值　（GNP）gross national product
国内生产总值　（GDP）gross domestic product
外商投资　foreign investment
市场潜力巨大　vast market potential
劳动力成本高　high costs of labor
销售战略　merchandising strategies
最大客户　best customer
获益匪浅　great benefits
很大的互补性　great complementarity
互通有无　to buy and exchange each other's goods and services
融资难　financing hurdles
再贷款　re-lending subloan
开放式基金　open-ended fund
流动资金　current capital
国际市场　international market
借贷市场　borrowing and loan market
亚洲金融危机　Asian economic crisis
市场渗透力　market penetration
降低成本　cost reduction
民间资本参股　private capital to invest in or hold shares
外国投资高潮　wave of foreign investment
汇率浮动区间　exchange rate floating range
东亚四小龙　four small dragons of East Asia
全球竞争力　global competitiveness
指导性贷款　directed credit
通货膨胀　inflation
低通货膨胀率　low inflation rate
控制通货膨胀　to control inflation
浮动汇率制　floating exchange rates
联系汇率　linked（or pegged）exchange rate
良好的投资环境　a sound investment environment
开展卓有成效的合作　to forge effective collaboration
电子商务博览会　E-Cmmerce Fair
国际产业转移　international industrial transfer
生产要素流动　flow of production factors
国际能源市场　global energy market
多哈回合谈判　Doha Round
南北对话　North-South dialogue
资金援助　financial assistance
减免债务　debt relief
优惠货款　concessional loans
有效的财政调控　effective fiscal control
经济持续快速增长　sustained rapid growth for economy
提升开放型经济水平　to make improvements to China's open economy
多种所有制经济共同发展　common development of economic

entities under diverse forms of ownership
整体经济（宏观经济） macroeconomic
个体经济（微观经济） microeconomic
财政和货币政策体系 fiscal and monetary policy frameworks
金融服务实体经济 Financial services to the real economy.
国际收支不平衡 global payments imbalances
经营范围 scope of business
价格刚性 price rigidity
经济型汽车 econobox
经济圈 economic rims
经济带 economic belts
经济衰退 recession / economic downturn
经济动荡 economic turmoil
经济扩张 economic expansion
经济互补 economically complementary
经济相互依从 economic interdependence
经济互利合作 mutually beneficial economic cooperation
经济转型 to transform the economic areas
经济增长极 poles of economic growth
经济低迷 economic downturn
经济前景 economic outlook
经济指标 economic indications
经济市场化 economic marketization
经济法制化 to manage the economic affairs according to laws
宏观经济管理 macroeconomic management
财政增收节支 to increase fiscal revenue and cut public spending
整顿市场经济 to regulate the market economy
规范市场经济 to standardize the market economy
自主经营经济 economic entities operating independently
扭住经济建设 to keep economic development
经济承包责任制 an economic contract responsibility system / system of contracted responsibility in economy
经济互助委员会 council of mutual economic assistance
经济技术开发区 economic and technological development zone
欧洲经济一体化 economic integration of Europe
丝绸之路经济带 a Silk Road economic belt
长三角地区经济一体化 economic integration in the Yangtze River Delta
泛珠三角区域经济合作 economic cooperation in the Pan-Pearl River Delta
环渤海及京津冀地区经济协作 to further coordinate economic development in the Bohai Rim region and the Beijing-Tianjin-Hebei regions
长江经济带 an economic development belt along the Yangtze River
区域经济增长极 new regional economic growth poles

区域经济支撑带	regional economic mainstay belts
孟中印缅经济走廊	Bangladesh-China-India-Myanmar Economic Corridor
中巴经济走廊	China-Pakestan Economic Corridor
经济联合体	an economic association
经济成分	a sector of the economy
经济合同	an economic contract
经济单位	a business accounting unit / the economic accounting units
经济基础	an economic base
经济昆虫	economic insects
经济立法	an economic legislation
经济林	an economic forest
经济模式	an economic mould
经济实体	an economic entity
经济效益	economic benefit / economic performance
经济援助	an economic aid
经济植物	economic plants
经济作物	an industrial crop / cash crop
计划经济	planned economy
外向型经济	export-oriented economy
欧洲共同体	European Community (EC)
欧洲经济区	European Economic Area (EEA)
经济业务	business transactions
经济全球化	economic globalization
经济改革	economic reform
经济活力	dynamism of the economy
经济控制力	leverage of the economy
经济影响力	influence of the economy
经济事务	economic matters
民营经济	private economy
民营企业	private enterprises
裙带经济	crony economy
主体经济	mainstay economy
虚拟经济	virtual economy
实体经济	a real economy
集体经济	collective economy
合作经济	cooperative economy
低碳经济	low-carbon economy
货币投资	investing money
资本充足	abundant capital funds
资金短缺	to lack capital funding
境外投资	to invest abroad
利用外资	to utilize foreign capital
中国外汇储备	China's foreign exchange reserve
主要经济指标	a main economic index
乌拉圭回合谈判	Uruguay Round Negotiations
中央经济工作会议	Central Economic Conference
中非合作论坛	Forum on China-Africa Cooperation
中非经济技术合作	China-Africa economic and technological cooperation
国际竞争与合作	international cooperation and competition
经济和金融突发事件	economic and financial eventualities
经济运行中突出问题	glaring problem in the economic operation
有条件的国内企业	qualified Chinese enterprises
交流经济情况	to share one's economic

| 贸易,商业,房地产,经济 |
| Trade, Business, Real Estate and Economy |

	development
交流经济政策	to exchange one's views on economic policy issues
宏观经济政策	a macro-economic policy
关税歧视	tariff discrimination
关税壁垒	tariff barriers
回合谈判	round of negotiation
专利	patents
国际支付转账	international transfer of payments
收支基本平衡	basic balance in payments
现代优惠待遇	preferences in force
优惠的幅度	margins of preference
关税同盟	customs union
亚太经济合作组织	Asia-Pacific Economic Cooperation (APEC)
地区经济合作组织	regional economic integration
《财富》500强	FORTUNJE 500
博鳌亚洲论坛	Boao Forum for Asia
国际商会	International Chamber of Commerce
世界商业组织	the world business organization
七国集团	Group of Seven (G-7)
亚太经济体	Asia Pacific economies
东南亚国家联盟	Association of Southeast Asian Nations
加勒比共同市场	Caribbean Community and Common Market
石油输出国组织	Organization of Petroleum Exporting Countries (OPEC)
经合组织	Organization for Economic Cooperation and Development
美元的坚挺	strong dollar
共同繁荣	common prosperity
次区域经济合作	Subregion Economic Cooperation Program
区域经济发展	regional and economical development
人与自然和谐发展	to keep human society and nature in harmony
经济形式多样性	various forms in economy
两元经济结构	urban-rural dual economy
统筹城乡发展	to achieve balanced development in rural and urban areas
开放包容的区域合作	open and inclusive regional cooperation
区域经济一体化	economic integration in the region
国际经济技术合作	international economic and technological cooperation
各国经济互利合作	mutual beneficial cooperation among various economies
经济增长的质量	quality of the economic growth
转变经济增长方式	to change the mode of economic growth
大力发展循环经济	to do a good job of developing circular economy
混合所有制经济	economic sector of mixed ownership
优化经济资源配置	to optimize the allocation of

067

涉外经济管理体系	foreign economic management system
经济更加发展	a more developed economy
经济良性互动	sound interactions of economy
以经济建设为中心	focus on economic development
推动经济全面发展	to economically achieve an all-round progress
防止国有资产流失	to prevent the loss (devaluation) of State assets
无缝区域经济	seamless regional economy
巩固合作成果	to consolidate cooperation achievements
提高合作水平	to raise cooperation levels
南北经济走廊	to transport links along the South-North
公私联营	public-private partnership
人民币汇率	RMB exchange rate
经济总量大	a large economic size

经济法制化
to manage economic affairs according to law / to put economic operation on a legal basis

经济发展全球化
globalization in economic development

经济市场化与私有化
marketization and privatization of the economy

经济发展新的推动力
a new engine of the economic growth

经济增长内生动力	internal force of the economic growth
经济发展良好势头	a good momentum of economic growth
给经济注入新活力	to give new impetus to economic growth
主要发达经济体	major developed economies
新兴市场经济体	an emerging market economies
宏观经济政策协调	macro-economic policy coordination

科技和经济紧密结合
to closely link science and technology with economic growth

科技创新和新兴产业发展
to foster innovation and emerging industries

经济的强劲内生动力
a strong home-grown driving force for growth

经济发展稳中有进	to make progress in economic growth
经济外部风险	the external risks of economy
使经济信息化	to informationize the economy
经济体制改革	a economic restructuring
全球经济增长	global economic growth
经济7%的增速	a 7% annual growth of economy
经济总体平衡	to be generally smooth in economy
靠消费需求拉动	to increase dependence

	on consumption
经济增长质量	quality of economic growth
经济增长效益	efficiency of economic growth
经济全球化趋势	trend of the economic globalization
发展中经济体	developing economies
亚太经济体	economies in the Asia Pacific
经济发展创新	innovative development of economy
经济发展联动	interconnected growth of economy
经济利益融合	converging interests of economy
经济的硬着陆	a hard landing of economy
经济的软着陆	a soft landing of economy
经济基本面	economic fundamentals
统筹推动经济	to press ahead with reforms in economic field
经济起飞	an economic takeoff
经济兴旺	an economic boom
经济萎缩	an economic depression (slump/recession)
经济转轨	a switch to a market economy
资源的高效	efficiency of resources
资源的开发	exploitation of resources
资源的节约	conservation of resources
再生能源回收和利用	recyclable use of renewable resources
节能技术服务体系	technical service system for more efficient use of energy
节能型交通运输工具	a new generation of energy-efficient means of transportation
能源结构以煤为主	predominant role of coal in our energy mix
资源环境约束	resources and environmental constraints
开发再生能源	to exploit renewable energy resources
资源有偿使用	compensation for use of resources
建设节能型社会	to build a energy-conscious society
建设资源节约型社会	to build a resource-efficient society
理顺能源价格体系	to base the energy pricing system on market supply and demand

4 金融, 融资, 货币
Finance, Financing and Currency

1. 金融 (Finance)

金融机构	banking institution
金融机关	financial institution
金融货币危机	financial and monetary crises
金融监管一体化	integration of financial regulations
局部性金融风波	local financial disturbance
金融中介机构	financial intermediary
金融衍生物	financial derivative
金融寡头	financial oligarch
金融界	financial circles
金融巨头	financial magnate / shark of finance
金融市场	money / financial market
金融工具	financial instrument
金融体系	financial system
金融体制	banking system
金融创新	financial innovation
金融监管	the financial regulation
金融改革	reform of the financial system
金融违纪	financial indiscipline
金融中心	financial / banking centre
金融资本	financial capital
金融资产	financial assets
金融媒介	financial intermediary
金融公司	finance company
金融危机	financial crisis
金融恐慌	financial panic
金融压抑	financial repression
金融风波	financial disturbance
金融脆弱	financial fragility
金融动荡	financial turbulence
金融诈骗	financial fraud
金融期货	financial future
金融兴旺	financial thriving
完善金融监督体制	to improve the financial regulation system
金融服务自由化	financial service liberalization
国际金融危机	global financial crisis
国际金融体系	international financial architecture
防范和化解金融风险	to guard against and defuse financial risks
金融机构贷款利率	loan interest rate of financial institutions
贷款利率7折下限	70 percent of the benchmark rate
防范金融风险能力	ability to guard against financial risks
金融市场波动	financial market fluctuation

金融，融资，货币
Finance, Financing and Currency

金融市场动荡	financial market volatility
整顿金融秩序	to rectify financial order
中小金融机构	middle and small financial institution
货币金融环境	monetary and financial environment
亚洲单一货币体制	Single Asian Currency
稳健的货币政策	prudent monetary policy
积极的财政政策	proactive fiscal policy
国际货币金融体系	international monetary and financial system
金融资产管理公司	financial asset management companies
构建组织多元金融体系	to develop a financial system featuring diverse organization
构建服务高效金融体系	to develop a financial system of efficient service
构建监管审慎金融体系	to develop a financial system of prudent supervision
构建风险可控金融体系	to develop a financial system of risk-control
金融保险业营业税	business tax for banking and insurance industries
互联网金融	Internet finance
结构性减税	selective tax cuts
低风险投资	a low risk investment
增值利益	value-added profits
财务总监	CFO
财务主管	financial executive
金融服务	financial services
双边贸易额	bilateral trade volume
分散投资	investing diversification
资本充足	abundant capital funds
资本净值	capital net worth
对冲基金	hedge-fund
数字现金	digital cash
财政赤字	budget deficit
阳光财政	transparency of public finance
地方财政收入	local fiscal revenues
单一共同货币	a single common currency
清算和结账程序	clearing and settlement procedures
游资	the idle money
理财	managing money
硬通货	hard money
美元价值	dollar value
商品货币	commodity money
信用货币	credit money
信用证结算	payment by L/C
民航发展基金	Civil Aviation Development Fund
非国有资本	non-state capital
多层次资本市场	a multilevel capital market
资本流动	capital flows
法定货币	fiat money
基准货币	basic money
本位币	standard money
人民币汇率	RMB exchanging rate
美元汇兑率	dollar-exchange standard
利率市场化	interest rate liberalization
税费改革	reform of taxes and charges
簿记制度	book keeping system
存款余额	bank balances

银行汇款	bank drafts	资金往来	capital exchange
配套资金	supporting funds	外汇储备	reserve of foreign currencies
建设资金	funds for construction	国际货币体系	international monetary system
资金短缺	shortage of funds		
资金外流	capital outflow	预算外资金	extrabudgetary funds
资本市场	capital market	涉农资金	funds for agricultural development
无形资产	intangible assets		
资产冻结	freezing of assets	国债资金	capital obtained from insurance of government bonds
资本货物	capital goods		
固定资产	fixed assets	资本充足率	capital adequacy
流动资产	liquid assets	流动资金	circulating funds
清点资产	to make an inventory of the assets	周转资金	operating funds / working fund / revolving fund
现金余额	cash balance	信用卡公司	credit-card company
长期贷款	a long-term loan	银行信用卡	bank credit cards
记账员	bookkeeper	旅游与娱乐信用卡	travel and entertainment cards
会计师	accountant		
版税收入	royalty income	识别码	identifying codes
应纳税收入	taxable income	分类账	ledgers
财政偿还能力	ability to serve debt	抵押贷款	mortgage
财政刺激政策	fiscal stimulus measures	不良贷款	non-performing loans
非常规货币政策	unconventional monetary policies	首付款	down / advance payment
		还债 / 消偿	to pay off
资产负债表	statement of assets and liabilities / balance sheet	按月分期付款	monthy installments
		转账 / 划拨	to transfer
财政收支基本平衡	to maintain a basic balance between revenue and expenditures	信托部	trust department
		志愿信托基金	voluntary trust funds
		信托公司	trust company
适当的财政赤字	to keep the deficit at appropriate level	人寿保险	life insurance
		受托机构	depository institutions
适当的国债规模	to keep the government bonds at appropriate level	单一亚洲货币	single Asian currency
		统一货币	a uniform currency
		存款保险制度	a deposit insurance system
拆迁补偿款	compensation for demolition		
财务报表	financial statement	银行存贷款利率	bank interest rates for

金融, 融资, 货币
Finance, Financing and Currency

	savings deposits and loans
免、抵、退税办法	tax exemption, deduction and rebate measures
银行体系流动性	liquidity in the banking system
国有独资商业银行	wholly state-funded commercial bank
国家银行	state bank
中国人民银行	People' Bank of China
中国银行	Bank of China
政策性银行	policy banks
中国工商银行	Industrial and Commercial Bank of China
中国人民建设银行	People's Construction Bank of China
中国农业银行	Agricultural Bank of China
交通银行	Communications Bank
中国招商银行	China Merchants Bank
汇丰银行	Hongkong and Shanghai Banking Corporation
花旗银行	CitiBank
非合作银行	single proprietorships and partnerships bank
中信银行	China Citic Bank
投资银行	investment bank
贸易银行	trading bank
信托银行	trust bank
兴业银行	Industrial Bank
代理银行	correspondent bank
储备银行	reserve bank
储蓄银行	savings bank
商业银行	commercial bank
建设银行	construction bank
中央银行	central bank
瑞丰银行	Ruifeng Bank
人民银行	Bank of People
农业银行	Agricultural Bank
股份银行	joint-stock bank
光大银行	China Everbright Bank
徽商银行	Huishang Bank
浙商银行	China Zheshang Bank
民生银行	China Minsheng Bank
结算银行	settling bank
道德银行	morality bank
亚洲银行	Asia Bank
大通银行	Chase Bank
实业银行	Industrial Bank
民营银行	Private Bank
地方银行	District Bank
国家银行	National Bank
世界银行	World Bank
联营银行	Associate Bank
开证银行	Issuing Bank / Open Bank
保证银行	Confirming Bank
美丰银行	American Oriental Banking Corporation
承兑银行	Bank of Acceptance
付款银行	Paying Bank
通知银行	Notifying Bank / Advising Bank
米兰银行	Midland Bank
省银行	Provincial Bank
信用社	credit union
中小银行	small and medium-sized banks
市场化银行	market-oriented banks
进出口银行	Export-Import Bank
出口代办行	export commission house

中小企业银行	Bank for Medium-scale Enterprises		Bank
邮政储蓄银行	Post Office Savings Bank	美国交通银行	American Express Communication Bank
广东发展银行	Guangdong Development Bank	美国进出口银行	Export-Import Bank of Washington
上海浦东发展银行	Shanghai Pudong Development Bank	美洲开发银行	Inter-American Development Bank
储蓄信贷银行	Savings and Trust Bank	信托投资银行	Trust Investment Bank
德累斯顿银行	Dresdner Bank A.G	国际经济合作银行	International Bank of Economic Cooperation
欧洲中央银行	European Central Bank		
亚洲开发银行	Asian Development Bank		
"免下车"银行	drive-in bank	银行承兑汇票	The Banker's Acceptance Bill
跨国银行分行	branches of multinational banks	国际货币基金	International Monetary Fund
泛美开发银行	Inter-American Development Bank	金融信托公司	Financial Trust Company
非洲开发银行	African Development Bank	外汇管理局	Foreign Exchange Control Bureau
国际结算银行	Bank for International Settlements	欧洲货币局	European Monetary Institute
		农业信用社	rural credit cooperative
世界开发银行	International Bank for Reconstructon and Development	银行每月结单	monthly statement
		银行票据贴现	bank discount
		银行手续费	bank handling charge
日本东京银行	Bank of Tokyo, Ltd.	银行信用卡	bank credit card
瑞士联合银行	United Bank of Switzerland	汇出汇款	outward remittance
		汇入汇款	inward remittance
国际投资银行	International Investment Bank	邮政汇票	postal money order
		定期汇票	time bill
恒信合作银行	Hengxin Cooperative Bank	远期支票	postdated check
		证券汇票	securities draft
加勒比开发银行	Caribbean Development Bank	银行汇票	bank draft
		支票存根	check stub
伊斯兰开发银行	Islamic Development Bank	转手支票	the third party check
		转账支出	transfer accounts to pay money
欧洲投资银行	European Investment	资金周转	financing

金融,融资,货币
Finance, Financing and Currency

自由现金	free cash	年利息	annual interest rate
作废支票	cancelled check	年息率	per annum interest rate
银行储备金	Bank Reserves	年息	yearly interest
城市信用社	urban credit cooperative	开户	to open an account
房地产贷款	real estate loans	存款	deposit
消费者贷款	consumer loans	进账	entry account
政策性亏损	policy mandated losses	面值	nominal value / par value / face value
账户已结清	account closed	面额	denomination
不良贷款	non-performing loan	结清	to close an account
信贷限额	a line credit	结算	to liquidate an account
逾期贷款	overdue loan	结汇	settlement of exchange
财税政策	the fiscal and tax policies	侨汇	overseas remittance
趋同标准	convergence criteria	汇兑	exchange
人民币资本项目	RMB capital account	支出	expense
地方收税政策	local charging policies	汇款	remittance
深化汇率改革	to deepen the reform of interest rate	收款	receipts
		汇票	exchange bill
人民币汇率弹性	flexible RMB exchange	汇费	remittance charge
银行利率	bank rate	退票	returned check
外汇管制	exchange control	筹贷	finance
外汇存款	foreign currency deposit	借方	debit
外汇利率	foreign exchange rate	贷方	credit
低利率	lower-interest rates	审计	audit
无记名支票	check without stating bearer's name	储户	depositor
		定金	down payment
同业往来	business relations within the same field	贷款	loan
		账号	account number
相对基金	counterpart fund	金库	treasury
美元区	dollar area	账本	books
汇款方式	remittance way / method	总账	general ledger
汇票票根	remittance stub	银行家	banker
汇票通知	remittance advice	借贷卡	debit cards
欧元区	Euro-currency area	无声卡	dumb cards
英镑区	the sterling area	智能卡	smart cards
纯利息	net interest	通用卡	all-purpose cards / general cards

现金代用品	a cash substitute	抵押贷款	mortgage loan
不固定利息	variable interest	存款到期	deposit maturity
转账/划拨	transfer	活期储蓄	demand savings
循环账户	revolving account	活期存单	demand-deposit slip
银行存款	bank account	活期存款	current deposit
储蓄存款	savings deposit	活期存折	demand passbook
储蓄存折	savings account book	活期贷款	demand loan
储蓄账户	savings account	银行信贷	bank loan
支票账户	checking account	信托存款	trust deposit
冻结账户	frozen account	信托资金	trust fund
定期存单	time certificate	信托贷款	load on credit
定期存款	fixed-time deposit	无息贷款	interest-free loan
信托存款	trust deposit	消费者贷款	consumer loans
消费贷款	consumptive loan	长期贷款	long-term loan
信用贷款	loan on credit	短期贷款	short-term loan
取款	withdraw money	信贷发放	credit supply
收款人	payee	夜间存款机	night deposit box
取款单	to withdraw slip	自动提款机	cash machine / ATM
存款簿	deposit passbook	银行经理/总裁	bank manager / bank president
存款单	deposit slip		
对账单	check bill / statement of account	银行高级职员	senior clerk of bank
保险柜	safe / strongbox	银行职员	bank clerk
保险箱	safty-deposit box	出纳员	teller
保险库	safe strong room	收银员	payee / cashier
提款机	cash dispenser	审核员	checker
通知存款	to call deposit	收账员	collector
同业存款	banker's deposit	付款联	sales slip
同业透支	banker's overdraft	支票	cheque
透支款项	overdraft money	开支票	to write a cheque
透支利息	interest on an overdraft	空白支票	blank cheque
存款收据	deposit receipt	空头支票	rubber cheque
存款转账	deposit transfer	保付支票	certified cheque
存款利率	deposit rate	转账支票	cheque for transfer
贷款利率	rate on loan	未兑现支票	outstanding cheque
贷款担保书	guarantee on loan	支票挂失	to report the loss of a cheque

金融，融资，货币
Finance, Financing and Currency

现金支票	cash cheque
旅行支票	traveller's cheque
个人用支票	personal cheque
付款通知	payment advice
法定利息	legal interest
银行储备金	bank reserve
保值储蓄	inflation-proof bank service
银行票据	bank money
付款条件到期	payment terms maturity
综合运用税收	to use a combination of a full range of tax
免除营业税	to exempt the business tax
税收减免政策	to reduce the business tax
综合运用信贷	to use a combination of a full range of credit

2. 融资（Financing）

企业融资成本	financing costs of enterprises
资金来源成本	costs of acquiring funds
资金拆借成本	costs of inter-bank borrowing
固定资产投资	fixed-asset investment
中央预算内投资	budgetary investment of the central government
投融资体系	investment and financing system
融资融券	securities margin trading
投资结构	investment structure
融资公司	financing company
民间资本	private capital
融券贷款	securities loan
融资渠道	financing channels
直接融资	direct financing
个人融资	personal financing
集体融资	collective financing
民间融资	private financing
融资规则	financing rules
融资政策	financing policy
获利套现	profit-taking
银行买价	buying rate of bank
通货紧缩	deflation
银根收缩	currency deflation
通货膨胀	inflation
通货升值	currency revaluation
浮动汇率	floating rate
固定汇率	fixed rate
买入汇率	buying rate
卖出汇率	selling rate
市场汇率	market exchange rate
收盘汇率	closing rate
官价汇率	official exchange rate
复汇率	multiple exchange rate
软贷款	soft loan

3. 货币（Currency）

（中国）人民币	Renminbi
（阿尔巴尼亚）列克	Lek
（阿尔及利亚）第纳尔	Algerian Dinar
（阿富汗）尼	Afghani
（阿根廷）奥斯特拉尔	Austral
（阿联酋）迪拉姆	Dirham
（阿曼）阿曼里亚尔	Omani Rial
（埃及）埃及镑	Egyptian Pound

（爱尔兰）爱尔兰镑　Irish Pound
（安哥拉）宽扎　Kwanza
（澳大利亚）元　Australian Dollar
（奥地利）先令　Austrian shilling
（巴基斯坦）卢比　Pakestan Rupee
（巴拉圭）瓜拉尼　Guarani
（巴林）第纳尔　Bahhrain Dinar
（巴西）克罗扎多　Cruzado
（白俄罗斯）卢布　Rouble
（俄罗斯）卢布　Russian Rouble
（保加利亚）列弗　Lev
（贝宁）法郎　Franc
（比利时）法郎　Franc Belge
（秘鲁）新索尔　New Sol
（冰岛）克朗　Icelandic Krona
（波黑）第纳尔　Dinar
（波兰）兹罗提　Zloty
（玻利维亚）诺　Boliviano
（安道尔）法郎　Spanish Peseta and French Franc
（博茨瓦纳）普拉　Pula
（不丹）努尔特鲁姆　Ngultrum
（布隆迪）法郎　Brundi Franc
（朝鲜）圆　Won
（库克群岛）新西兰元　New Zealand Dollar
（肯利亚）镑　Pound
（拉脱维亚）卢布　Rupee
（科特迪瓦）法郎　Franc
（科摩罗）法郎　Franc
（卡塔尔）里拉尔　Riyal
（喀麦隆）法郎　Franc
（克罗地亚）第纳尔　Dinar
（科威特）第纳尔　Dinar
（赤道几内亚）法郎　Franc

（斐济）斐济元　Fiji Dollar
（芬兰）马克　Markka
（冈比亚）达拉西　Dalasi
（哥伦比亚）比索　Peso
（格鲁吉亚）卢布　Rouble
（哥斯达黎加）科朗　Colon
（刚果）法郎　Franc
（关岛）美元　U.S dollar
（古巴）比索　Peso
（丹麦）克朗　Danish Krone
（德国）马克　Deutsche Mark
（多哥）法郎　Franc
（圭亚那）元　Guyana Dollar
（菲律宾）比索　Philippine Peso
（梵蒂冈）意大利里拉　Italian lira
（东帝汶）盾　Indonesian Rupiah
（哈萨克斯坦）卢布　Rouble
（法国）法郎　Franc
（英国）英镑　Pound Sterling
（美国）美元　United States Dollar
（多米尼加共和国）比索　Peso
（巴布亚新几利亚）基那　Kina
（厄瓜多尔）苏克雷　Sucres
（巴拿马）巴波亚　Balboa
（巴巴多斯）元　Barbados Dollar
（佛得角）埃斯库多　Escudo
（阿塞拜疆）卢布　Rouble
（爱沙尼亚）卢布　Rouble
（埃塞俄比亚）比尔　Birr
（海地）古德　Gourde
（韩国）元　Won
（荷兰）荷兰盾　Guilder / Florin
（洪都拉斯）伦皮拉　Lemppira
（基里巴斯）元　Australian Dollar
（吉布提）法郎　Djibouti Franc

金融，融资，货币
Finance, Financing and Currency

（几内亚）法郎　Guinea Franc
（加拿大）元　Canadian Dollar
（加纳）赛迪　Cedi
（加蓬）法郎　Franc
（柬埔寨）瑞尔　Riel
（捷克）克朗　Koruna
（利比亚）第纳尔　Libyan Dinar
（立陶宛）卢布　Rouble
（津巴布韦）元　Zimbabwe Dollar
（喀麦隆）法郎　Franc
（卡塔尔）里亚尔　Qatar Riyal
（格林纳达）元　East Caribbean Dollar
（格陵兰）克朗　Danish Krone
（黎巴嫩）镑　Lebanese Pound
（老挝）基普　Kip
（越南）越盾　Dong
（扎伊尔）扎伊尔　Zaire
（乍得）法郎　Franc
（智利）比索　Peso
（中非）法郎　Franc
（中途岛）美元　United States Dollar
（直布罗陀）镑和比萨塔　Pound and Peseta
（印度尼西亚）盾　Indonesian Rupiah
（印度）卢比　Indian Rupee
（意大利）里拉　Lira
（新西兰）元　New Zealand Dollar
（约旦）第纳尔　Jordanian Dinar
（匈牙利）福林　Forint
（叙利亚）镑　Syrian Pound
（以色列）谢克尔　Shekel
（伊朗）里亚尔　Rial
（伊拉克）第纳尔　Dinar
（牙买加）元　Dollar
（也门）里亚尔/第纳尔　Rial (north)/ the Dinar (South)
（亚美尼亚）卢布　Rouble
（新加坡）元　Singapore Dollar
（希腊）德拉克马　Drachma
（西班牙）比塞塔　Peseta
（乌拉圭）新比索　New Peso
（乌克兰）卢布　Rouble
（乌干达）新先令　New Uganda shilling
（乌兹别克斯坦）卢布　Rouble
（塔吉克斯坦）卢布　Rouble
（土耳其）里拉　Turkish Lira
（突尼斯）第纳尔　Dinar
（汤加）元　Tongan Dinar
（坦桑尼亚）先令　Tanzania Shilling
（文莱）元　Brunel Dollar
（委内瑞拉）玻利瓦尔　Bolivar
（危地马拉）格查尔　Quetzal
（瓦努阿图）瓦图　Vatu
（图瓦卢）元和硬币　Dollar and Tuvaluan Dollar
（泰国）铢　Baht
（索马里）先令　Somali Shilling
（所罗门群岛）元　Dollar
（苏里南）盾或弗罗林　Guilder or Florin
（苏丹）苏丹镑　Sudanese Pound
（塞浦路斯）镑　Pound
（斯威士兰）里兰吉尔　Lilangeni
（塞舌尔）卢比　Rupee
（斯里兰卡）卢比　Rupee
（沙特阿拉伯）沙特利亚尔　Saudi Riyal
（斯洛文尼亚）第纳尔　Dinar
（斯洛伐克）克朗　Koruna
（圣马力诺）里拉　Lira
（塞内加尔）法郎　Franc
（塞拉利昂）里昂　Leone

（尼加拉瓜）科多巴　Cordoba
（尼日利亚）奈拉　the Naira
（尼泊尔）卢比　Rupee
（尼日尔）法郎　Franc
（日本）日元　Yen
（瑞典）克朗　Krona
（瑞士）法郎　Franc
（塞尔瓦多）科朗　Colon
（葡萄牙）埃斯库多　Escudo
（挪威）克朗　Krona
（毛里塔尼亚）乌吉亚　Ouguiya
（蒙古）图格里克　Togrog
（孟加拉国）塔卡　Taka
（缅甸）缅元　Kyat
（摩尔多瓦）卢布　Rupee
（摩洛哥）迪拉姆　Dirham
（摩纳哥）法郎　Franc
（密克罗尼西亚）美元　United States Dollar
（毛里求斯）卢比　Rupee
（马其顿共和国）第纳尔　Dinar
（马绍尔群岛）美元　United States Dollar
（马里）法郎　Franc
（马来西亚）元　Malaysian Dollar
（马拉维）克瓦查　Kwacha
（马耳他）里拉　Lira
（马尔代夫）拉菲亚　Rufiyaa
（马达加斯加）法郎　Franc
（罗马尼亚）列伊　Leu
（卢旺达）法郎　Franc
（卢森堡）法郎　Franc
（莫桑比克）梅蒂卡尔　Metical
（墨西哥）比索　Peso
（纳米比亚）兰特　Rand
（南非）兰特　Rand

（南斯拉夫）第纳尔　Dinar
（瑙鲁）元　Dollar
（莱索托）洛蒂　Loti
纸币制度　paper monetary system
储存货币　reserve currency
代用货币　token
法定货币　legal tender
瑞士法郎　Swiss Franc
南非兰特　South African rand
加拿大元　Canaddian dollar
芬兰马克　markka
梅蒂卡尔　metical
第纳尔　Dinar
拉菲亚　Rufiyaa
荷兰盾　Florin
伦皮拉　Lempira
洛蒂　Loti
汇率　exchange rate
金券　gold certificate
造币　coinage
外币　foreign currency
外汇　foreign exchange
金币　gold coin
银币　silver coin
硬币　coin
纸币　paper money
假币　fake money
年息　annual interest
月息　monthly interest
定息　fixed interest
低息　low interest
纯利息　net interest
存款　deposit
面值　nominal amount
面额　denomination

金融, 融资, 货币
Finance, Financing and Currency

港币	Hong Kong dollar
克朗	krone
软货币	soft currency
兑换	change
镍币	nickel coin
钞票	banknote
欧元	Eurodollar
英镑	pound sterling
法郎	franc
先令	Shilling
欧元	Euro
卢比	rupee
卢布	Rouble
马克	mark
美元	U.S dollar / American dollar
日元	yen
先令	shilling
缅元	Kyat
奈拉	naira
索尔	sol
利昂	leone
塞迪	Cedi
瑞尔	Riel
比索	Peso
古德	Gourde
里奥	Rial
里尔	Riel
兰特	Rand
比尔	Birr
里拉	Lira
列弗	Lev
列克	Lek
塔拉	Tala
塔卡	Taka
铢	Baht

侨汇	overseas remittance
货币	currency / money / monetary
国币	national currency
升水	premium
贴水	agio
货币发行局	currency board
货币当局	monetary authority
货币单位	monetary unit
货币平价	par value of currency
货币升值	appreciation of currency
货币市场	money market
货币期货	currency futures
货币危机	monetary crisis
货币收益率	currency yield
货币交换	exchange through money
货币基础	monetary base
货币回笼	withdrawal of currency from circulation
货币篮子	currency basket
货币供应量	money supply
金本位制度	gold standard
黄金外汇储备	foreign exchange reserve of gold
黄金市场	gold market
黄金双价	dual gold price
黄金外流	gold outflow
黄金保值	gold guarantee
黄金储备	gold reserve
黄金官价	official gold price
国际货币基金	international monetary fund
货币市场基金	money market fund
信用货币	credit money
货币互换	currency swap
货币幻觉	money illusion

货币贬值	devaluation of currency
货币发行	issurance of monetary
货币风险	currency risk
货币政策	monetary policy
货币资本	money capital
流通货币	circulation currency
基本货币	key currency
法定货币	lawful money / legal monetary
国际货币	international currency
欧洲货币	Eruo-currency
强势货币	strong currency
商品货币	commodity currency
土地货币	land money
自由兑换货币	convertible currency
自由外汇	free foreign exchange
进口外汇	import exchange of keeping account
记账外汇	foreign exchange
即期外汇	spot (immediate) foreign exchange
货币信用	confidence in currency
货币中性	monetary neutrality
货币主义	monetarism
铸币平价	mint par
直接标价	direct quotation
间接标价	indirect quotation
银根收紧	currency deflation
信用膨胀	credit inflation
黄金输送点	gold points
现金管理	cash control
支付手段	medium for payment
通货紧缩	deflation
通货升值	currency revaluation
硬通货	hard currency
融券贷款	securities loan
软贷款	soft loan
软通货	soft currency
金平价	gold standard
外汇兑换券	foreign exchange certificate
官价汇率	official exchange rate
自由汇率	free foreign exchange
出口外汇	export exchange
法定贬值	devaluation
法定升值	revaluation
浮动汇率	floating rate
市场汇率	market exchange rate
收盘汇率	closing rate
卖出汇率	selling rate
买入汇率	buying rate
留成汇率	to retain a portion of one's foreign exchange rate
进口汇率	import exchange rate
复汇率	multiple exchange rate
固定汇率	fixed rate
外逃资本	flight capital
外汇动态	exchange position
外汇波动	foreign exchange fluctuation
外汇银行	foreign exchange bank
外汇储备	foreign exchange reserve
外汇条款	foreign exchange clauses
外汇收入	earnings in foreign exchange
外汇交易	transaction in foreign exchange
外汇市场	foreign exchange market
外汇牌价	foreign exchange rate
外汇行情	exchange quotations
外汇管理	exchange control
外汇官价	official exchange rate
外汇平价	par of exchange / exchange parity

5 企业及管理
Enterprise and Management

1. 企业（Enterprise）

产业	industry
企业化	to run an enterprise on a commercial basis
合资企业	joint venture
独资企业	sole proprietorship
企业集团	enterprise group
财务总裁	chief financial officer（CFO）
企业会计	enterprise accounting
企业年金	supplementary pension
企业家	entrepreneur / big businessman
自由职业	private professions
民营企业	private enterprise
二次创业	to start a new undertaking
企业结构	structure（or set-up）of enterprises
环保产业	environmental protection industry
生态农业	environment-friendly agriculture
科技企业	science-and-technology enterprises
权势企业	enterprises in positions of power and authority
非国有企业	non-state enterprises
合同制企业	enterprises of contract system
企业自主权	power of decision of enterprise
私人企业主	private entrepreneurs
大企业集团	large-scale conglomerates
大型联合企业	conglomerate
利益关联企业	well-connected enterprises with interests
中小微企业	micro, small and medio-sized enterprises
夕阳产业	sunset industry
三股企业	three-share-enterprises
产权单位	owner of property rights
国有大中型企业	large and medium-sized state-owned enterprises

2. 企业管理（Enterprise Management）

国有资产管理体制	system for managing state assets
现代金融企业制度	a modern financial enterprise system
降低企业准入门槛	lower the threshold for market entry
企业经营管理	enterprise management
换算风险管理	management of

083

	translation exposure
国际存货管理	management of international inventory
现金管理	cash control
风险管理	risk management
目标管理	management by objectives
需求管理	demand management
管理能力	management capacity
管理水平	management level
管理措施	management measures
管理不善	mismanagement
管理费用	costs of management
管理财务	to be in charge of financial affairs
管理人员	management personnel
经营规划	business plan
物流中心	logistics center
订立合同	to make a contract
撕毁合同	to tear up a contract
线性规划	linear programming
项目记载	item recording
物料项目	material item
物料清单	material bill
集中预测	focus forecasting
财务清查	financial inventory
财产清查	asset inventory
财务预测	financial forecasting
财务报告	financial report
财务机构	setup for financial affairs and accounting
价值工程	to value engineering
经济批量	economic lot size
可签约量	available to promise
独立需求	independent demand
订货承诺	order promising
安全库存	safety stock
合资经营	jointly owned business
偿债基金	funds for paying a debt
反馈价值	feedback value
对应账户	corresponding accounts
周期盘点	cycle counting
零基预算	zero based budgeting
损耗系数	shrinkage factor
应付账款	payable accounts
应收账款	receivable accounts
长期借款	long-term loans
长期应付款	long-term payable money
主生产计划	master production schedule
准时制生产	just in-time production
按需订货法	lot for lot
订单输入	order entry
采购计划法	vendor scheduling
拖期预报	anticipated delay report
加强企业管理	to strengthen the management of enterprises
企业信息化建设	IT promotion in enterprises
加强金融管理	to tighten financial supervision
流动性管理	liquidity management
财务杠杆系数	degree of financial leverage
车间作业管理	floor control at shop
成本效益分析	cost-benefit analysis
分类法管理	classification in management
生产管理原则	manufacturing management practice
生产规划编制	production planning

经济订货批量	economic ordering quantity
现在库存量	on-hand balance
物料需求计划	material demand planning
资源需求计划	resource demand planning
预计可用库存	projected available balance
预计入库量	scheduled receipt
非独立需求	dependent demand
投入/产出控制	input / output control
库存周转次数	inventory turnover
成本回收制度	cost recovery system
会计信息系统	accounting information system
保税物流园区	bonded logistic parks
固定订货批量法	fixed ordering quantity
固定资产重估价	revaluations of fixed assets
固定资产更换	replacement of fixed assets
固定资产改良	improvement of fixed assets
固定资产扩建	addition of fixed assets
固定资产修理	maintenance of fixed assets
固定资产折旧	depreciation of fixed assets
确认计划订单	to confirm planned order
拨定留存收益	appropriate retained earnings
财务状况表	statement of financial position
财务报表要素	elements of financial affairs
标准成本法	standard costing
变本成本法	variable costing
不定期检查	non-periodic check
备查账簿	memorandum
定期检查	periodic check
配送货物	to distribute goods
提取货物	to take delivery of goods
退运手续	returning formalities
存储期限	storage time
国际物流业	international logistics

3. 科技管理用语 (Common Terms of Management in Science and Technology)

目标管理	objective management
科学管理	scientific management
主管人员	supervisor
主要决定	major decision
批准程序	approval procedure
评价工具	appraisal tool
强化理论	to reinforce theory
紧缩政策	to retrench strategy
可考核目标	verifiable objective
管理任务法	managerial roles approach
管理方格图	managerial grid
市场占有率	market share
随机制宜法	contingency approach
投入原则	commitment principle
投资回报	return on investment
管理决策	managerial decision
管理职能	managerial function
激励方法	motivational techniques
激励因素	motivator
集体目标	group objective

检查记录	inspection record	经验法	empirical approach
考绩制度	merit system	可行性	feasibility
控制手段	control device	领先性	primacy
人力投入	human input	进取性	aggressiveness
破产政策	liquidation strategy	缺勤率	absenteeism
派生政策	derivative policy	利润率	profitability
劳资纠纷	labor dispute	董事会	board of director
竞争对手	rival of competition	自主权	latitude
共同作用	synergy	总预算	overall budget
顾客服务	customer service	安全	safety
产品系列	product line / series	报酬	compensation
产品质量	quality of products	采购	procurement
专利产品	patented product	成本	cost
资本货物	capital goods	程序	procedure
定量目标	quantitative objective	创新	innovation
定性目标	qualitative objective	法规	regulation
增长目标	growth goal	反馈	feedback
多种经营	diversification	奉献	devotion
公共关系	public relation	福利	welfare
误工记录	record about labor-hours lost	概率	probability
公司效益	company's profits	股息	dividend
工作效率	work efficiency	规划	program
个人价值	personal worth	机时	machine-hour
个人利益	personal interest	计划	planning
个人责任	personal responsibility	鉴定	appraisal
生产能力	capacity to produce	奖金	bonus
先进技术	advanced technology	奖励	reward
资本支出	capital outlay	解雇	layoff
内部环境	internal environmenet	控制	controlling
外部环境	external environment	优势	strength
行为科学	behavior science	预算	budget
应变策略	consistency strategy	招聘	recruit
生产率	productitivity	职责	responsibility
税收率	tax rate	培训	training
系统法	system approach	评估	assessment

设备	equipment	业绩	performance
资源	resources	盈余	surplus

4. 资金管理 (Fund Management)

经营资金	management fund	利润预测	profit prediction
流动资金	circulating capital	应付账款	accounts payable
企业基金	enterprise fund	往来账户	current accounts
生产资金	production capital	现金账簿	cash book
特种基金	special fund	主要账簿	main account book
储备资金	reserve capital	原始单据	original document
货币资金	money capital	信汇结算	M/T settlement
结算资金	settlement capital	现金结算	cash settlement
专用资金	capital for special use	银行结算	bank settlement
成品资金	finished product capital	票汇结算	bill remittance settlement
厂长基金	director's fund	余额式账	reducing balance accounts
公用经费	public expenditure	现金管理	cash management
财政拨款	financial allocation	有形损耗	material loss
基建借款	loan for capital construction	无形损耗	invisible waste
应收款项	fund receivable	无形资本	incorporeal capital
财务检查	financial examination	基本工资	basic wages
固定资产	fixed assets	计时工资	payment by hour
国家投资	state investment	计件工资	piece rate wages
集体投资	collective investment	平均工资	average wages
个人投资	personal investment	职务工资	post salary
企业纯收入	net income of an enterprise	退休金	retirement pay
固定资产周转	turnover of fixed assets	生活费	living expense
生产费用预算	budget of productive expense	月工资	monthly salary
		余额表	balance sheet
商品总销售额	total sales of commodity	预支款	prepaid fund
商品流通费	circulating expenses for commodity	利润率	profit rate
		工资单	payroll
资金占用费	amount of capital occupied	算细账	to break down accounts
资金利用率	utilization ratio of capital	统制账	controlling account
销售利润	sales profit	试算表	trial balance
资金循环	cycling of capital	流水账	journal account

损益表	profit and loss statement	开支	expenditure
资金表	fund statement	亏损	loss
负债	liability	摊付	allotment
工资	wages	盈亏	profit and loss
奖金	bonus		

6 信息技术术语
Terms of Information Technology

信息学	information science
信息子	informofer
信息体	informosome
信息论	information theory
信息技术	information technology
信息科学	information science
信息产业	information industry
信息经济	information economy
信息编码	information encoding
信息载体	information carrier
信息储备	store of information
信息检索	information retrieval
信息传递	information transmission
信息中心	information centre
信息交流	information exchange
信息共享	to share more information
市场信息	market information
信息培训	information training
中央处理器	Central Processing Unit
固定控制器	Firmware Controller
嵌入式控制器	Embedded Controller
16位存储器	Rambus DRAM
频率鉴别	Frequency Identification
指令解码	Decode
数据前送	Data Forwarding
指令缓存	Instructions Cache
内存插槽	Dual-Inline-Memory-Modules
局域互联	local interconnect
新指令集	Katmai New Instructions
无效超频	No-Account Over Clock
分支预测	branch prediction
浮点操作	floating point operation
浮点减	floating point subtraction
浮点加	floating point addition
浮点乘	floating point multiplication
浮点除	floating point division
内存控制中心	Memory Controller Hub
同步突发内存	Synchronous Burst RAM
芯片内集缓存	Cache on Die
并行指令代码	Explicitly Parallel Instruction Code
英特尔移动模块	Intel Mobile Module
特别模块寄存器	Model-Specific Registers
常规视觉处理器	Generic Visual Perception Processor
多重处理器架构	multi-processing
快速进入多媒体状态	fast entry multimedia state
复杂指令集计算机	Complex Instruction Set Computing
销售点信息系统	point of sale

退出多媒体状态	exit multimedia state
输入控制器中心	Input Controller Hub
输出控制器中心	Output Controller Hub
分支处理单元	branch processing unit
浮点运算单元	floating point unit
指令执行单元	Integer Execution Unit
指令控制单元	Instructions Controller Unit
地址产成单元	Address Generation Unit
多媒体单元	Multi-Media Unit
多重处理器规格	multi-processor specification
基本输入系统	Basic Input System
基本输出系统	Basic Ouput System
管理信息系统	management information system
信息存储器	computer Information Storing Device
信息高速公路	information superhighway
信息资源管理	information resource management

7 证券，保险
Securities and Insurance

1. 证券 (Securities)

证券法	securities law
证券交易所	securities exchange
票据交易所	clearing house
证券交易	securities transaction
长期证券	long-term securities
发行股票,债券	issue shares and bonds
股票与证券交易	trading stock and bonds
股票发行注册制	stock issuing registration system
注册证券交易所	registered stock exchange
有价证券投资	portfolio investment
哄抬证券价格	bull campaign
认购新股款项	application moneys
通胀挂钩债券	inflation-linked bond / inflation-indexed bond
股份合作制	cooperative system of the joint stock
控股公司	holding company
股份制	share-holding system
期货市场	future market
股票上市	floatation of shares (or stocks)
债券市场	bond market
大额交易	block traders
现金交易	cash transactions
票面价值	par value
票证交换	clearing stock
普通股票	ordinary share
股票交易所	stock exchange house
公用事业股票	utility share
股票公开上市	going public
股东股本利益	share holder's equity
实行股份制	to enforce stockholding system
股票指数	stock index
股票反弹	stocks rebound
股票市场	stock market
股票行市	current prices of stock
股票价格	stock prices
股东价值	shareholder value
股东权益	shareholder's equity
股价上扬	stock bounce
股票投机	stock speculation
股票信托	share trust
股市动荡	stocks fluctuation
股份与股票	stocks and shares
股份回购	share buyback
股票证书	stock certificate
股票暴跌	stock breaking
股票暴涨	stock rising
股市疲软	stocks sluggish /dull

股利/股息	dividents	优先股	preference share
股票登记簿	stock register	产权股	equity stock/share
发行股票	to issue shares	蓝筹股	blue chip share
疲软股票	soft stock	工业股	industrial stocks
热门股票	glamour share	农业股	agricultural stocks
配股	allotment of shares	红筹股	red chip share
股东	stockholder/shareholder	股本金	equity capital
股份	a share/shares/stocks	股市行情表	share list
让股	the transfer of share	票据贴现	discounted note
供股	right issue	招股书	prospectus
批股	share placement	保持国有股	to keep the state-held shares
让股人	transferor	上市股份有限公司	public limited companies
供股权	rights		
普通股	common stock/ordinary share	证券信息公司	securities data co./securities information company
让予股份	denoted share		
在册股东	stock holders of record		
招股价	public offering price	债券清算公司	stock clearing corporation
募股书	prospectus	定息债券	fixed income securities
换手率	turnover rate	核定股本	the authorized capital
盘档	dull	债券持有人	bond holder
开盘	opening	债权人	creditor
看跌	bear market	注资	asset injection
看涨	bull market	回报	return
空头	bear	价内	in the money
股本	capital stock	价外	out of the money
配股	right issue	成交	to strike a bargain/to clinch a deal
过户	the assigned	利率	interest rate
控股	share holding	息率	dividend
A股	A stock/share	交叉盘	cross trade
B股	B stock/share	市价盘	market order
H股	H stock	期票	promising note
法人股	corporate share	发行成本	flotation cost
跌停板	falling limit	双方拍卖	double auction
成分股	constituent stock	议价市场	negiotiation market
金边股	gift-edged share/stock	牛市	bull market

证券，保险
Securities and Insurance

熊市	bear market	反向市场	backwardation
汇率波动	daily trading band	多头市场	bull market
清新指数	fresh air index	多头	long position
恒生指数	Heng Seng Index	逼仓	force selling
互惠基金	mutual funds	波幅	range
资本得利	capital gain	结算	settle
储备公债	savings bonds	交割	delivery
公司债券	corporation bonds	开仓	open position
点心债券	dim sum bonds	开盘 / 开市	open
可换股债券	convertible bonds	开盘价	opening price
市盈率	price-to-earnings ratio (p/e ratio)	收盘价	closing price
流动比率	current ratio	空头	short position
流动负债	current liabilities	卖空	short selling
流动资产	current asset	跳空	gap
固定资产	fixed asset	暴跌	tumble
最优惠利率	prime rate	暴涨	bulge
名义利率	nominal interest rate	飙升	soar
入限价买盘	to buy limit order	狂跌	collapse
行使价	exercising price	下跌	sink
收市价	closing price	下跃	reaction
收盘价	closing price	走弱	weak
每日波幅限额	daily fluctuation limit	升水 / 贴水	premium
指数备兑证	index covered warrants	收盘 / 收市	close
特别成交	special trade	反弹 / 上涨	rally
大手成交	large transaction	涨停板	raising limit
上升轨	upward trendline	空头回补	short covering
上升旗型	rising flag	买进冲销	to buy to close
上升风险	upside risk	买进建仓	to buy to open
下跌风险	downside risk	买入期权	to call option
系统性风险	systematic risk	欧式期权	European-style options
自动对盘	automatching	基差合约	basis contract
止蚀盘	to stop loss order	技术分析	technical analysis
止赚盘	to stop profit order	正向市场	normal market
期货	futures	平均值下移	average down
成交量	volume	商品期货	commodity futures

金融期货	finance futures	蝶式套利	butterfly spread
期货合同	futures contract	融资套利	credit spread
期货交易所	futures exchange	套期保值	hedging
商品经纪人	commodity broker	套保者	hedger
公司保证人	corporate surety	支撑位	to support levels
期末库存	ending stocks	阻力线	resistance line
变形套利	crush spread	趋势线	trend line
盒式套利	box spread	支撑线	to support line
牛市套利	bull spread		

2. 保险 (Insurance)

保险公司	insurance company	船体保险	hull insurance
保险合同	insurance treaty	免费保险	insurance for waiver of premium
保险客户	insured / policy holder		
保险类别	varieties of insurance	森林火灾险	insurance for forest fire
商业保险	commercial insurance	受潮受热险	insurance for the damage caused by wetting and heating
社会保险	social insurance		
失业保险	unemployment insurance		
财产保险	property insurance	碰损破碎险	insurance for risk of clashing & breakage
货物保险	cargo insurance		
健康保险	health insurance	安装工程险	insurance for erection all risk
人寿保险	life insurance		
人身保险	personal insurance	进口关税险	insurance for import duty
医药保险	medicine insurance	空中旅行险	insurance of air trip accident
工伤保险	insurance against workplace injury		
老年保险	services for the elderly	航空运输险	insurance for air transportation risk
劳工保险	labor insurance	陆运综合险	insurance for overland transportation all risk
旅行保险	traveller's insurance		
投资保险	investment insurance	特别附加险	insurance for special addition
定期保险	term insurance	码头检验险	survey insurance at jetty risk
分期保险	instalment insurance	预付保险费	deposit premium
海损保险	maritime insurance	邮包综合险	insurance for parcel post all risk
汽车保险	automobile insurance		
雾霾险	smog insurance	交货不到险	insurance for failure to

	delivery
海关检验险	survey insurance in customs risk
农村养老保险	pension insurance for rural residents
定额保险合同	sum insurance contract
保险商	underwriter
保险经纪人	insurance broker
保险费	insurance premium
保险单	insurance policy
拒收险	rejection insurance
保险人	insurer / assurer
被保人	insured person
承保人	insurer
承兑人	acceptor
综合险	comprehensive insurance
意外险	casualty insurance
损害险	damage insurance
全损险	insurance for total loss only
邮包险	insurance for parcel post risk
战争险	insurance for war risk
盗窃险	burglary insurance
地震险	earthquake insurance
陆运险	insurance for overland transportation risk
洪水险	flood insurance
火灾险	fire insurance
附加险	insurance for additional risk
住家险	residence insurance
自燃险	insurance for the risk of spontaneous combustion
停车保险	waiting insurance
全额赔偿	full settlement
保险凭证	insurance certificate
保险单据	insurance document
保险收益	insurance yield
保险范围	insurance coverage
保险金额	insured sum
保险收入	premium proceeds
保险总额	insurance coverage
保险索赔	insurance claim
保险条款	insurance clauses
单独保单	specific policy
浮动保单	floating policy
不定价保险单	open policy
定价保险单	valued policy
综合保险单	comprehensive policy
总括保险单	blanket policy
附加保险费	additional premium
投保单	application form for insurance
损失额	amount of loss
年利息	annual interest rate
年息率	per annum interest rate
超息期	date of value
退保金	surrender value
准备金	reserve value
担保书	guarantee
分保条	reinsurance slip
分保	reinsurance
承保	cover
索赔	claim
大病医疗保险试点	a trial programs of medical insurance for major diseases
婚姻保险	marriage protection insurance
个人保险	personal belongs insurance
团体保险	group insurance
团体人寿险	group life insurance
责任保险	liability insurance
终身人寿保险	whole life insurance

航班延误险	flight delay insurance	平安险	peaceful insurance / free from particular average
养老保险	endowment insurance		
基本医保	basic medical insurance	损害险	damage insurance
儿童保险	kids insurance	年保费	annual premium
产业保险	industrial insurance	保险金	insurance benefit
住宅保险	residence insurance	退款金额	surrender value
房租保险	rent insurance	赔款	indemnity
房产保险	house property insurance	全额赔偿	full settlement
抵押保险	hypothecation insurance	部分赔偿	partial settlement
自动保险	volunntary insurance	加倍赔偿	double indemnity
过期保险	extended-term insurance	减赔	deductible settlement
短期保险	short-term insurance	补偿赔款	recovery
信贷基金保险	credit and bond insurance	保险索赔	insurance claim
意外事故保险	accident insurance	保险法规	insurance laws
重大疾病保险	critical illness insurance program	保险契约	insurance contract
		保险商	underwriter
旅行平安保险	travel accident insurance	保险期	period of insurance
受托人保证保险	fiduciary bond	保险物	insured objet
投标保证保险	to bid bond insurance	保险箱	safety-deposit box
存款保险	deposit insrance	索赔人	claimant
运输保险	transportation insurance	仲裁人	arbitrator
旅游保险	travel insurance	承保方	insurer
防盗保险	insurance against theft	赔偿者	indemnitor
政策保险	policy insurance	退保	surrender
投资保险	investment insurance		

3. 其他（Others）

限价指示单	limit orders	债权，产权	claim
市价指示单	market orders	净资产（资产净值）	net assets (net worth)
价格暴涨	jump	利率	interest rates
价格下跌	to lose ground	股票经济人	broker
价格略回落	slight firming	投资经纪人	investment broker
价格浮动	price fluctuation	坐收坐支	to obtain and use funds without authorization
多头和空头	bulls and bears		
投机性短期性炒卖股票	go-go	报价	quote

证券，保险
Securities and Insurance

报盘	offer	交易台	posts
实盘	firm offer	电子交易	electronic trading
虚盘	no-firm offer	抛股票	to sell stocks
还盘	counter offer		

8 旅游
Tourism

1. 旅游机构 (Tourism Agency)

世界旅游组织	World Tourism Organization
国家旅游局	National Tourism Adminstration
省旅游局	Provincial Tourism Bueau
市旅游局	Municipal Tourism Bueau
县旅游局	County Tourism Bueau
中国青年旅行社	China Youth Travel Agency
中国国际旅行社	China Intrnational Travel Service
旅行社	travel agency
旅游公司	travel company
旅游观光团	tour group / tour sightseeing party
旅游团	tourist group / touring party
旅游接待站	touristy stop
旅游战略组	tourism strategy group
团队旅游	group tour
旅游企业	tourism enterprises / business

2. 旅游地 (Tourist Destination)

避暑胜地	summer resort
旅游胜地	tourist attraction
旅游目的地	travel destination
国家 A 级旅游风景区	the National A-class tourist spot
自然保护区	nature reserve
国家森林公园	national forest park
旅游度假村	tourist holiday resort
旅游假日野营地	tourist holiday camp
旅游避暑胜地	tourist summer resort
旅游客店	tourist home
旅店 / 旅馆	hotel / inn
两地旅游	twin center breaks

3. 中国著名旅游景点 (China's Famous Tourist Attractions)

1) 北京市 (Beijing)

天安门广场及城楼	Tian'anmen Square & Rostrum
人民英雄纪念碑	Monument to the People's Heroes
故宫博物馆 / 紫禁城	Palace Museum / The Forbidden City
太和殿及殿前广场	The Hall of Supreme Harmony and the Courtyard in front of it

Tourism

养心殿及御花园	Hall of Mental Cultivation & Imperial Garden
颐和园	Summer Palace
长廊和石舫	Long Corridor & Marble Boat
园中园/谐趣园	Garden of Harmonious Interest
祈年殿	Hall of Prayer for Good Harvests
天坛	Temple of Heaven
丹陛桥和圜丘坛	Red Stairway Bridge and Circular Mound Altar
名胜古迹	scenic spots and historical sights
劳动人民文化宫	Working People's Cultural Palace
国家级文物	national-grade relics
毛主席纪念堂	Chairman Mao Memorial Hall
人民大会堂	Great Hall of the People
革命历史博物馆	Museum of Revolutionary History
八达岭长城	Great Wall at Pedaling
明十三陵	Ming Tombs
民族文化宫	Cultural Palace for Nationalities
中华世纪坛	China Century Altar
北京工人体育馆	Beijing Worker's Stadium
中华民族园	Chinese Ethnic Culture Park
周口店遗址	Zhoukoudian Ancient Site
北京孔庙	Beijing Confucius Temple
九龙壁	Nine Dragon Screen
北京猿人博物馆	Museum of Beijing Men
北海公园	Beihai Park
香山公园	Fragrant Hill Park
圆明园遗迹	Ruins of Yuanmingyuan

2）天津市（Tianjin）

水路风光游	tour via water route
名人故居游	former residence of the celebrities
民俗大院	Folk Custom Residences
精武元祖霍元甲故居	the Former Residence of Huo Yuanjia
天津妈祖庙	Tianjin Mazu Temple
杨柳青年画馆	Yangliuqing Spring Festival Paintings Museum
名街休闲游	famous street travelling
渔阳山野游	outing to Yuyang Mount
西青民俗游	Xiqing folk custom travelling
滨海风情游	tour to Binhai New Area

3）黑龙江省（Heilongjiang Province）

哈尔滨	Harbin City—The Ice City
镜泊湖	Jingbo Lake
五大连池	Five Connected Lakes
漠河北极村	Arctic Pole Village in Mohe
北极村——临江小镇	Arctic Pole Village—The Northern-most Town in the Mainland, China
北极村石碑	Stele in the Arctic Pole Village
北极哨所	Post in the North Pole Sentry
冰雾奇观	freezing fog—A Unique Natural Wonder
李金庸祠堂	Li Jinyong Memorial Temple
大冰雪游	abundant snow and ice tour

大平原游　vast plains tour
大森林游　vast forestry tour
大湿地游　wetlands tour
4) 吉林省 (Jilin Province)
长白山景区　Changbai Mountain Tourist Resort
长白山自然保护区　Changbai Mountain Natural Reserve
长白山天池　Changbai Mountain's Heavenly Lake
长白山温泉群　Changbaishan Hot Spring Cluster
长春净月潭风景名胜区
Changchun Jinyuetan Forest Park
吉林松花湖风景名胜区
Jilin Songhua Lake scenic zone
通化高句丽古文化游览区
Tonghua Gaojuli ancient cultural tourist zone
仙景台风景名胜区　Xiianjingtai scienic spot
通榆向海草原湿地旅游区
Tongyu and Xianghai grasslands and wetlands
5) 辽宁省 (Liaoning Province)
沈阳故宫　Shenyang Imperial Palace
沈阳世博园　Shenyang International Horticultural Exposition
大连 (浪漫之都)　Dalian (A City of Romance)
北方明珠　bright pearl in the north
老虎滩极地馆　Laohutan Pole Aquarium
圣亚海洋世界　Sunasia Ocean World
珊瑚馆　Coral Hall
贝壳馆　Shell Museum

蛇博物馆　Snake Museum
服装节　Fashion Festival
女骑警　Mounted policewomen
滨海风光　seaside scenery
森林动物园　forest zoo
国家级旅游度假区——金石滩
National Tourism and Holiday Resort—Jinshitan
国家级风景名胜区——旅顺
National Scenery Resort Zone—Lushun
中国最大的海洋公园
China's largest ocean park
6) 内蒙古自治区 (Inner Mongolian Autonomous Region)
呼伦贝尔大草原　Hulun Buir grasslands
鄂尔多斯世珍园　Erdos Shizhenyuan
赤峰阿斯哈图石林景区
Chifeng Asihatu Stone Forest
大青沟自然保护区　Daqing Gully Nature Reserve
海拉尔国家森林公园　Hailar National Forest Park
哈达门国家森林公园
Hadamen National Forest Park
南山生态百亭园
One-Hundred-Pavilion Ecological Park
百彦哈达草原　Baiyanhada Grasslands
葛根塔拉大草原　Gegentala Grasslands
希拉穆仁大草原　Xilamuren Grasslands
哈素海旅游度假村　Hashuhai Tourist and Holiday Resort
乌素图旅游开发区　Wusutu Tourist Development Zone
呼和浩特——历史文化名城
Hohhot city—a famous Chinese historical

and cultural city
成吉思汗陵　Genghis Khan Mausoleum
响沙湾　Dalad Banna Sand Gorge
呼伦湖　Hulun Lake

7）河北省（Hebei Province）
革命教育基地——西柏坡
the famous site of revolutionary education—Xibaipo
承德避暑山庄　Chengde Mountain Resort
北戴河海滨　Beidaihe Beach
清西陵　Western Qing Mausoleum
清东陵　Eastern Qing Mausoleum
山海关古城墙　Shanhaiguan ancient wall
山海关古城　Shanhaiguan ancient town

8）山西省（Shanxi Province）
八路军太行纪念馆　Taihang Memorial Hall of the Eighth Route Army
大同云冈石窟　Datong Yungang Grottoes
壶口瀑布　Hukou Waterfall
平遥古城　Pingyao Ancient City
乔家大院　Qiao Family's Living Quarter
杏花村　Xinghua Village
五台山　Mount Wutai
晋祠　Memorial Temple of Jin
恒山　Mount Hengshan

9）陕西省（Shanxi Province）
兵马俑　Terra-cotta Warriors
延安宝塔山　Yanan Pagoda Hill
黄河壶口瀑布　Hukou Waterfall lying on the Yellow River
半坡遗址　Banpo Ruins
八路军西安办事处纪念馆
Memorial Museum of the Eighth Route Army Xi'an Office
秦始皇陵　Emperor Qin Shi Huang's Tomb
秦始皇兵马俑
Museum of Qin Shi Huang's Terracotta Warriors
华清池　Huaqing Hot Spring
黄帝陵　Mausoleum of the Yellow Emperor
古城墙　Ancient City Wall
阿房宫　E'Fang Palace
大雁塔　Big Wild Goose Pagoda
小雁塔　Small Wild Goose Pagoda
法门寺　Famen Temple
华山　Mount Huashan
碑林　Forest of Stone Steles
昭陵　Zhaoling Mausoleum
乾陵　Qianling Mausoleum
茂陵　Emperor Wu's Maoling Tomb
钟楼　Bell Tower
鼓楼　Drum Tower

10）甘肃省（Gansu Province）
敦煌莫高窟　Mo Gao Grotto at Dunhuang
敦煌雅丹——国家地质公园
The Dunhuang Yadan—National Geology Park
敦煌鸣沙山月牙湖
Dunhuang Mingsha Mountain Yueya Spring
平凉崆峒山　Pingliang Kongtong Mountain
永靖黄河三门峡景区
Yongjing Yellow River Three Gorges scenic area
嘉峪关　Jiayuguan Fortress

甘南大草原　Gannan Plateau Grassland
天水麦积山　Tianshuimaiji Mountain
武威擂台汉墓　Wuwei Leitai Han Dynasty Tomb
张掖大佛寺　Zhangye Great Buddhist Temple

11) 宁夏回族自治区（Ningxia Huizu Autonomous Region）

沙湖　Sand Lake
中卫沙坡头　Zhongwei Shapotou
西夏王陵　Emperial Tombs of Western Xia
贺兰山岩画　Rock Carvings in Helan Mountain
六盘山　Liupan Mountain
西部影城　Western Movie Studio
水洞沟古人类遗址　Ancient Shuidonggou Relics
银川南关清真寺　Yinchuan South Gate Mosque
须弥山石窟　Xumi Mountain Grotto
青铜峡108塔　One Hundred and Eight Pagodas in Qingtongxia

12) 新疆维吾尔自治区（Xinjiang Uygur Autonomous Region）

吐鲁番葡萄沟　Turpan Grape Valley
楼兰古城　Loulan Ancient City
喀纳斯湖　Kanas Lake
一号冰川　No.1 Glacier
博斯腾湖　Bosten Lake
天池　Heavenly Lake
红山　Red Hill
坎儿井　Karez Well
火焰山　Flaming Mountain
乌尔禾魔鬼城　Urho Ghost Castle

克孜尔千佛洞　Kezil Thousand-Buddha Grottoes
交河古城　Jiaohe Ancient City
高昌古城　Gaochang Ancient City
果子沟　Fruit Valley
香妃墓　Apak Hoja Tomb

13) 青海省（Qinghai Province）

青海湖　Qinghai Lake
塔尔寺　Taer Lamasery
三江源　Source of Three Rivers
玉树地区民俗　Yushu Regional Customs
结古寺　Jiegu Lamasery
文成公主庙　Princess Wencheng Temple
勒巴沟岩画　Lebagou Rock Drawing

14) 四川省（Sichuan Province）

都江堰灌溉系统　Dujiangyan Irrigation System
九寨沟国家公园　Jiuzhaigou National Park
黄龙国家公园　Huanglong National Park
峨眉山风景区　Mount Emei Scenic Area
成都小吃城　Chengdu's Snack City
乐山大佛　Leshan Giant Buddha
卧龙国家级自然保护区　Wolong National Nature Reserve
三星堆考古遗址　Sanxingdui Archaeological Ruins
四川博物馆　Sichuan Museum
金沙博物馆　Jinsha Museum
大熊猫繁育研究中心　Giant Panda Breeding Research Center
西岭雪山　Xiling Snow Mountain
青城山　Mount Qingcheng
望江公园　River Viewing Pavilion Park
刘氏庄园　Liu Mansion

杜甫草堂　Du Fu Thatched Cottage
武侯祠　Marquis Wu Shrine
文殊院　Wenshu Temple / Monastery
青羊宫　Qingyang Taoist Temple
安仁古镇　Anren Ancient Town
黄龙古镇　Huanglong Ancient Town
洛带客家古镇　Luodai Hakka Ancient Town

15）重庆市（Chongqing）
奉节白帝城　Baidi City in Fengjie
重庆人民大会堂　Chongqing People's Great Hall
大足石刻　Dazu Stone Carvings
红星亭　Red Star Pavilion
瞰胜楼　Two-River Tower
山城夜景　Mountain City Night Scene
朝天门水景　Chaotianmen's River View
四面山的瀑布　Waterfalls in Four Sides' Mountains
南北温泉　South and North Hot Springs
黄山官邸　Huangshan Official Residence
红岩村　Hongyan Village
解放碑　Jiefangbei's Urban View
张飞庙　Zhang Fei Temple
神秘悬棺　Mysterious Suspended Coffins
桂园　Gui Garden

16）西藏自治区（Tibetan Autonomous Region）
布达拉宫　Potala Palace
大昭寺　Jokhang Temple
青藏铁路　Qinghai-Tibet Railway
雅鲁藏布大峡谷　Yarlung Zangbo Grand Canyon
昆仑雪山　Kunlung Snow Mountain
藏北羌塘草原　Changtang Grassland
温泉胜地羊八井　Yangpajing Hot Springs
唐古拉山　Tangula Mountain
天湖纳木错　Lake Namtso
青海湖　Qinghai Lake
鸟岛　Bird Island

17）贵州省（Guizhou Province）
黄果树瀑布　Huangguoshu Waterfall
犀牛潭峡谷　Xiniu Pond Gorge
水帘洞　Water Curtain Cavern
龙宫　Dragon Palace
竹海　Bamboo Sea
凤凰山　Mount Phoenix
瑶人山　Mount Yaoren
红枫湖　Hongfeng Lake
织金洞　Zhijin Cave
梵净山　Mount Fanjing
茂兰喀斯特森林　Maolan Karst Forest
咸宁草海　Xianning Grass Sea
遵义会议会址　Zunyi Meeting Site
遵义杨粲墓　Zunyi Yangcan Tomb
安顺符文庙　Anshun Fuwen Temple
民族文化旅游村寨　Villages with Cultural Tour of National Minority
7 个国家森林公园　seven State-Level Forest Parks
19 个全国重点文物保护单位　nineteen State-Level Key Cultural Relic Protection Sites
57 个省级风景名胜区　Fifty-seven Province-Level Scenic Areas
12 个国家级风景名胜区　Twelve State-Level Scenic Areas

6个国家级自然保护区
Six State-Level National Protection Zones
18) 河南省 (Henan Province)
嵩山少年寺　Songshan Shaolin Temple
龙门石窟　Longmen Grottoes
东周王陵　Eastern Zhou Dynasty Imperial Mausoleum
北宋皇陵　Northern Song Dynasty Imperial Mausoleum
洛阳白马寺　White Horse Temple in Luoyang
开封相国寺　Chancellor Temple in Kaifeng
杜甫故里　Du Fu Former Residence
玄奘故里　Xuan Zang Former Residence
苏秦故里　Suqin Former Residence
洛阳太学　Luoyang Imperial College
嵩阳书院　Songyang Academies of Classical Learning
应天府书院　Yingtian Academies of Classical Learning
19) 上海市 (Shanghai)
上海外滩　Bund in Shanghai
东方明珠　Oriental Pearl
城隍庙　Chenghuan Temple
豫园　Yuyuan Garden
朱家角古镇　Zhujiajiao Ancient Town
南京路街市　Nanjinglu Downtown Streets
20) 安徽省 (Anhui Province)
合肥逍遥津　the Leisure Ford in Hefei
合肥明教寺　Mingjiao Temple in Hefei
合肥包公祠　Memorial Temple of Bao Zheng in Hefei
黄山景区　Mt. Huang Scenic Areas
九华山景区　Mt. Jiuhua Scenic Areas
天柱山景区　Mt. Tianzhu Scenic Areas
齐云山景区　Mt. Qiyun Scenic Areas
天坛寨景区　Mt. Tiantangzhai Scenic Areas
皖南新四军纪念馆　New fourth Army Memorial Hall in the south of Anhui
皖南古村落　The Ancient Villages in Southern Anhui Province
巢湖风景区　Chaohu Scenic Areas
21) 浙江省 (Zhejiang Province)
杭州西湖　The West Lake in Hangzhou
千岛湖　Qiandao Lake
普陀山景区　The Putuo Mountain Scenic Areas
奉化溪口雪窦山　Fenghuaxikou Xuedou Mountain
横店影视城　Hengdian Movie City
中国茶叶博物馆　Chinese Tea Museum
雁荡山　Yandang Mountain
灵隐寺　Lingyin Temple
杭州宋城　Song Dynasty City in Hangzhou
岳飞庙　General Yue Fei's Temple
双龙洞　Shuanglong Cave
南太湖　South Tai Lake
楠溪江　The Nanxi River
绍兴兰亭　Lan Pavilion in Shaoxing
绍兴会稽山　The Mt. Kuaiji in Shaoxing
鲁迅纪念馆　Luxun Memorial Hall
蔡元培纪念馆　Caiyuanpei Memorial Hall
秋瑾纪念馆　Qiujing Memorial Hall
周恩来故居　Zhouenlai Former Residence
22) 江苏省 (Jiangsu Province)
古都南京　The Ancient Capital—

Nanjing City

中山陵	Dr. Sun Yat-sen's Mausoleum
秦淮河	The Qinhuai River in Nanjing
玄武湖	Xuanwu Lake in Nanjing
莫愁湖	Mou Chou Lake in Nanjing
夫子庙	Confucius Temple in Nanjing
洪秀全纪念馆	Hongxiuquan Memorial Hall in Nanjing
阅江楼	Viewing River on the Pavilion in Nanjing
南京钟山	Nanjing's Bell Mountain
清凉山	Qingliang Mountain in Nanjing
北固山	Beigu Mountain in Zhenjiang
金山	Jin Mountain in Zhenjiang
焦山	Jiao Mountain in Zhenjiang
苏州城	Suzhou City—the Oriental Venice
苏州园林	Suzhou's Classical Gardens
京杭大运河	the Beijing-Hangzhou Grand Canal
无锡太湖	the Tai Lake in Wuxi
苏北洪泽湖	Hongze Lake in northern Jiangsu Province
扬州瘦西湖	Yangzhou's Slim West Lake
徐州云龙湖	Yunlong Lake in Xuzhou
常州恐龙园	Dinosaur Garden in Changzhou

23）江西省（Jiangxi Province）

庐山景区	Mt. Lu Scenic Areas
滕王阁	Tengwang Pavilion
婺源景区	Wuyuan Scenic Areas
石钟山	Mt. Shizhon Scenic Area
彭泽龙宫洞	Longgong Cave in Pengze County
八一南昌起义纪念馆	August 1 Nanchang Uprising Museum
井冈山革命烈士陵园	Revolutionary Martyrs' Mausoleum in Jinggang Mountain
井岗山纪念馆	Jinganshan Memorial Hall
庐山锦绣谷景区	Beautiful Valley Scenic Area in Mt. Lushan
景德镇陶瓷旅游项目	Ceramic Travelling Program in Jingdezhen

24）福建省（Fujian Province）

武夷山	Mount. Wuyi
鼓浪屿	Gulangyu—the Garden on the Sea
泰宁	Taining—the World Geology Park
妈祖庙	Holy Mazu Temple
古田会址	the Site of Glorious Gutian Meeting
白水洋	Mysterious Baishuiyang
滨海火山	Coastal Volcano
礜石山	Mt. Tanshishan

25）湖北省（Hubei Province）

二七纪念馆	"Twenty-seven" Memorial Hall
武汉起义军政府旧址	The Former Site of the Wuchang Insurgent Army Government
武汉古琴台	Wuhan Guqin Pavilion
秭归屈原祠	Zigui Qu Yuan Temple
秭归屈原故里	Zigui Qu Yuan Former Residence
襄樊古隆中	Xiangfan Gulongzhong
纪南古城	Jinan Old City
昭君故里	Zhaojun's Hometown
武汉东湖	the Wuhan's East Lake

江汉古城	Jianghan ancient city
蒲圻赤壁	Puqi Cliff
长江三峡	Three Gorges over the Yangtze River
三峡大坝	grand dam over the Three Gorges
黄鹤楼	Yellow Crane Tower
归元寺	Guiyuan Temple
九宫山	Mt. Jiugongshan
武当山	Mt. Wudangshan
神农架	Mt. Shennong

26）湖南省（Hunan Province）

毛泽东故居	Mao Zedong's Former Residence
湖南省博物馆	Hunan Provincial Museum
马王堆汉墓	Han Tombs of Mawangdui
南岳衡山	Nanyue Hengyang Mountain
湘西猛洞河景区	Scenic Area of Xiangxi Mengdong River
张家界风景区	Scenic Areas of Zhangjiajie Mountains
武陵源风景区	Wulingyuan Scenic Area
岳麓山风景名胜区	The Yuelu Mountain Scenic Resort Areas
莨山风景区	Liangshan Scenic Area
炎帝陵	Emperor Yan's Mausoleum
凤凰古城	Fenghuang Ancient Town
岳阳楼	Yueyang Tower in Yueyang city
桃花源	Peach Blossom Garden
苏仙岭	Suxian Mountain
万花岩	Wanhua Rock
南长城	South Great Wall of China

27）广东省（Guangdong Province）

孙中山故居	Former Residence of Dr. Sun Yat-sen
梁思成故居	Former Residence of Dr. Liang Sicheng
锦绣中华	Splendid China
中国民族文化村	Chinese Folk Cultural Village
丹霞山	Danxia Mountain
罗浮山	Luofu Mountain
西樵山	Xiqiao Mountain
鼎湖山	Dinghu Mountain

28）广西省（Guangxi Province）

桂林漓江	Lijiang River in Guilin City
阳朔风景区	Yangshuo Scenic Area
象鼻山风景区	Elephant Trunk Hill
北海银滩	Beihai Silver Beach

29）海南省（Hainan Province）

海口风景区	Haikou Scenic Areas
野菠萝岛	Wild Pineapple Island
海底村庄	Benthic Villages
万绿园	Evergreen Garden
海口黄金西海岸公园	Haikou Western Coastal Park
桂林洋海滨旅游区	Guilin Seaside Tourism Zone
海南热带海洋世界	Hainan Tropical Oceanic World
东寨港红树林自然保护区	Dongzhaigang National Mango Forest National Reserve
三亚之旅	Sanya Tourism
天涯海角	End of the Earth
大东海	Dadong Sea
亚龙湾	Yalong Bay
南山寺	Nanshan Temple
蝴蝶谷	Butterfly Valley

大小洞天	Paradise Caves for Celestial Beings
鹿回头公园	Luhuitou Park
兴隆热带植物园	Xinglong Tropical Botanical Garden

文昌东郊椰林风景区
Wenchang Eastern suburb Coconut Grove Scenic Areas

居丁珍稀动物园	Juding Zoo of Rare Birds and Animals
博鳌水城	Boao Aquapolis
南湾猴岛	Nanwan Monkey Peninsula
蜈支州岛	Wuzhizhou Island
六大温泉	Six Famous Hot Springs
万泉河漂流	Drifting about over the Wanquan River
五指山	The Wuzhishan Mountain

30）云南省（Yunnan Province）

| 石林景区 | Stone Forest Scenic Areas |
| 世博园景区 | The World Horti-Expo Garden |

西双版纳勐仑热带植物园
Xishuangbanna Menglun Tropical Botanical Garden

西双版纳傣族园	Daizu Garden in Xishuangbanna
南诏故都大理	Capital of Nanzhao Kingdom—Dali
玉龙雪山	Jade Dragon Snow Mountain
丽江城	Ancient Lijiang Town
和顺古镇	Heshun Ancient Town
香格里拉	Shangri-la
腾冲地热火山	Tengchong Hot Sea Volcano

31）山东省（Shandong Province）

泰山景区	Taishan Scenic Areas
青岛之旅	Tourism of Qingdao City
青岛海滨	Qingdao Sea Beach
古城曲阜	Ancient City—Qufu
孔庙	Confucius Temple
孔府	Living Quarters of the Confucius Family
孔林	Graveyard of the Confucius Family
蓬莱阁	Penglai Pavilion

32）台湾省（Taiwan）

阿里山风景区	Alishan Scenic Area
阿里山森林游乐区	Alishan Forest Recreation Area
北关海潮公园	Beiguan Tidal Park
北港朝天宫	Beigang Chao Tian Temple

北海岸及观音山风景区
North Coast & Guanyinshan Scenic Area

| 八仙洞 | Baxian Caves |

东眼山森林游乐区
Dongyanshan Forest Recreation Area

八仙山森林游乐区	Baxianshan Forest Recreation Area
鲤鱼潭风景特定区	Liyu Lake Special Scenic Area
碧潭风景特定区	Bitan Special Scenic Area
布洛湾游甜区	Pulowan Recreation Area
垦丁森林游乐区	Kending Forest Recreation Area
琉球风景区	Liuqiu Scenic Area
澎湖风景区	Penghu Scenic Area

梨山风景区	Lishan Scenic Area
满月园森林游乐区	Manyueyuan Forest Recreation Area
青洲滨海游息区	Qingzhou Ocean Recreation Area
茂林风景区	Maolin Scenic Area
富源森林游乐区	Fuyuan Forest Recreation Area
池内森林游乐区	Chinei Forest Recreation Area
日月潭风景区	Sun Moon Lake Scenic Area
狮头山风景区	lion's head mountain scenic area
草岭古道系统	Caoling historic trail system
莲池潭	Lotus pond
龙潭湖	Longtan lake
梅花湖	plum blossom lake
澄清湖	Chengqing lake
大湖	Dahu lake
兰潭	lan pond
大佛风景区	Dafoshan Buddha scenic area
大鹏湾风景区	Dapeng Bay scenic area
东部海岸风景区	East coast scenic area
观音瀑布风景区	Guanyin waterfall scenic area
龟山岛海域游息区	turtle island coast recreation area
佳乐水风景区	Jialeshui scenic area
内洞森林游乐区	Neidong forest recreation area
东方夏威夷	East Hawaii amusement park
东山乐园	Dongshan paradise
东埔温泉	Dongpu hot-spring
翡翠湾海水浴场	green bay
和平岛滨海公园	Hepingdao seashore park
凤凰谷鸟园	Phoenix valley bird park
阳明公园	Yangming park
雪霸公园	Xueba park
台中公园	Taizhong park
情人湖公园	Qingrenhu park
社顶自然公园	Sheding nature park
田中森林公园	Tianzhong forest park
垦丁公园	Kending park
金门公园	Jinmen park
安平古堡	Anping fort
大天后宫	Great Empress of Heaven Temple
佛光山	Foguangshan
高雄史迹文物陈列馆	Gaoxiong Museum of History
顺益台湾原住民博物馆	Shungyi Museum of Formosan Aborigines
台湾科学教育馆	science and education centre of Taiwan
台湾民俗北投文物馆	folk custom museum of Beitou
科学工艺博物馆	Science and Technology Museum
自然科学博物馆	Museum of Natural Science
金山温泉馆	Jinshan hot-spring gym pool
澎湖水族馆	Penghu Aquarium
排云山庄	Paiyun lodge

九九山庄　Jiujiu villa
九族文化村　Culture Village of the nine degrees of kindred
中华民俗村　China folk custom village
西湖度假村　West Lake resort
中山纪念林　Sun Yat Sen Memorial Forest
万和宫　Wanhe Temple
五妃庙　Five Concubines Temple
忠烈祠　Revolutionary Martyrs Shrine
五峰旗瀑布　Wufengqi Waterfall
新光摩天展望台　Topview Observatory of Taibei

33）香港（Hong Kong）
中英街　Zhonying Street
海洋公园　Ocean Park
新界　New Territories
总督府　Government House
香港仔　Aberdeen
尖沙嘴　Tsim Sha Tsui
九龙　Kowloon
跑马地　Happy Valley
香港岛　Hong Kong Island
浅水湾　Repulse Bay
维多利亚港　Victoria Harbor
黄大仙　Wong Tai Sin
合和中心　Hopewell Centre
海港城　Harbor City
香港迪斯尼乐园　Hong Kong Disneyland
香港会展中心　Hong Kong Convention and Exhibition Center
大屿山　Lantau Island
扯旗山　Victoria Peak

34）澳门（Macao）
大炮台　Monte Fortress
妈祖庙　Barra Temple / Mazu Temple
莲峰庙　Linfeng Temple
观音堂　Gunying Temple
阿婆井　Lilau Square
仁慈堂　Santa Casa da Misericordia
十字公　Marques Esparteiro Garden
议事亭　Leal Senado Square
文化中心　cultural centre
艺术公园　arts garden
妈祖雕像　Statue of the Goddess Kun Iam
圣玫瑰教堂　St. Dominic's Church
圣母雪地教堂　Chapel of our Lady of Guia
嘉思栏花园　St. Francis Garden
澳门大三巴牌坊　Ruins of St. Paul
澳门博物馆　Macao City Museum
东望洋灯塔　Guia Lighthouse
大赛车博物馆　Grand Prix Museum
海事博物馆　Maritime Museum
葡萄酒博物馆　Wine Museum

4. 名胜古迹（Scenic Spots and Historical Sites）

人造景观　artificial scenery
民俗村　folk custom park
半坡村　6000-year-old Banpo Village
赤壁古战场　Chibi ancient battlefield
佛教胜地　Buddha scenic spot
宗教胜地　sacred sites
佛像　statue of Buddha
碑林　Forest of Steles

钟楼	Bell Tower	古城遗迹	ruins of an ancient city

5. 著名自然风光 (Famous Natural Scenery)

西湖	the West Lake		resort
桂林山水	Guilin Mountains and Waters	度假胜地	holiday resort
瀑布	waterfall	古建筑群	ancient architectural complex
日月潭	Sun Moon Lake	园林建筑	garden architecture
敦煌莫高窟	Mogao Grotto in Dunhuang	山水风光	scenery with mountains and rivers
景点	scenic spots		
旅游观光点	tourist spots	城市风光	cityscape
热带风光	tropical scenery	诱人景色	inviting views
游乐园	amusement park	湖光山色	landscape of lakes and hills
旅游野餐区	picnic area for tourists	青山绿水	green hills and clear waters
春/秋游	spring / autumn outing	石舫	stone boat
假日旅行	vacation tour	主题游乐园	theme park
自然保护区	national reserves	海滨浴场	bathing beach
有吸引力的名胜	attractive sights	海滨胜地	seaside resort
风景如画	picturesque scenery	海滩	beach
自然景观	natural scenery / attraction; natural landscape	海滨沙滩	sand beach
		避暑胜地	summer resort
人文景观	places of historic figures and cutural heritage	海滨休息地	seaside resort
		山水风光	landscape scenery
名山大川	famous mountains and great rivers	田园风光	idyllic scenery
		山区胜地	mountain resort
名胜古迹	scenic spots and historical sites	穴洞	grotto
		石笋	stalagmite
佛教名山	famous Buddhist mountains	主要名胜	chief sights
避暑山庄	summer resort / mountain		

6. 国外著名旅游景点 (The Famous Tourist Attractions of Foreign Countries)

1) 亚洲其他国家 (Asian other countries)

泰国曼谷——天使之城 Bangkok, Thailand—the City of Angels

马尔代夫——情人天堂 Maldives—the Lover's Paradise

新加坡——花园城 Singapore—the Garden City

马来西亚槟城 Penang, Malaysia

印度泰姬陵	Taj Maha—The Great Monument to the Love of the Emperor and the Empress
阿联酋迪拜	Dubai, the UAE—The Luxurious Star City
日本富士山	Fu Shi Mountain in Japan—the Snow Scenery
韩国济州岛	Jeju Island in South Korea—the Famous Island of Honeymoon and of Celebration
芭提雅（泰国）	Pattaya（scenic area）
巴厘岛风光	Bali Island scenery

2）欧洲（Europe）

巴黎圣母院	Notre Dame de Paris—the birthplace of the world-famous literary works
德国无忧宫	Sans souci Palace in Germany—the Summer Palace on the Dunes
巴塞罗那	Barcelona in Spain—the European Flower
白金汉宫	Buckingham Palace in Britain—the Miserable and Beautiful Love in the British Palace
维罗纳	Verona—the Secret Wedding Place of Romeo and Juliet
爱情海	Aegean Sea—the young bride was born for love
布拉格	Prague City—the City with the Thousand Towers
普罗旺斯	Provence—the Romantic Story with Lavender
雪浓梭堡	Chateau de Chenonceau—the Six Women's Love and Hate
剑桥大学	University of Cambridge—the famous university in the world

3）大洋洲（Oceania）

达尔文	Darwin—the City of Heartbeat
墨尔本	Melbourne—the Garden City
悉尼歌剧院	Sydney Opera House—the Sydney's Soul of the Culture and Art
海姆斯沙滩	Hyams Beach
关岛恋人岬	Two Lovers Point in Guam—Romantic Lovers Here
爱丽斯泉	Alice Springs
皇后镇	Queens town—the Capital of Exploration

4）非洲（Africa）

萨哈拉大沙漠	Sahara Vast Desert
约翰内斯堡	Johannesburg—The Golden City
卡萨布兰卡	Casablanca—Atlantic Bride
好旺角	Cape of Good Hope—The Dangerous Waterway
南非太阳城	Sun City in South Africa—Legendary Charm
埃及金字塔	Egyptian Pyramids—The Miracle of Architecture
肯尼亚树顶旅馆	Treetop's Hotel in Kenniya
毛里求斯岛国	Island Nation—Mauritius

5）南美洲（South America）

利马唐人街	Lima's China's Town—Chinese-style Architectures

and Delicious food
智利复活节岛　Easter Island in Chile—The Hometown of Stone Statues
亚马逊雨林　Amazon Rainforest—The Scenery of Tropical Forest
哥伦比亚五色河　Cano Cristales—The Beautiful Rainbows
阿根廷门多萨　Mendoza in Argentina—Typical Kingdom of Wine
科尔多瓦花之巷　Cordoba—Flower Lane
马丘比丘　Machu Pichu—The Lost City

6）北美洲（North America）

加拿大渥太华　Ottawa in Canada—Tulip City
加拿大多伦多　Toroto in Canada—The North Hollywood
美国夏威夷　American Hawaii—Dream Heaven
美国好莱坞　American Hollywood—Dream Factory of the Film Stars
金斯顿　Kingston—Pirateland
拉斯维加斯　Las Vegas in America—Entertainment Capital of the World
爱德华王子岛　Edward Prince Island—Rural Life and Picturesque Ocean Scenery

7. 旅游方式（Tourist Ways）

文明之旅　journey of civilization
周游世界　globe trotter /world traveler
国际旅游　international tourism
漫游世界　world tour
国内游　home tourism
地方旅游　local tour
海上游　sea journey
乘车游　bus tour
乘游览车　to take tourist coach
乘旅游大巴　to take sightseeing bus
乘空中游览车　to take skyride
乘缆车　to take cable car
豪华游　luxurious tour
自驾游　driving travel
公费游　public expense tourism / junket
自费游　tourism at one's own expense / self-financed tour
观光旅游　sightseeing tour
文化旅游　cultural tourism
文化遗产旅游　cultural heritage tourism
生态旅游　eco-tourism
登山旅游　mountaineering tour
城市观光游　city breaks
粉色旅游　pink tourism
郊游　outing
环球旅游　around the world trip
蜜月游　honeymoon tour / bridal tour
相亲游　dating tours
免费旅游　free travel tour
业余导游　amateur guide
短期游　short breaks
全包旅游线路　all inclusive itineraries
家庭度假游　family holidays tourism
外国婚礼游　weddings abroad
别墅度假　villa holidays

探险度假　adventure holidays
陪同游　escorted tours
乘飞机旅游　air traveller
电子旅游　electronic tourism
徒步旅游　hiker / wayfarer
经济游　economical travel
包价旅游　package tour
国外游　foreign tour
短途游　outing / journey
长途旅游　long journey
一日游　one-day tour / day excursion
二日游　two-day tour
八日游　eight-day tour
假日游　holiday travel

周末游　weekend trip
春游　spring outing
夏季旅游　summer tour
秋游　autumn outing
冬季游　winter tour
游园　to visit a park or garden
游山玩水　to make a sightseeing tour
水上游　voyage tour / cruises
滑雪度假　ski holidays
度假游客　holiday maker
海上旅游者　seafarer
旅游观光者　travel sightseer
骑自行车旅游者　bicycle tourer
外国游客　foreign tourist

8. 其他旅游词语 (Other Tourist Terms)

旅游计划　travel program / itinerary
旅游服务　travel service
导游　courier / tourist guide
旅行家　veteran traveller
旅游天地　travelling scope
国际导游　global guide
旅游证件　travel documents
导游手册　guidebook
旅游指南　tourist guide / travel brochure
旅游纪念品　tourist souvenir
旅游图　tourist map
旅行指南　itinerary
旅游线路　tourist track (or route)
旅游护照　tourist card
旅行支票　traveller's cheque
旅游日记　itinerary
旅程　itinerary
旅费　travelling expenses
旅游旺季　tourist season / high season

旅游淡季　slack season of tour
旅游高峰季　peak-travel period
旅游萧条　tourist drought
旅游陷阱　tourist trap
旅游纪念品　tourist souvenir
旅游住宿地　tourist home
旅游旅馆　tourist hotel
电子旅游企业　electronic tourism enterprises
旅伴　travel companion
旅友　tourist friend
旅游用品　travel kit
旅游服　outing dress
旅游鞋　hiking boots
登山鞋　mountaineering boots
旅行箱　travelling case
手提旅行包　hold-all / gladstone bag
小提箱　gripsack
旅行袋　travelling bag

睡袋	sleeping bag
旅行折叠床	camp bed for travel
游览船	excursion-boat
游览车	tourist coach（car）
高空索道	rope way
景点门票	admission ticket
免门票	admission free
门票费	admission fee
长途跋涉	to travel a long way
旅游外汇	tourist foreign exchange
旅游资源	tourism assets (or resource)
旅游运营商	tour operator
休闲度假行业	the leisure vacation industry
即刻度假	last minute holidays
即刻订票	last minute flights
限时特价	last availability discounts
个人旅游顾问	personal travel agent
旅游宿营帐篷	tourist camp
旅游数字化	digitalization of tourism

9 产业经济
Industrial Economy

发展特色产业	to develop specialty industries
多种产业经济	multi-industrial economy
个体经济 / 私营经济	self-employed and private business
转变经济发展方式	shift of the economic growth model
出口加工区	export processing areas
保税区	bonded zones
独立核算工业企业	independent accounting unit enterprises
中外合资企业	Sino-foreign joint ventures
装备产业升级	to upgrade equipment and manufacturing industry
经济技术开发区	an economic and technological development zone
高新技术产业	high-tech industry
国有企业改革	reform of state-owned enterprises
外资企业	foreign funded enterprises / foreign invested enterprises
龙头企业	leading enterprises
环保产业	environmental protection industries
生态农业	environment-friendly agriculture
循环经济	circular economy
绿色经济	green economy
低碳经济	low carbon economy
误导性品牌	derivative trademarks
转基因食品	genetically modified food
拳头产品	knockout products / competitive products
高科技产品	the high-tech products
长线产品	products in excessive supply
畅销产品	marketable products / products with good market
IT 企业群	a cluster of IT enterprises
新能源新材料	new energy and materials
成长型企业市场	growing enterprise market
高附加值产业	high value industries
产业集群	industrial clusters
以企业为主体	to let enterprises be the main players
支柱产业	pillar industry
新兴企业	start-up company
小微企业	small and micro business
红帽子企业	red cap enterprise
振兴支柱产业	to invigorate pillar industry

发展环保产业	to develop environmental conservation industries	新型农业经营体系	a new type of system for intensive agricultural operations
信息技术产业	information technology industry	新型经营主体	new types of business entities
物流业	logistics	对外工程承包	overseas projects contracting
博彩业	lottery industry	劳务合作营业额	turnover of labour contract
高技术产业化	high-tech industrialization		
农业产业化	industrtrialized agriculture	振兴装备制造业	to invigorate our equipment manufacturing industry
白色农业	white agriculture /white engineering agriculture	技术密集型产业	technology-intensive industries
教育产业化	a market-oriented education		
知识社会化	a knowledge-driven society	产能产量过剩产业	excess industries in production capacity and output
国民经济信息化	an information-based national economy		
科技成果产业化	to apply scientific research results to industrial production	取消福利分房	to abolish the welfare-oriented house distribution
企业化管理	to manage in the same manner as what is done to an enterprise	政策性住房	policy-related house / policy-based house
物业管理	property management	社区服务业	community-based services
归口管理	centralized management by specialized departments	天然林保护	to protect natural forests
续建项目	ongoing projects	防沙治沙	to prevent futher desertification
收尾项目	projects of near completion	南水北调工程	the irrigation works of diverting water from the south to the north
支持强强联合	to support association between strong enterprises	东线一期工程	the first-phase project of the eastern route
实现优势互补	to realize taking advantage of each other's strengths	中线一期工程	the first-phase project of the central route
采取市场多元化战略	to adopt the strategy of multi-outlet market	非化石能源发电量	electricity generation from non-fossil energy
产销直接挂钩	directly link production with marketing	新型工业化之路	new path of

产业经济 / Industrial Economy

	industrialization
战略性新型产业	strategic emerging industries
企业核心竞争力	core competency of enterprises
产业核心竞争力	core competitiveness of industries
产业升级	to upgrade industries
产业结构升级	upgrading of an industrial structure
产业衔接状况	the ratio of sales to production
产业升级换代	upgrading of industries
优势产业	competitive industries
窗口行业	various service trade
文化产业	cultural sector
创业园	high-tech business incubator / pioneer park
第一产业	primary industry
第二产业	secondary industry
第三产业	tertiary industry / service sector
第四产业	quaternary industry / information industry
房屋改造	renovation of old residential buildings
产业结构	industrial structure
产品结构	product mix
市政工程	civil engineering projects
集资房	housing of raising funds / housing of collecting money
商品房	commercial residential building
硬件行业	hardware sector
软件行业	software sector
中小企业	small and medium-sized enterprises
实体经济	real economy
独资	wholly-owned venture
联营	joint operations
营运利润率	operating margin
原油生产量	crude output
资源税	resource tax
现代物流	modern logistics
农产品流通	farm products distribution
西部大开发	to develop the western regions
西电东送	transmission of electricity from the western to the eastern regions

10 电脑, 网络语言
Computer and Network Language

携式电脑	laptops / notebook computer
台式电脑	desktop computer
苹果电脑	apple computer
物联网	Internet of things
桌面 pc 机	desktop PC
奔腾 111 型电脑	Pentium 111 computer
彩色 imac 电脑	colourful apple iMac computer
个人电脑	personal computer
兼容机	compatible computer
品牌机	brand name computer
康柏电脑	compag computer
国产电脑	domestically-made computer
数字电脑	digital computer
电子电脑	electronic computer
苹果机	apple macintosh (PC)
光学计算机	optical computer
大型集成电路计算机	large integrated circuit computer
终端计算机	terminal computer
超级计算机	super computer
超小型计算机	micro-minicomputer
微处理机	micro-processor
英特尔奔腾	Intel Pentium
微处理器	microprocessor
电脑主机	computer main frame
操作系统	operating system
数据处理	data processing
文字处理	word processing
文字处理系统	word processing system
终端操作系统	terminal operating system
网络公开课	massive open course online
看电视发微博	chatterboxing
硬盘操作系统	dos
接口	interface
网上浏览	to surf online
商业软件	business software
电脑软件	computer software
电脑硬盘	computer hard drive
软盘空间	disk space
机箱	case
软件	software
光盘	CD (computer disk)
软盘	floppy disk
阅读器	reader
服务端(器)	server
存储块区	bank
警告过程	beacon
关键/阻塞	bottleneck
磁泡	bubble
掩码	mask
存储桶	pocket

Computer and Network Language

网桥	bridge	存储器	memory
汇流排	bus	存储量	memory space / storage size
界址	fence	修饰器	metaphor
标志	flag	中央处理器	central processing unit
集成器	hub	监视器/监控程序	monitor
位平面	plane	显示器	monitor
数据流	stream	信息变换	information conversion
端口	port	信息反馈	information feedback
求反	negate	输入信息	input information
硬件	hardware	输入程序	input programme
应用软件	application software	制造程序	maker
病毒	virus	出错显示程序	panic
死机	freeze	磁盘的磁头	head
单线索	single thread	祖节点	ancestor
指令	instruction	后继节点	descendent
索程	thread	友元	friend
窗口	window	主机	host
内存	RAM	键盘	keyboard
数组	array	鼠标	mouse
群集器	cluster	主/从结构	master / slave
关闭	disable	孤立单元	orphan
回送	echoing	节点	node
换码	escape	电子游戏	PC game
升级	upgrade	电子邮件	E-mail
转发	forwarding	电子附件	electronic attachment
信关/网关	gateway	电子表格	spread sheets
17吋显示器	17 inch monitor	安装软件	load the software
调制解调器	modem	用户端软件	client software
硬盘驱动器	hard drive	超级应用软件	killer applications
磁盘驱动器	disk drive	图像处理软件	graphics
信号交换	handshaking	计算机辅助设计	computer-aided design（CAD）
因特网服务	Internet service		
网上服务	service on-line	信息高速公路	information highway
存取/访问	access	综合业务数字网	integrated service digital network
记账程序	account		

远程导航系统	long-range aid to navigation
虚拟数据网络	virtual data network
移动无线电网络	mobile radio network
人工电源网络	artificial mains network
虚拟存储系统	virtual memory system
虚拟存储器	virtual storage
网络分析仪	network analyzer
虚拟终端机	virtual terminal
计算机代码	computer code
计算机电缆	computer cable
安全系统	fail-safe system
安全锁	security key-lock
功能键	function key
指令	instruction
上网	surf on Internet
网址 / 网站	website
网点	a network of commercial establishments
网络	network
网巾	hairnet
宽带	broadband network
网吧	intenet bar
网友	network friend
网民	netizen
网虫	internet buff / internet geek
网恋	romance on the internet
网速	speed of network
信息亭	information booths
互联网络协议	Internet Protocol
商业网络	commerce network
企业网络	enterprise network
信息网络	information networks
邮政网络	postal service networks
水运网络	water transport networks
网络审查	sensor the Internet / Internet censorship / online supervision
网络广告	advertisement online
网络安全	cyber security
网络环境	network environment
网络社区	web community
网络结构	network configuration
网络经济	cyber economy
网络空间	cyber space
网络礼仪	netiquette
网络语言	network languages
网络连接	network interconnectivity
网络社区	online community
网络新手	newbie
网络新闻	network news
网络电话	internet phone
网络"黑话"	network cant
网络运行中心	network operation center
网络信息中心	network information center
网络消费者	consumer online
网络经济学家	web economist
网络计算机	network computer / NC
网上银行	e-bank
网上教育	e-learning
网上购物	online shopping
网上支付	onling payment
网路钟点工	virtual troubleshooter
网络日记 / 博客	blogs
网上中间商	reseller online
网络投资者	network investor
网络基础设施	internet infrastructure
内部网关协议	interior gateway protocol
外部互联网	external network
三网融合	to deliver telecommunications,

Computer and Network Language

	radio and television, and Internet services over a single broadband connection		villages
网上电子结算		online electronic settlement	
在线娱乐	online entertainment	网络交换服务	switched services by Internet Network
网上卖线路	online route purchasing		
网上订线路	online route reserving	网上集体议价	to buy in group on internet
网上品牌	website brand	网上求职中心	online career center
网络账号	network accounts	宽带中国	China's broadband
网上促销	promotion on internet	电子商务	E-commerce
网上调查	to investigate on internet	网上空间	cyberspace
网上求职	to ask / to hunt for job on internet	网民	cyber citizen
		网络犯罪	cyber crime
八卦网站	gossip site	数字鸿沟	digital gap
网上信用卡支付	payment by online credit card	数字准入	digital access
		数据影子	data shadow
企业电子邮件系统	project E-mail system	家庭办公族	Small Office Home Office (SOHO)
客户服务器	Client-Server	Wi-Fi 蹭网族	Wi-Fi squatter
局域网络协议	LAN Protocol	脑图	mind map
宽带综合业务数字网	broadband ISDN / B-ISDN	红色网站	politically-minded / oriented web
互联网络信息中心	Internet Network Information Center	白帽子黑客	white hat hacker
		黑帽子黑客	black hat hacker
第四代移动通讯	4G mobile telecommunications	灰帽子黑客	grey hat hacker
		访问	access / visiting
宽带网村乡工程	project for broadband connection to rural	下载	download

121

11 文化和思想教育
Culture and Education in Thought

1. 思想教育 (Education in Thought)

中国先进文化的前进方向 orientation of China's advanced culture

三讲教育 three emphasises' education

讲学习,讲政治,讲正气 to stress theoretical study, political awareness and good conduct

有理想,有道德,有文化 people with lofty ideals, moral integrity, a good education

有纪律的人民 people with a strong sense of discipline

加强精神文明建设 to enhance the social construction of ideological infrastructure

青少年思想道德 ideals and ethics among young people

公民道德建设工程 program for improving civic morality

博采各种文明之长 to draw upon the strength of other civilizations

向人民交出满意的答卷 to deliver a good report to the people

关心中国现代化建设 to care about China's modernizations

社会主义政治文明 socialist political civilization

共产主义道德 communist morality /ethics

旧道德观念 old moral concepts

道德品质 moral character

体育道德 sportsmanship

商业道德 business ethics

道德败坏 morally degenerate

思想道德建设 to promote ideological and ethical progress

思想道德教育 education in ideology and ethics

坚持拒腐防变 to adhere to resist corruption, prevent degeneration

2. 文化 (Culture)

文化体制改革 reform of cultural administrative system

大力发展文化产业 vigorously develop the cultural industry

公益性文化事业 non-profit cultural undertakings

加强文化建设 to strengthen cultural development efforts

文化和思想教育
Culture and Education in Thought

文化整体实力	overall cultural strength
公益文化活动	nonprofit cultural programs
文化更加繁荣	a more prosperous culture
文化共同繁荣	cultural common prosperity
丰富的文化内涵	to be rich in culture
中国传统艺术	Chinese traditional art
传承文化	to carry forward Chinese culture
文化创意	cultural design
文化精髓	cultural quintessence
文化精品	high-quality cultural works
建立繁荣的文化市场	to create a thriving cultural market
对外文化交流格局	a pattern of foreign cultural exchange
有地方特色的文化产业	cultural industries with regional features
公共文化服务标准化	public cultural services in a standard and equitable way
继承中原文化正统	to inherit cultural tradition of central plains
非物质文化遗产	intangible cultural heritage
保护历史文化遗址	to protect sites of historical and cultural relic
促进文化创意	to integrate the development of cultural and creative industries
文化下乡活动	culture-to-the-countryside drive
培养文化市场	to foster a market for cultural goods
规范文化市场	a well-regulated market for cultural goods
文化软实力	cultural soft power
文化竞争力	cultural competitiveness
文化产业	cultural industries
文化产业基础	cultural industry bases
文化工作者	cultural workers
文化设施	cultural facilities
人类文化	human culture
文化人	man of letters
文化交流	culture exchange
文化沟	culture gap
文化事业	cultural undertakings
文化建设	cultural development
文化制度	cultural system
文化渗透	cultural penetration
文化遗产	cultural heritage
文化污染	cultural contamination/cultural pollution
文化多样性	cultural diversity
文化大省	culturally advanced province
文化音乐	culture music
中华民乐	Chinese folk music
古典名乐	famous classic pieces of Chinese music
中国文化	Chinese culture
外国文化	foreign culture
民族文化	national culture
古代文化	ancient culture
东方文化	oriental culture
西方文化	western culture
物质文化	material culture
传统文化	traditional culture
先进文化	advanced culture
落后文化	backward culture

123

文化逆差	cultural deficit	文化经济联合体	cultural-economic venture
亚文化	sub-culture	物质文化需求	material and cultural needs
本地文化	local culture		
社区文化	community culture		
文化积淀	rich in cultural heritage	弘扬文化传统	carry forward cultural heritage
人文交流	cultural and people-to-people exchange		
		优秀文化传统	fine cultural traditions
精神文化生活	spiritual and cultural life	音乐节	music festival

3. 节日文化 (Festivals and Culture)

元旦	New Year's Day	父亲节	Father's Day
春节	Spring Festival	万圣节	All Saint's Day
元宵节	Lantern Festival	教师节	Teacher's Day
清明节	Qingming Festival	护士节	Nurses' Day
端午节	Dragon-boat Festival	国际妇女节	International Women's Day
中秋节	Mid-autumn Festival		
重阳节	Chongyang Festival	狂欢节	Carnival
圣诞节	Christmas Day	建军节	Army Day
感恩节	Thanksgiving Day	泼水节	Water Sprinkling Day
愚人节	April Fool's Day	斋戒节	Fast Day
复活节	Easter Holiday	公假日	Public Holiday
情人节	St. Valentine's Day	吉日	Auspicious Day
母亲节	Mother's Day	好日子	Lucky Day

4. 常用文化术语 (Useful Cultural Terms)

文化合作	cultural cooperation	文化进化	cultural evolution
文化程度	cultural standard / level	文化交往	cultural contact
精神文化	spiritual culture	文化革命	cultural revulotion
文化遗址	a site of ancient cultural remains	通俗文化	popular culture
文房四宝	the four treasures of the study	文化差别	cultural difference
文化课	literacy class	文化进步	cultural progress
大众文化	mass culture	文化扩展	culture expansion / extension
风俗文化	customs culture	文化冲击	cultural shock
民间文化	folk culture	文化传播	cultural diffusion
文化复兴	cultural revitalization	文化内涵	cultural connotation

文化专制	cultural autocracy	三个一百	"a hundred patriotic films (or songs / books)" list
文化侵略	cultural aggression		
文化渗透	cultural infiltration	经营性文化	cultural enterprises
文化占领	cultural occupation	经营性文艺	commercial art and culture
文化模式	culture pattern	文艺复兴	the Renaissance
文化偏见	cultural bias	精彩的文艺表演	a wonderful artistic performance
文化中心	cultural center		
文化区域	culture region	文化事业单位	cultural institutions
文化学	culturology	文化扶贫计划	culture-aid program
文化退化	cultural devolution	文化建设项目	cultural development items
文化特质	culture trait		
文化停滞	cultural lag	文化精品工程	cultural works of excellence
文化统一	cultural unity		
文化多元论	cultural pluralism	文化信息资源	cultural information and resources
文化相对论	culture relativism		
文物保护	preservation of cultural relics	对外文化宣传	internationally cultural publicity
社会文化	community culture		
文化下乡	bringing culture to the countryside	对外文化贸易	internationally cultural trade
文化机制	cultural mechanism	对外文化传播	internationally cultural communication
文化宫	palace of culture		
文化馆	cultural centre	县县都有文化站	Every county has cultural center.
文史馆	Research Institute of Culture and History		
		乡乡都有文化站	Every township has cultural station.
文化节	cultural festival		
文化界	cultural circles	小额文化援助	small-fund aid for cultural development
文化水平	cultural level		
文化专员	cultural attache	有文化的农民	a farmer with a basic education and some knowledge
文化机关	cultural institution		
文化用品	stationery		

5. 文化团体与机构 (Culture Group and Organization)

文工团	art ensemble	乐队	band
剧团	troupe	民乐队	folk orchestra
音乐团体	musical organization	军乐队	military band

管乐队	wind band		流行乐队	pop group
钢管乐队	brass band		爵士乐队	jazz orchestra
管弦乐队	orchestra		摇滚乐队	rock and roll band
弦乐队	string band		专业乐队	professional band
交响乐队	symphony orchestra		业余乐队	amateur band
轻音乐队	light music band		巡回乐队	touring band

6. 文化多样性（Cultural Diversity）

喜剧	comedy		民歌	folk song
悲剧	tragedy		歌剧	opera
戏剧	drama		声乐	vocal music
杂剧	Zaju		古乐	ancient music
木偶剧	puppet show		音色	tone / timbre
皮影剧	shadow play		音调	tone
活报剧	street performance		音长	duration of a sound
复仇剧	revenge drama		音程	interval
样板戏	model opera (drama)		音符	note
抒情歌剧	lyric theater		音高	pitch
现代戏剧	modern drama		音阶	scale
性格喜剧	comedy of humors		音量	volume
古典悲剧	classical tragedy		音律	temperament
家庭悲剧	domestic tragedy		音频	audio frequency
学院戏剧	academic drama		音速	velocity of sound
革命戏剧	revolutionary drama		格调	tone
音乐公爵	musical duke		贝多芬	Beethoven
管弦乐曲	orchestral music		电子音乐	electronic music
音乐节奏	musical beat		旋律	melody
合奏	ensemble		新摇滚	new rock
伴奏/伴唱	accompaniment		喜剧小品	comedy skit
合唱	chorus/ensemble		独奏曲	solo
二重奏/二重唱	duet		喜剧表演	comedy performanc
即兴演奏	improvisation		流行歌曲	pop song
舞步	dance steps		前奏曲	prelude
舞会	dance ball		序曲	overture
民乐	folk music		交响曲	symphony

协奏曲	concerto	女中音	mezzo-soprano
狂想曲	rhapsody	女低音	contralto
幻想曲	fantasia	音乐喜剧	music comedy
随想曲	caprice	独唱音乐会	recital
夜曲	nocturne	流行歌曲音乐会	pop concert
组曲	suite	实景歌舞演出	real-scene musical extravaganza
进行曲	march		
编曲	arrangement	歌手大赛	singing competition
男高音	tenor	国际电影节	Intenational Film Festival
男中音	baritone	黄色音乐	vulgar music
男低音	bass	黄色电影	blue-films (or pornographic pictures)
女高音	soprano		

7. 音乐人（Musician）

制片人	producer	领唱者	accentor
乐队指挥	orchestra conductor	主角	leading character
合唱队指挥	chorus master	男主角	leading man
乐队领队	band leader	男配角	male supporting role
客座指挥	guest conductor	女主角	leading lady
指挥棒	baton	女配角	female supporting role
作曲家	composer	主题歌手	theme singer
独奏者	soloist	歌手	singer
演奏者	player	舞女	dancing girls
钢琴手	pianist	流行歌手	pop singer
领奏者	leader	获奖者	prize-winner

8. 文化娱乐场所（Culture and Entertainment Place）

音乐厅	music hall	舞厅	dance hall
娱乐厅	pleasure-house	舞池	dance floor
游乐场	pleasure-ground	露天游乐场	fun fair

9. 乐器（Musical Instrument）

西洋乐器	western instrument	民间乐器	folk instrument
中国乐器	Chinese instrument	民族乐器	national instrument
现代乐器	modern instrument	古乐器	ancient instrument

传统乐器	traditional instrument	扬琴	dulcimer
管乐器	wind instrument	月琴	yueqin
木管乐器	woodwind instrument	吉他	guitar
铜管乐器	brass instrument	琵琶	pipa /Chinese lute
电子乐器	electronic instrument	二胡	erhu
管弦乐器	stringed instrument	高胡	gaohu
打击乐器	percussion instrument	笛子	bamboo flute
口琴	mouth organ	筝	zheng
小提琴	violin	笙	sheng
中提琴	viola	箫	xiao / Chinese vertical bamboo flute
大提琴	cello	单弦	one-string fiddle
钢琴	piano	二弦	two-string fiddle
大钢琴	grand piano	三弦	three-string fiddle
手风琴	accordion / piano accordion	竹板	bamboo clappers
古钢琴	harpsichord	锣鼓	gong and drum
竖琴	harp	腰鼓	waist drum

10. 美术类 (Fine Arts)

肖像画	portrait painting	毛笔画	brush drawing
人物画	figure drawing	水彩画	water-color painting
裸体画	nudity	水墨画	wash painting
山水画	landscape painting	贴裱画	collage drawing
风景画	landscape painting	蚀刻画	etching painting
花鸟画	flower-and-bird painting	写生画	skech drawing / sketch
花卉画	flower-and-plant painting	写意画	painting in impressionistic style
讽刺画	caricature	自画像	self-protrait
宫廷画	imperial academy painting	石板画	lithograph painting
古典画	classical painting	仕女画	painting of the beautiful women
工笔画	painting in the elaborate style	水墨杂画	monochrome in painting
钢笔画	pen drawing	禽兽杂画	animal drawing
稻草画	straw drawing	古迹壁画	graffiti painting
蛋壳画	eggshell art painting	粉蜡笔画	pastel drawing
蜡笔画	crayon drawing	国画技巧	technique in the traditional Chinese painting
蜡染画	batik painting		
铅笔画	pencil drawing	道释人物画	Taoist-Buddhist figure

	drawing	临摹	imitation
创意山水画	creative landscape	轮廓	outline sketch
金碧山水画	gold-and-green landscape	构图	compositional stretch
青山绿水画	blue-and-green landscape	画笔	painting brush
素描	charcoal drawing	画稿	preliminary sketch to be painted
临裱	warped silk mounting	画题	painting theme
纸裱	paper mounting	扇画	fan drawing
装裱	mounting	年画	new year picture
云书	yun script	镜画	mirror drawing
篆字	seal characters	指画	finger painting
篆刻	carving in seal script	古画	old painting
书法	penmanship	瓷画	encaustic painting
题签	a label with the title of a book on it	壁画	fresco painting
		版画	woodcut painting
题匾	inscription fronting hall	藏画	painting collection

11. 奖项（Prize）

群星奖	Galaxy Award	最佳影片奖	Best Film Award
百花奖	Hundred Flowers Award	最佳男主角奖	Best Actor Award
孔雀奖	Peacock Award	最佳女主角奖	Best Actress Award
金马奖	Golden Horse Prize	金像奖提名	Nomination for Academy Award
文华奖	Splendor Award		
荷花奖	Lotus Award	导演技术奖	Directing Technique Award
金鸡奖	Golden Rooster Award	导演风格奖	Directing Style Award
奥斯卡奖	Oscar Award	优秀电影奖	Outstanding Film Award
香港金像奖	HK Gold Statue Award	五个一工程奖	Five Top Project Award

12 文明
Civilization

全社会文明程度	educational and ethical standards of the whole society
社会主义物质文明进步	to achieve progress in the social construction of material
社会主义政治文明进步	to achieve progress in the social construction of politics
社会主义精神文明进步	to achieve progress in the social construction of ideological infrastructure
全民族文明素质	educational and ethical standards of the whole nation
做文明人开文明车	to be a courteous person and a defensive driver
避免冲突,得让人处且让人	to avoid all conflicts, even if you are right
宁晚三分不抢一秒	better late than the late
遵守交通法规	to obey the traffic laws
为了自己也为他人	for yourself as well as for others
文质彬彬	gentle, urbane and suave
文明驾驶	defensive driving
文明城市	model city of social development
文明单位	model units
文明个人	civilized person
文明举止	civilized manners
精神文明	spiritual civilization
物质文明	material civilization
精神污染	spiritual contamination
五讲四美	five merits to advocate and four virtues to promote
文明戏	early form of spoken drama
讲文明	to stress on decorum
讲礼貌	to stress on manners
讲政治	to speak of politics / pay heed to politics
讲正气	to pay heed to healthy trends
讲学习	to pay heed to study
讲卫生	to stress on hygiene
讲纪律	to stress on discipline
讲道德	to stress on morals
心灵美	beauty of the mind
语言美	beauty of the language
行为美	beauty of the behavior
环境美	beauty of the environment
精神家园	spiritual home

文明
Civilization

团队精神	a team spirit		peace and harmony
优质服务日	quality service day	平等相待	to treat each other as equals
公开,公正,公平	open, fair and just	自强自立	self-reliance and self-improvement
现代文明强国	a strong modern civilized nation	尊重对方	to respect one's opponent
清正廉洁	honest and upright	自尊自重	self-esteem
清廉政府	corruption-free government	扫黄打非	to struggle against pornographic and illegal publications
和睦相处	to live with each other in		

13 教育及人才
Education & Talents

1. 教育（Education）

1）教育术语（Educational Terms）

教育工作	educational work
教育公平	equal access to education
教育水平	educational level
教育方式	educational mode
教育方法	educational method
教育模式	educational pattern
教育方针	educational principle
教育政策	educational policy
教育制度	educational system
教育经费	educational expenditure
教育投资	educational investment
教育拨款	education allocation
教育改革	education reform
教育创新	educational innovation
教育质量	educational quality
素质教育	quality education
教育观念	concept of education
教育资源	education resources
全民教育	education for the whole people
全面教育	comprehensive education
全日制教育	full-time education
义务教育	compulsory education
普及教育	universal education
学前教育	preschool education
职业教育	vocational education
职业培训	vocational training
应试教育	examination oriented education
成人教育	adult education
政治教育	ideological education
国民教育	national education
德育及国民教育	moral and national education
高等教育"211工程"	the "211" project for higher education
高等教育"985工程"	the "985" project for higher education
九年制义务教育	nine-year compulsory education
普及义务教育	universal compulsory education
规范民办教育	to standardize non-government funded schools
中等职业教育	secondary vocational education
提高教育水平	to enchance teaching level
提高教育质量	to improve teaching quality
因材施教原则	individualized instruction principle

学校管理体系	administration system for schools
教学质量评估	assessment plan of instruction performance quality
教师资格认定	accreditation of teacher's qualification
研究生课程班	non-degree postgraduate course
教育乱收费	unauthorized collections of fees by educational institutions
教育综合改革	comprehensive education reform
考试招生制度	examination and enrollment systems
高校办学自主权	Institutions of higher learning enjoy more decision-making power
学生营养改善计划	the project to improve nutrition of rural students
特困地区乡村教师	the rural teachers in contiguous poor areas
教育扶贫工程	the project to alleviate poverty through education
农村义务教育	the compulsory education in rural areas
在家教育	home schooling
毛入学率	gross enrollment rate
伦理教育	ethical education
高等教育	higher education
中等教育	secondary school education
小学教育	primary school education
启蒙教育	primary education
幼儿教育	preschool education
幼儿园教育	kindergarten education
职业教育体系	vocational education system
远程教育	distance education
函授教育	correspondence education
正规教育	formal education
网络教育	online education
品德教育	moral education
学前教育	preschool education
特殊教育	special education
品学兼优	excellent in character and learning
必考科目	exam-compulsory course
开除学籍	expulsion
教学原则	teaching principles
教学实习	field practice
教学计划	teaching plan
教学管理	teaching administration
教学大纲	teaching syllabus (or program)
评教评学	assessment on teaching and learning
课程体系	curriculum system
自我教育	self-education
中途退学	dropout
自动退学	withdrawal
勒令退学	to be ordered to quit school
升级考试	promotion examination
毕业考试	graduation examination
期中考试	mid-term examination
期终考试	final examination

普通考试	ordinary examination
全国统考	national unified examination
全国统一高考	national unified college and university entrance examination
文科综合考试	integrated examination for social science
综合考试成绩	integrated examination scores
考查学生成绩	to check students' work
社会力量办学	to manage shools by social resources
考上大学	to be admitted to a university
考大学	to take a college entrance examination
定向招生	recruitment of students from selected departments or regions
定向培养	to provide training to selected students
同等学历	academic qualification equivalent
毕业实习	graduation field work
毕业鉴定	graduation appraisal
毕业证书	graduation certificate
毕业典礼	graduation ceremony
毕业分配	job assignment on graduation
毕业设计	graduation project
毕业论文	graduation dissertation
速成班	crash course
毕业班	graduation class
进修班	class for advanced studies
学分制	credit system
必修课	compulsory course
基础课	basic course
选修课	optional course
专业课	course within one's major (or special course)
主要课	major course
进修课	refresher course
成教课	course for adults
补习课	a make-up course
复试	final test
考评	evaluation of one's professional work
考分	marks in a test (or grades)
考勤	to check on work attendance
考核	to assess sb's proficiency
考题	examination questions
考试	to take an examination
考卷	examination paper
考取	to pass an entrance examination
考生	examinee / a candidate for an entrance examination
考课	to assess the service of sb.
补课	to make up a missed course
学制	school system
休学	schooling suspension
逃学	skip class
学科	discipline / a school subject
学界	educational circles
学籍	one's status as a student
学海	sea of learning
学报	learned journal
学费	tuition fee
学分	credit
学风	academic atmosphere
学府	institution of higher learning
学监	proctor
学会	learned society
学究	pedant

学派	school of thought
学术	systematic learning
学历	academic credentials
学力	educational level
学名	scientific name
学时	class hour
学年	academic year
学人	a learned man
学识	learning / scholarly attainments
学龄	school age
学术	systematic learning / learning
学位	academic degree
学问	systematic learning / scholarship / knowledge
学衔	academic rank (or title)
学者	scholar / a learned man
学子	student

2）教育机构（Educational Institutions）

联合国教科文组织 United Nations Educational, Scientific and Cultural Organization

教育部	Ministry of Education
教育局	bureau of education
教会学校	mission school
重点高校	key colleges and universities
基础教育	basic education
社会办学	non-government schools
幼儿园	kindergarten
小学	primary school
中学	high school
初级中学	junior middle school
高级中学	senior middle school
大学	university
学院	college /institute
中等职业学校	secondary vocational schools
中等专业学校	secondary specialized school
中等技术学校	secondary technical school
高等专科教育	higher specialized school
高等职业技术学院	higher vocational and technical college
特殊教育学校	special education school
幼儿师范学校	school of training kindergarten teachers
函授学校	correspondence school
重点中学	key middle school
专科学校	training (or vocational) school
业余学校	spare-time school
民办学校	non-publicly funded schools
附属学校	affiliated school
技工学校	vestibule school
护士学校	nurse's training school
私立中学	private middle school
示范中学	model middle school
文科大学	university of liberal arts
补习学校	continuation school
老年大学	college for the aged
财经学院	institute of finance and economics
师范学院	teacher's college / Normal College
师范大学	normal university
农学院	agricultural college
农业大学	agricultural university
理学院	college of science
理工科大学	university of science and

	engineering
电子工学院	institute of electronic engineering
电子工程大学	university of electronic engineering
电力工程学院	institute of electrical engineering
电讯工程学院	institrute of telecommunications engineering
轻工业学院	institute of light industry
城建学院	institute of urban construction
测绘学院	institute of geodesy
铁道学院	railway institute
航空学院	aeronautical engineering institute
航空大学	aeronautical engineering university
邮电学院	institute of post and telecommunications
邮电大学	university of post and telecommunications
化工学院	institute of chemical engineering
化工大学	university of chemical engineering
法学院	college of law
政法大学	university of political science and laws
医学院	college of medicine
医科大学	medical university / university of medicine
海洋学院	oceanography college
海洋大学	oceanography university
水产大学	university of aquatic products
水利学院	institute of water-conservancy
气象学院	meteorological institute
机械学院	college of mechanical engineering
机械工程大学	university of mechanical engineering
石油学院	petroleum collge
石油大学	petroleum university
矿业学院	college of mining technology
矿业大学	university of mining technology
煤炭学院	coal institute
工业学院	college of industrial engineering
工业大学	polytechnic university
林学院	forestry institute
林业大学	forestry university
药学院	pharmaceutical institute
药科大学	pharmaceutical university
体育学院	institute of physical culture
体育大学	university of physical culture
商学院	college of commerce
工商大学	university of industry and commerce (business)
民族学院	institute for nationalities
民族大学	university for nationalities
广播学院	institute of radio broadcasting
广播电视大学	university of radio and television
外语学院	foreign languages college
外国语大学	foreign languages university
警官学院	college for police officers
警官大学	university for policy officers
军医大学	university of army medicine

中医学院	institute of Chinese traditional medicine
中医药大学	university of Chinese traditional medicine
文理学院	college of arts and science
教育学院	educational college
艺术学院	academy of arts
美术学院	academy of fine arts
戏曲学院	opera college
舞蹈学院	dancing college
纺织工学院	institute of textile engineering
粮食工学院	institute of grain industry
船舶工学院	institute of ship-building engineering
冶金学院	metallurgy institute
丝绸工学院	institute of silk textile engineering
民用航空学院	institute for civil aviation
国际关系学院	college of international relations
教师进修学院	teacher's college for vocational studies
高等学校	institutions of higher learning /colleges and universities
教务处长办公室	Deans' Office
大学校长办公室	president's office
校务委员会	university affairs committee
研究生院	postgraduate shool
留学生部	overseas student's department
校董事会	school board of directors
研究所	research institute
教研室	teaching and research section
教研组	teaching and research group
系办公室	department office
招生办公室	admission office
学校人事处	school personnel department
学校外事办	foreign affairs office of school
资产管理处	office of asset management
函授部	correspondence department
教务处	studies of department / Dean's Office
教务科	studies of section
科研处	office of scientific research
基建处	office of capital construction
审计处	audit office
保卫处	security office
总务处	general affairs office
膳食科	catering section
学生处	students affairs office
学生科	student's section
招生办	admission office / enrolment office
招生制度	enrolment system
招生简章	school admission brochure

3）985 工程大学出版社

北京大学出版社	Beijing University Press
清华大学出版社	Qinghua University Press
北京师范大学出版社	Beijing Normal University Press
北京航空航天大学出版社	Beihang University Press
北京理工大学出版社	Beijing University of Science and Technology Press
中国人民大学出版社	China Renmin University Press
中国农业大学出版社	China Agricultural University Press

东南大学出版社	Southeast University Press	厦门大学出版社	Xiamen University Press
南京大学出版社	Nanjing University Press	湖南大学出版社	Hunan University Press
复旦大学出版社	Fudan University Press	国防科技大学出版社	National Defense Science and Technology University Press
上海交通大学出版社	Shanghai Jiaotong University Press	中山大学出版社	Zhonshan University Press
华东师范大学出版社	Huadon Normal University Press	华南理工大学出版社	Huanan Science and Technology University Press
同济大学出版社	Tongji University Press		
吉林大学出版社	Jilin University Press		
哈尔滨工业大学出版社	Haerbing Industrial University Press		
大连理工大学出版社	Dalian University of Science and Technology Press		
南开大学出版社	Nankai University Press		
天津大学出版社	Tianjin University Press		
山东大学出版社	Shandong University Press		
兰州大学出版社	Lanzhou University Press		
西安交通大学出版社	Xian Jiaotong University Press		
四川大学出版社	Sichuan University Press		
武汉大学出版社	Wuhan University Press		
华中科技大学出版社	Huazhong Science and Techology University Press		
中国科技大学出版社	China Science and Technology University Press		
浙江大学出版社	Zhejiang University Press		

4）职务（post）

幼儿园老师	teachers of kindergarten
小学老师	teachers of primary school
中学老师	teachers of middle school
大学老师	university teachers
助教	teaching assistant
讲师	lecturer
副教授	associate professor
教授	(full) professor
兼职教授	part-time professor
名誉教授	honorary professor
客座教授	guest professor /visiting professor
返聘教授	professor of returning to one's post
特聘教授	specially employed professor /specially invited professor/ chair professor
访问学者	visiting scholar
外籍教师	foreign teacher / foreign instructor
博士生导师	doctoral supervisor
硕士生导师	graduate supervisor
高级讲师	senior lecturer

指导教师	tutor
专职教师	full-time teacher
大学校长	president
副校长	vice-president
中学（小学）校长	schoolmaster
院长	college leader
教务长	dean of studies
总务长	dean of general affairs
政治辅导员	political assistant / political counselor
少先队辅导员	counselor for the Young Pioneers
班主任	head teacher

5）学生与学位（Students and Academic Degree）

小学生	primary school pupil
中学生	middle school pupil /student
大学生	（college）student
中专生	secondary specialized school student
大专生	professional training college student /junior college student
大学本科生	（university/college）undergraduate
进修生	visiting scholar
硕士研究生	master postgraduate
博士研究生	doctor postgraduate
法学博士	doctor of law / DL
文学博士	doctor of arts /DA
哲学博士	doctor of philosophy
理学博士	doctor of science
医学博士	doctor of medicine
博士后	postdoctoral student /researcher
文学硕士	master of arts
理学硕士	master of science
医学硕士	master of medicine
工程硕士	master of engineering
工学硕士	master of engineering
建筑硕士	master of architecture
农学硕士	master of agriculture
法学硕士	master of law
美术硕士	master of fine arts
哲学硕士	master of philosophy
药学硕士	master of pharmacy
新闻硕士	master of journalism
会计学硕士	master of accounting
工商管理硕士	master of business administration
图书馆学硕士	master of library science
公共卫生硕士	master of public health
大学学历	college/university degree
工学学士	bachelor of engineering
学士学位	bachelor's degree
硕士学位	master's degree
博士学位	doctoral degree
文学学士	bachelor of arts（BA）
理学学士	bachelor of science（BS）
法学学士	bachelor of law（BL）
医学学士	bachelor of medicine（BM）
药学学士	bachelor of pharmacy（BP）
农学学士	bachelor of agriculture（BA）
美术学士	bachelor of fine arts（BFA）
音乐学士	bachelor of music（BM）
工商学士	bachelor of business administration
一年级学生	freshman
二年级学生	sophomore
三年级学生	junior
四年级学生	senior
文凭	diploma

大专文凭　associate degree / diploma for college of professional training

2. 人才 (Talents)

人才政策	personnel policy	中级人才	middle rank talents
人才战略	human resources strategy	尊重人才	value talents
人才发展	talent development	科技人才	talents in science and technology
人才培养	talent fostering		
人才培训	personnel training	青年英才	young talents
人才管理	human resources management	党管人才	human resources under the Party leadership
人才队伍	talent team		
人才选拔	personnel selection	管理人才	talents in management
人才工程	human resources project	党政人才	Party and government officials
人才投资	talent investment	军事人才	military talents
人才考察	talent observation	拔尖人才	tip-top talents
人才类型	personnel types	新人才	fresh talents
人才使用	talent use	复合型人才	versatile professionals
人才之家	home for talents	海外高层次人才	high-quality overseas professionals
人才流失	brain drain		
人才辈出	people of talent coming forth in large numbers	高素质军事人才	high-quality military talents
人才出众	personnel with exceptional ability	农业技术人才	technical talents of agriculture
人才荟萃	a galaxy of talent	专业医药人才	professional medical personnels
人才群体	talent group		
人才济济	an abundance of capable people	创新型科技人才	innovative skilled sci-tech workers
人才外流	flow of trained personnel		
人才储备	reserve of talents	健康卫生人才	health professionals
人才高地	talent highland	紧缺专门人才	professionals in short supply
人才交流	talent exchange		
人才库	talent pool	专业技术人才	professional and technical talents
海外人才	overseas talents		
国内人才	domestic talents	高素质信息技术人才	high-quality IT talents
高级人才	top talents		
初级人才	primary talents	高素质教育人才	high-quality educators

高技能人才　highly-skilled workers
企业管理人才　enterprise management
　　　　　　　talents
人才管理机制　talent administration
　　　　　　　mechanism
人才发展纲要　program for talent
　　　　　　　development
人才队伍建设　qualified personnel
　　　　　　　development
人才交流协会　Association for
　　　　　　　Exchange of Personnel
人才交流大会　Conference on exchange
　　　　　　　of professionals
留学生之家　overseas Chinese student's
　　　　　　home
人才强国战略　strategy of reinvigorating
　　　　　　　China through human
　　　　　　　resources
优化教育资源　quality education resources
研究人员报酬　researcher's pay
重大人才工程　major projects for talent
　　　　　　　development
各类型人才队伍　a diversified workforce
多层次人才队伍　a multilevel workforce

3. 出国留学（Overseas Study）

出国深造　to go abroad for further
　　　　　pursuing study
申请签证　to apply for a visa
护照　passport
签证　visa
申请费用　application fee
支持人　sponsor
财务支持　financial support
财务申明书　financial statement
财务支持担保书　affidavit for financial
　　　　　　　　support
赞助人　sponsor
奖学金申请表　application form for
　　　　　　　financial support
奖学金　scholarship/fellowship
自费留学　self-supporting study abroad
公费留学　state-supporting overseas
　　　　　study
临时入境学生申请表
student application for temporary admission
临时身份　provisional status
入学许可证　certificate of admission
入学申请书　application for admission
个人简历　personal resume
工作简历　professional / work
　　　　　experience
个人成绩　personal academic records
学历记录表　instruction record
家庭成员情况表　family composition
　　　　　　　　information sheet
推荐信　letter of recommendation /
　　　　letter of reference
体检表　health form
健康证明　health certificate
身体健康　physical health
精神健康　mental health
责任感　sense of responsibility
心理成熟　emotional maturity
生理缺陷　physical defects
情绪适应能力　emotional adjustment
耐心　patience
性格　personality

受过处分或品行不良记录
record of disciplinary action or misconduct
动机　motivation
托福测试　TOEFL（Test of English as a Foreign Language）

研究生资格考试　GRE（Graduate Record Examination）
管理研究生入学测试
GMAT（Graduate Management Admission Test）

14 医疗卫生
Medical Treatment and Health

1. 医疗机构 (Medical Establishment)

医学科学院	academy of medical sciences	教学医院	training hospital
儿童医院	children's hospital	部队医院	military hospital
综合医院	general hospital	肿瘤医院	tumor hospital
省立医院	provincial hospital	结核病医院	tuberculosis hospital
市立医院	municipal hospital	骨科医院	orthopaedic hospital
城镇公立医院	urban public hospital	传染病医院	infectious hospital
民营医院	private hospital	妇幼保健院	health center for women and children
县医院	county's hospital		
乡镇医院	town's hospital	整形外科医院	plastic surgery hospital
产科医院	maternity hospital	联合诊疗所	polyclinic
妇科医院	gynecology hospital	医院	hospital
精神病院	mental hospital	医疗站	medical station / health centre
口腔医院	stomatological hospital	医务所	clinic
眼科医院	hospital of ophthalmology	诊疗所	clinic
胸科医院	chest hospital	疗养院	sanatorium
分科医院	polyclinic	防疫站	epidemic prevention station
附属医院	affiliated hospital	急救站	the first-aid station
麻风病院	hospital for lepers	休养所	rest house

2. 医院科室 (Departments in Hospital)

按摩科	massage clinic		obstetrics
呼吸科	department of respiratory disease	口腔科	department of stomatology
放射科	X-ray department	理疗科	physiotherapy department
传染科	department of infectious disease	麻醉科	department of anesthesiology
风湿科	department of rheumatism	泌尿科	urological department
妇产科	department of gynecology and	脑外科	department of cerebral surgery

胸内科	chest internal department	门诊妇产科	outpatient department for obstetrics and gynecology
老年科	department for the old age disease	神经外科	neurosurgery department
普外科	department of general surgery	泌尿外科	urology department
皮肤科	department of dermatology	内分泌科	endocrinology department
烧伤科	burning department	性病专科	venereology department
肾病科	department of nephropathy	妇科	department for the women's disease
小儿科	department of pediatrics		
针灸科	department for acupuncture and moxibustion	骨科	department of orthopedics
		男科	department for the man's disease
中医科	department of traditional Chinese medicine	眼科	department for ophthalmology
		诊室	consulting room
急诊科	department for emergency	治疗室	therapeutic room
急诊儿科	department for pediatric emergency	质控室	quality control room
		制片室	slide making room
急诊外科	emergency surgery	候诊室	waiting for consulting room
急诊内科	internal medicine for emergency	急诊室	emergency room
		检查室	examination room
矫形外科	department for orthopedic surgery	手术室	operation room
		生化室	biochemical laboratory
整形外科	department for plastic surgery	石膏室	plaster room
口腔外科	stomatological surgery	输液室	transfusion room
耳鼻喉科	ENT department	血液室	blood laboratory
腹部外科	abdominal surgery	消毒室	disinfection room
肝胆外科	department for hepatobiliary surgery	细胞室	cell room
		碎石室	stone manipulation room
肛肠外科	department for anus & intestine surgery	洗婴室	bathing room for baby
		洗涤室	washing room
低温外科	cryosurgery	无菌室	asepsis room
心血管内科	department for cardiovascular disease	胃镜室	gastroscope room
		窥镜室	endoscope room
心血管外科	department for cardiovascular surgery	理疗室	physiotherapy room / department
医学整形科	department for plastic surgery	免疫室	immunology laboratory
		拍片室	X-ray room

医疗卫生
Medical Treatment and Health

取片室	taking film room	膀胱镜室	cystoscopy room
抢救室	resuscitation room	纤维镜室	fiberscope room
配置室	collocation room	CT 检查室	CT examination room
化验室	laboratory	小手术室	outpatient operation room
化疗室	chemotherapy room	胎心监护室	fetal monitor room
换药室	room for changing bandage	外科治疗室	surgery therapeutic room
隔离室	isolation room	血压监控室	monitoring room for ambulatory blood pressure
供应室	supply room		
妇检室	room for gynecological examination	细菌检验室	bacteriological laboratory
		超声波检查室	ultrasonic wave examination room
待产室	labour room		
肠镜室	enteroscopy room	急诊治疗室	therapeutic room for emergency
测听室	audiometric room		
电疗室	electrotherapy room	门诊治疗室	room for medical treatment
心电室	electrocardiogram room	门诊观察室	observation ward
B 超室	B ultrasonic room	重症监护室	intensive care unit
病案室	recording room	急诊值班室	duty room for emergency
储藏室	store room	计生指导室	guiding room for birth control
脑电图室	electroencephalogram room		
		家属等待室	waiting room for relations

3. 医务人员称呼(Names for Medical and Nursing Staff)

医院院长	director of hospital	内科主任	head of the medical department
医务部主任	head of the medical administration department	外科医生	surgeon
		内科医生	physician
门诊部主任	head of out-patient department	心外科医生	cardiac surgeon
		心血管医生	cardiovascular doctor
住院部主任	head of in-patient department	神经科医生	neurologist
		神经外科医生	neurosurgeon
护理部主任	head of the nursing department	心脏病专家	heart specialist
		结核科医生	doctor for tuberculosis
护士长	head nurse	流行病医生	epidemiologist
内科主治医生	physician in charge	脑科医生	brain doctor
外科主治医生	surgeon in charge	麻醉医生	anesthetist
外科主任	head of the surgical department	助产医师	midwife

泌尿科医生	urologist	放射科医生	radiologist
皮肤科医生	dermatologist	眼科医生	eye doctor
泌尿外科医生	urological surgeon	产科医生	obstetrician
耳鼻喉科医生	ear-nose-throat doctor	儿科医生	pediatrician
整形外科医生	plastic surgeon	药剂医生	pharmaceutical doctor
肿瘤科医生	oncologist	营养医生	dietician
全科医生	general practitioners	实习医生	intern
牙科医生	dentist	住院医生	resident physician
妇科医生	gynecologist		

4. 常见病 (Common Diseases)

心脏病	heart disease	过敏性皮炎	allergic dermatitis
胃病	gastropathy	接触性皮炎	dermatitis
冠心病	coronary heart disease	流行性腮腺炎	mumps
糖尿病	diabetes	流行性乙型肝炎	epidemic hepatitis B
风湿病	rheumatism	流行性脑膜炎	epidemic encephalitis
败血病	septicemia	风湿性关节炎	rheumarthritis
白血病	leukemia	病毒性心肌炎	viral myocarditis
结核病	tuberculosis	脊髓灰质炎	poliomyelitis
狂犬病	rabies	输卵管炎	salpingitis
艾滋病	AIDs	前列腺炎	prostatitis
精神病	insanity	阑尾炎	appendicitis
疯牛病	mad cow disease	肾炎	nephritis
黑死病	black death	肺炎	pneumonia
黄热病	yellow fever	气管炎	tracheitis
外科病	surgical disease	食管炎	esophagus
高血压病	hypertension	喉头炎	laryngitis
白化病	albinism	神经炎	neuritis
肾盂肾炎	pyelonephritis	腮腺炎	parotiditis
急性胃炎	acute gastritis	乳腺炎	mastitis
胃肠炎	gastroenteritis	皮肤炎	dermatitis
支气管炎	bronchitis	脑膜炎	cerebral meningitis
扁桃体炎	tonsillitis	盆腔炎	pelvic inflammatatory
神经性皮炎	neurodermatitis	宫颈炎	cervicitis
过敏性鼻炎	allergic rhinitis	睾丸炎	orchitis

卵巢炎	oophoritis	甲状腺功能亢进	hyperthyroidism
膀胱炎	urocystitis	再生障碍性贫血	aplastic anemia
肠胃炎	enterogastritis	人感染禽流感	avian flu. to humans
胆囊炎	cholecystitis	扁桃体肥大	hypertrophy of tonsils
尿道炎	urethritis	单纯性肥胖	simple obesity
阴道炎	vaginitis	支气管哮喘	bronchitis asthma
腹膜炎	peritonitis	上呼吸道感染	upper respiratory infection
关节炎	arthritis	坐骨神经痛	sciatica
黏膜炎	catarrh	精神分裂症	schizophrenia
结膜炎	conjunctivitis	斑疹伤寒	typhus
鼻窦炎	sinusitis	卒中后遗症	sequela of wind stroke
角膜炎	keratitis	神经过敏症	neuroticism
口角炎	angular stomatitis	开放性骨折	compound fracture
中耳炎	otitis media	粉碎性骨折	comminuted fracture
外耳炎	otitis externa	良性肿瘤	benign tumor
牙周炎	periodontitis	恶性肿瘤	malignant tumor
牙龈炎	gingivitis	肝硬化	cirrhosis
牙髓炎	pulpitis	骨瘤	osteoma
肺结核	pulmonary tuberculosis	神经瘤	neuroma
肺气肿	pulmonary emphysema	脂肪瘤	adipoma
偏头痛	migraine	荨麻疹	urticaria
心绞痛	angina pectoris	牛皮癣	psoriasis
神经错乱	mental disorder	抑郁症	depression
神经衰弱	neurasthenia	肥胖症	obesity
心律不齐	arrhythmia	鼻过敏	nasal allergy
心肌梗死	miocardial infarction	猩红热	scarlet fever
血栓形成	thrombosis	风湿热	rheumatic fever
高脂血症	hyperlipidemia	黄褐斑	chloasma
慢性菌痢	chronic bacillary dysentery	胃溃疡	gastric ulcer
皮肤过敏	allergic skin reaction	肾结石	kidney stone
婴儿腹泻	infantile diarrhea	破伤风	tetanus
膀胱结石	vesical calculus	白癜风	vitiligo
习惯性流产	habitual abortion	白内障	cataract
先兆性流产	threatened abortion	百日咳	whooping cough
甲状腺肿大	goiter	青光眼	glaucoma

禽流感　bird flu.

5. 医疗常用词语（Common Terms in Medical Treatment）

医疗救助	a medical assistance
缺医少药	shortage of medical services and medicines
国产疫苗	domestically produced vaccine
医药补医	to compensate for low medical service charges
社会资本办医	to run hospitals by non-governmental capital
基本药物制度	system of basic medicines
疾病应急救助	emergence assistance
基本医保财政补助	financial subsidy for basic medical insurance
基本医疗卫生机构	mechanism for operating community-level clinics
全民基本医保	national basic medical insurance
医疗卫生体制	medical and health care system
分级诊疗体系	system of tiered medical services
医师多点执业	doctors work in more than one medical institution
常规检查	routine examination
超声波检查	ultrasonic diagnosis
X线检查	X-ray examination
穿刺检查	examination by centesis
粪便检查	examination of stool
活组织检查	biopsy
临床机能检查	clinical function tests
免疫学检查	immunological examination
内窥镜检查	endoscopy
尿液检查	examination for urine
生化检查	biochemical examination
随访检查	follow-up examination
实验室检查	laboratory examination
体格检查	physical examination
体液和分泌液检查	examination for body fluids and secretions
微生物检查	microbiological examination
心电图检查	electrocardiogram examination
血液学检查	hematological examination
针刺疗法	acupuncture therapy
诊断法	diagnostic
电疗法	electrotherapy
对症疗法	symptomatic treatment
保守疗法	conservative therapy
综合疗法	combined therapy
支持疗法	supporting treatment
治疗方法	therapies
物理疗法	therapy treatment
手术疗法	operation treatment
皮肉投药法	endermatic medication
皮下投药法	hypodermatic
肌肉投药法	intramuscular
放射性疗法	radio-therapy
高压氧疗法	hyperbaric therapy
姑息疗法	alleviative treatment
电休克疗法	electroshock treatment
全身疗法	constitutional therapy

医疗卫生
Medical Treatment and Health

连续冲洗法	continuous irrigation
间接冲洗法	mediate irrigation
精神疗法	psychotherapy
饮食疗法	dietetic therapy
封闭疗法	block therapy
胰岛素休克疗法	insulin-shock treatment
白内障手术	cataract surgery
鼻息肉切除术	nasal polypectomy
扁导体切除术	tonsillectomy
大手术	major operation
小手术	minor operation
导尿术	urethral catheterization
刮宫术	uterine curettage
减压术	decompression
绝育术	sterilization
剖腹术	laparotomy
引产术	induction of labor
助产术	midwifery
痔切除术	hemorrhoidectomy
疝修补术	herniorrhaphy
胃切除术	nephrectomy
脾切除术	splenectomy
肾造口术	nephrostomy
子宫切除术	hysterectomy
气管切开术	tracheotomy
直肠切除术	proctectomy
开腹探查术	exploratory laparotomy
开颅探查术	exploratory craniotomy
关节固定术	arthrodesis for joint
牙矫正术	orthodontic treatment
羊膜穿刺术	amniocentesis
子宫颈切除术	cervicectomy
前列腺切除术	prostatectomy
子宫肌瘤切除术	hysteromyomectomy
人工关节置换术	prosthetic replacement
静脉肾盂造影术	intravenous pyelography
口对鼻循环复苏术	mouth-nose resuscitation
口对口循环复苏术	mouth-mouth resuscitation
胃十二指肠吻合术	gastroduodenostomy
肾造口肾镜取石术	nephrolithotomy
心脏循环复苏术	cardiopulmonary resuscitation
甲状腺切除术	thyroidectomy
心导管插入术	cardiac catheterization
心包切除术	pericardiectomy
乳房切除术	mastectomy
阑尾切除术	appendectomy
脑瘤切除术	excision for brain tumor
脓肿切开术	incision for abscess
胆囊切除术	cholecystectomy
导管插入术	catheterization
肺切除术	pneumonectomy
肝管切除术	hepaticotomy
肝叶切除术	hepatolobectomy
骨瘤刮除术	curettage of bone tumor
最后诊断	final diagnosis
暂定诊断	tentative diagnosis
直肠指诊	rectal touch
阴道指诊	vaginal touch
鉴别诊断	differential diagnosis
护理诊断	nursing diagnosis
伴发症状	concomitant symptom
典型症状	classical symptom
间接症状	indirect symptom
局部症状	local symptom
全身症状	systemic symptom

精神症状	mental symptom	止痛药	analgesic medicine
诱发症状	induced symptom	止血药	hemostatic medicine
主要症状	cardinal symptom	止泻药	antidiarrheal medicine
血管舒张药	vasodilator	阿托品	atropine
血管收缩药	vasoconstrictor medicine	盘尼西林	penicillin
抗癫痫药	antiepileptic medicine	及时消毒	concurrent disinfection
抗风湿药	antirheumatic medicine	紫外线消毒	disinfection by ultraviolet
民族医药	traditional medicines of ethnic minorities	用弹性绷带	to apply elastic bandages
病毒灵	anti-bacterial pills	引流预防措施	precautions for secretion
抗菌素	antibiotics	血液预防措施	precautions for body-fluid
中医药	traditional Chinese medicines	医学无菌操作	medical asepsis
咳嗽药	medicine for cough	测量生命体征	to measure the vital signs
激素药	hormone medicine	保护性隔离	protective isolation
药剂量	medicine dose	胸膜腔灌洗	pleural lavage
腹泻药	medicine for diarrhea	鼻骨闭合复位	closed reduction of nasal bone
退烧药	antipyretic medicine		
葡萄糖	glucose	关节脱位复位	reduction of joint dislocation
开药方	to prescribe		
抗癌药	anticarcinogen medicine	石膏夹板固定	plaster splintage
药粉	medical powder	高渗盐水注射	hypertonic
药膏	medical ointment	日常护理	daily care for patients
药片	medical tablet	急救护理	emergency care
药水	liquid medicine	手术后护理	postoperative care
配药	to make up a prescription	晨间护理	morning care
中草药	Chinese herbal medicine	晚间护理	to care in the evening
利尿药	diuretic medicine	量口腔体温	to measure / take oral temperature
麻醉药	anesthetic medicine		
解毒药	antidote medicine	量腋下体温	to take axillary temperature
解痉挛药	antispasmodic medicine	量直肠体温	to take rectal temperature
祛痰药	expectorant	临床表现	clinical manifestation
强心药	cardiac tonic	颅骨切开	craniotomy
镇静药	sedative medicine	严密隔离	strict isolation
止咳药	antitussive medicine	病理切片	pathological section
止痒药	antipruritic medicine	胸廓开刀	thoracotomy

血常规分析	routine analysis of blood	断指再植	replantation of amputated finger
尿常规分析	routine urinalysis		
血液透析	hemodialysis	适当热量饮食	eucaloric diet
盐水输注	saline infusion	糖尿病饮食	diabetic diet
间接输血	indirect transfusion	半流质饮食	semi-liquid diet
动脉输血	arterial transfusion	病弱者饮食	invalid diet
滴注输血	to drip transfusion	低蛋白饮食	low protein diet
静脉输血	venous transfusion	高蛋白饮食	high-protein diet
静脉输液	venous transfusion	高热量饮食	high caloric diet
点滴注射	fluid infusion	低热量饮食	low caloric diet
静脉注射	intravenous injection	高糖类饮食	high-carbohydrate diet
肌肉注射	intramuscular injection	易消化饮食	light diet
葡萄糖输注	glucose-saline infusion	孕期饮食	prenatal / pregnant diet
躯体无力	somasthenia	滋补饮食	nourishing diet
骨折复位	reduction of fracture	特定饮食	special diet
焦急不安	agitation	无盐饮食	salt-free diet
角膜移植	corneal grafting	细软饮食	soft diet
接触隔离	contact isolation	低渣饮食	low-residue diet
痉挛性痛	cramp-like pain	高脂饮食	high-fat diet
全身麻醉	general anesthesia	固体饮食	solid diet
吞吐困难	dysphagia	流质饮食	liquid diet
呼吸困难	dyspnea	普通饮食	full diet
呼吸急促	tachypnea	均衡饮食	balanced diet
端坐呼吸	orthopnea	规定食谱	regimen diet
呼吸隔离	respiratory isolation	低脂肪饮食	low-fat diet
晚期疾病	advanced disease	恢复期饮食	convalescent diet
随时消毒	concomitant disinfection	生化检查	biochemical examination
灭菌消毒	sterilization	缺氧	anoxia
大便失禁	copracrasia	热敷	hot compress
大量出汗	diaphoresis	失明	blindness
带血的痰	bloody sputum	失语	aphasia
尿失禁	urinary incontinence	石膏	plaster
膀胱冲洗	bladder irrigation	厌食	appetite loss
发病机制	pathogenesis	输血	blood transfusion
缝合切开	to sew up the incision	水肿	edema

栓剂	suppository	隔离	isolation
膨胀	distention	根治	radical treatment
喷嚏	sneeze	梗死	infarction
鼻涕	nasal discharge	瘙痒	itching
鼻塞	nasal obstruction	诱因	inducement
排尿	micturation	心悸	palpitation
排便	defecation	震颤	thrilling
尿频	urination frequency	诊断	diagnosis
尿急	urgent urination	粘连	adhesion
呕血	hematemesis	性病	sexual disease
气胀	flatulence	休克	shock
气胸	pneumothorax	虚弱	weakness
气喘	asthma	胸痛	chest pain
注射	injection	牙痛	toothache
灼痛	burning pain	镶牙	dental prosthetics
窒息	suffocation	洗胃	gastric lavage
治疗	treatment	洗剂	lotion
止血	hemostasis	剂量	dose
知觉	consciousness	激素	hormone
症状	symptom	冲洗	irrigation
蒸馏水	distilled water	出汗	sweating
月经史	menstrual history	初潮	menarche
原发病	primary disease	洗肠	intestinal lavage
慢性病	chronic diseases	体征	signs
职业病	occupational diseases	体重	body weight
防治吸血虫	to prevent and cure schistosomiasis	急诊	emergency
地方病	endemic diseases	会诊	consultation
传染病	communical diseases	听诊	auscultation
咽喉痛	sore throat	问诊	inquiry
神经痛	neuralgia	叩诊	percussion
肾活检	renal biopsy	触诊	palpation
肾移植	renal transplantation	传染	infection
炎症	inflammation	处方	prescription
肛裂	anal fissure	昏迷	coma
		昏厥	faint

Medical Treatment and Health

无菌	asepsis	碘酒	iodine
无力	fatigue	恶心	nausea
无尿	anuria	复发	relapse
消瘦	emaciation	骨折	fracture
消毒	disinfection	骨瘤	osteoma
痛经	dysmenorrhea	胰腺癌	cancer of pancreas
头痛	headache	子宫癌	cancer of cervix
脱水	dehydration	神经瘤	neuroma
望诊	inspection	脂肪瘤	adipoma
胃痛	stomachache	荨麻疹	urticaria
溃疡	ulceration	牛皮癣	psoriasis
冷敷	cold compress	胆石症	cholelithiasis
疗程	treatment course	抗凝剂	anticoagulant
耳聋	deafness	心搏骤停	cardiac arrest
麻木	numbness	黄疸	jaundice
麻醉	anesthesia	烧伤	burn
胶囊	capsule	痱子	sudamen
结石	calculus	霍乱	cholera
绞痛	colic	贫血	anaemia
截肢	amputation	偏瘫	hemiplegia
禁食	absolute diet	癔症	hysteria
康复	recovery	白喉	diphtheria
咳嗽	cough	感冒	cold
干咳	dry cough	沙眼	trachoma
咳痰	expectoration	近视	near sight
耳鸣	tinnitus	流感	influenza
耳痛	earache	痢疾	dysentery
发烧	fever	麻疹	measles
发热	pyrexia	梅毒	syphilis
发作	attack	面瘫	facial paralysis
猝死	sudden death	痛风	gout
打针	injection	癫痫	epilepsy
盗汗	night sweat	冻伤	frostbite
低热	low-grade fever	疥疮	scabies
低氧	hypoxia	肛瘘	anal fistula

便秘	constipation	肠癌	intestinal cancer
天花	smallpox	肺癌	lung cancer
水痘	varicella	肝癌	liver cancer
湿疹	eczema	胃癌	gastric carcinoma
中风	stroke	胬肉	a triangle mass of mucous membrane growing from the inner corner of the eye
风疹	German measles		
疱疹	herpes		
痤疮	acne	贫血	anaemia
痔疮	hemorrhoid	癣	ringworm
遗尿	enuresis	疣	wart
遗精	emission	缓解	remission
阳痿	impotence	充血	congestion
疟疾	malaria	便血	hematochezia
非典	Sars (Severe Acute Respiratory Syndrome)	病程	course of disease
		包扎	dressing
麻痹	paralysis	拆线	to remove (or to take out) the stitches
胃炎	gastritis		

6. 医疗器械和器具名称 (Names of Medical Machinery & Instruments)

心电图机	electrocardiograph	开睑器	eye speculum
心音图机	phonocardiograph	插管器	intubator
脑电图机	electroencephalograph	冲洗器	irrigator
呼吸机	respirator	除颤器	defibrillator
吸吮机	suction machine	食管镜	esophagoscope
正压呼吸机	positive pressure respirator	头镜	head mirror
超声波机	ultrasonic wave apparatus	纤维食管镜	esophagofiberscope
壁式输氧机	wall oxygen outlet	乙型结肠镜	sigmoidoscope
吸奶器	breast pump	支气管镜	bronchoscope
透析器	dialyzator	纤维胃镜	gastrofiberscope
张口器	speculum oris	直肠窥镜	rectal speculum
助行器	walker	直接喉镜	direct laryngoscope
起搏器	pacemaker	阴道窥器	vaginal speculum
耳窥器	aural speculum	机器吸吮器	mechanical suction
干燥器	drying baker	箱式呼吸器	cabinet respirator
灌肠器	enemator	皮下注射器	hypodermic syringe

Medical Treatment and Health

自动呼吸器	automatic respirator	保温箱	incubator
胸甲式呼吸器	cuirass respirator	止血带	tourniquet
肛门张开器	anal speculum	止血钳	hemostatic forceps
高压蒸汽灭菌器	high-pressure steam sterilizer	直腹带	straight abdominal binder
		蒸汽帷	steam tent
橡皮头止血器	rubber-topped hemostat	阴囊托	scrotal support
膀胱镜	cystoscope	氧气筒	oxygen tank
眼底镜	ophthalmoscope	压舌板	spatula
直肠镜	proctoscope	血管夹	vascular clamp
腹腔镜	peritoneoscope	悬带	sling
插管	cannula	腹带	binder
套管	cannula	钳子	forceps
胃管	stomach tube	沙袋	sand bag
吸管	sucker	纱布	gauze
滴管	dropper	冰袋	ice bag
肛管	rectal tube	产钳	obstetric forceps
试管	test tube	肠线	ribbon gut
心导管	cardiac catheter	弯盆	kidney basin
引导管	drainage-tube	担架	stretcher
软导管	flexible catheter	拐杖	crutch
三腔管	three channel tube	夹板	splint
灌注导管	perfusion cannula	剪刀	scissors
双腔导管	two-way catheter	胶布	adhesive
墨菲滴管	murphy's drip bulb	漏斗	funnel
冲洗套管	wash-out cannula	轮椅	wheelchair
橡皮引流管	elastic drainage-tube	棉球	cotton wood balls
女用导尿管	female catheter	急诊锤	percussion hammer
皮下导尿管	hypodermic catheter	酒精灯	alcohol burner
玻璃引导管	glass drainage-tube	灌肠筒	enemator
槽式导尿管	railway catheter	裹胸带	breast binder
留置导尿管	indwelling catheter	消毒箱	disinfect box
自流引导管	self-retaining catheter	药水瓶	vial
气管吸引导管	tracheal catheter	扫描仪	scanner
前列腺导尿管	prostatic catheter	手术刀	scalpel
一次性采尿袋	disposable collecting bag	体温表	thermometer

腿支架	leg brace	弹力绷带	elastic bandage
消毒包	surgical isolator	纱布绷带	gauze bandage
透析膜	dialyser	橡皮手套	rubber gloves
吸水棉	absorbent cotton	床上便盆	bedpan
核磁共振	nuclear magnetic resonance	取样器皿	specimen container
高压氧舱	hyperbaric oxygen chamber	男用尿壶	male urinal
线行探子	filiform sound	紫外线灯	ultraviolet lamp
吸水纱布	absorbent gauze	肺活量计	spirometer
急救绷带	first-aid bandage		

7. 诊断术语(Diagnosis Terms)

细脉	fine pulse	少气	rough breath
弦脉	stringy pulse	高热	high fever
结脉	knotted pulse	潮热	tidal fever
疾脉	swift pulse	望色	to inspect the colour
切脉	to feel one's pulse	治法	treatment
散脉	scattered pulse	正治法	orthodox treatment
牢脉	tight pulse	内治法	internal treatment
涩脉	hesitant pulse	涌吐法	emesis method
紧脉	tense pulse	治未病	preventive treatment of disease
滑脉	slippery pulse	问月经	inquiry of menstruation
缓脉	slow pulse	问寒热	to inquire about chill and fever
沉脉	sinking pulse	问白带	to inquire about leucorrhea
寸脉	cun pulse	问二便	to inquire about urination and defecation
代脉	intermittent pulse		
大脉	large pulse	问声音	to auscultate the sound
促脉	running pulse	望舌苔	to observe the tongue coating
浮脉	floating pulse	望舌态	to observe the tongue condition
数脉	rapid pulse	歪斜舌	deviated tongue
四诊	four examination methods	瘦薄舌	thin tongue
失神	loss of vitality	裂纹舌	cracked tongue
低热	low fever	芒刺舌	thorny tongue
嗳气	seam heat / warm gas / warm air	强硬舌	rigid tongue
喘气	dyspnea with wheezing	厚舌苔	thick tongue coating
短气	shortness of breath	颤动舌	tremulous tongue

医疗卫生
Medical Treatment and Health

调整阴阳	coordinating yin and yan		descendant
剥脱舌苔	to shed tongue coating	疏风透疹	to dispel wind to promote eruption
标本兼治	to treat both the principal and the secondary	异病同治	to treat different diseases with same methods
扶正固本	to strengthen body resistance		
扶正祛邪	to strengthen the genuine and eliminate the evil	治病求本	to treat aiming at its pathogenesis
缓则治本	to treat the fundamental aspect of the disease	同病异治	to treat the same diseases with different methods
解肌清热	to expel pathogenic factors from muscles for clearing heat	温阳通便	to warm yang for relaxing bowels
攻补兼施	to reinforce and eliminate in combination	辛凉清热	to clear heat with pungent and cool-natured drugs
清肃肺气	lung-qi being kept pure and		

157

15 媒体
Media

1. 电台，电视台（Broadcasting / Radio Station，TV. Station）

中央电视台　China Central Television Station
中央电视台综合频道　CCTV Comprehensive Channel
中央电视台新闻频道　CCTV News Channel
中央电视台文艺频道　CCTV Entertainment Channel
中央电视台戏曲频道　CCTV Opera Channel
中央电视台体育频道　CCTV Sports Channel
中央电视台经济频道　CCTV Economy Channel
中央电视台国际频道　CCTV International Channel
中央电视台电视剧频道　CCTV Serial Channel
中央电视台电影频道　CCTV Film Channel
中央电视台英语频道　CCTV English Channel
中央电视台军事频道　CCTV Military Channel
中央电视台少儿频道　CCTV Children Channel
中央电视台教育频道　CCTV Education Channel
外国电视台　Foreign TV. Station
无线电视台　Television Broadcasting Ltd.（TVB）
中央人民广播电台　Central People's Broadcasting Station
无线电广播转播台　Radio Relay Station
电视广播台　TV. Broadcasting Station
电视转播台　TV. Relay Station
调频广播电台　Frequency Modulation Broadcasting Station
外国电台　Foreign Radio Station
地方电视台　Local TV. Station
教育电视台　Educational Television Station
有线电视台　Cable TV. Station
凤凰卫视　Phoenix TV
澳门电视台　Macao TV Station
有线电视台　Cable TV. Station
省电视台　Provincial TV. Station
市电视台　Municipal TV. Station
地方人民广播台　Local People' Broadcasting Station
省广播电台　Provincial Broadcasting Station

媒体 Media

市广播电台　Municipal Broadcasting Station
干扰台　Jamming Station
有线电视网　cable news network
电视网　Television Network
电视厅　television hall
电视中心　Television Centre
电视播放　televise
广播中心　Broadcasting Centre
电视台大楼　telecasting building
环球影视公司　universal film and TV Co.
广播塔　radio tower
电视塔　television tower
广播网　broadcasting network
录音室／播音室　studio
实况转播车　obvehicle
调音室　mixer
电视转播车　mobile TV obvehicle
录像室／演播室　Studio
新闻编辑室　Newsroom
电视录像组　Camera Crew
监听室／监视室　Monitor Room

2. 广播电视人（Personnel）

编导　playwright-director /choreographer-director
编审　senior editor
编剧　screenwriter
导演　director
导播　program director
节目主持人　host /master of ceremonies
副导播　associate director
策划者　production engineer
经纪人　agent
电视观众　television viewers
广播听众　broadcasting listeners
电视节目男主持人　TV host
电视节目女主持人　TV hostess
电视录像员　camera man
电台记者　radio reporter
电视录像制作人　video grapher
电台广播员　radio broadcaster
电视台记者　TV reporter
电台采访记者　radio interviewer
电视台采访记者　TV interviewer
电台台长　head of radio station
电视台台长　head of TV station
电台节目制作人　radio packager
电视节目制作人　TV packager
电视片的监制人　television producer
节目编排负责人　programming chief
电视节目舞台监督　floor manager /TV stage manager
节目制作人　programme producer
电视明星　TV star
广播稿编辑员　script editor
广播电视节目撰稿者　TV script writer
成音操作员　audio operator
录音操作员　recording operator
灯光控制员　lighting engineer
道具管理员　property man
节目部经理　president for program
技术指导员　technical director
剧装设计师　costume designer
基本演员　regular player
音效制作人　sound effect man
制片人　producer

静片摄影师　still photo man　　　　　特效师　special effect man

3. 栏目, 节目 (Column, Programme)

电台节目	radio programme	电视大学节目	TV university programme
电台广播剧	radio play	专题报道节目	special report programme
电台音乐节目	music programme on the radio	欢乐周末	happy weekend
电台相声节目	comic dialogue on the radio	相声节目	comic dialogue programme
电视相声节目	comic dialogue on TV	插播节目	cut-in program
电视节目	TV programme / show	时事节目	current affairs programme
节目编排	programming	妇女节目	women's programme
电视节目单	TV guide	比赛节目	contest show
新闻节目	news programme	暴力节目	violent program
实况广播节目	live programme	动画片节目	cartoon programme
英语节目	English programme	儿童节目	kid show
教育节目	educational programme	教学节目	educational programme
娱乐性节目	entertainment programme	烹饪节目	cooking program
采访节目	interview programme	社教节目	syndicated program
音乐节目	music programme	神幻节目	mystery program
体育节目	physical culture (or sports) programme	特技节目	stunt show
军事节目	military programme	专题节目	special topic programme (or feature)
农业节目	agriculture programme	重播节目	to repeat show
文化节目	cultural programme	宗教节目	religious program
访谈节目脱口秀	talk show	侦探节目	detective program
联播节目	chain programme	有奖节目	giveaway show
天气预报节目	weather forecast programme	译制节目	foreign release
特别节目	special programme	气象节目	weather program
连播节目	serial programme	新闻节目	news program
点播节目	request program	抢答节目	quiz show
收听广播节目	listen-in programme	与你同行	Going along with you
数字电视节目	digital TV programme	戏剧人生	Dramatic life
现场节目	live show	东方时空	Oriental time and space
		热门话题	Hot-discussed subject
		朝闻天下	Morning news

夜间新闻	Nightly news	功夫片	Kungfu film
短波广播	shortwave broadcasting	电视连续剧	TV series
无线电广播	radio broadcasting	电视片	video film
视频点播	video on demand	枪战片	shoot-'em-up
现场直播	live broadcasting	伦理片	ethical film
有线转播	rediffusion on wire	国产片	film made in China
有线广播	broadcasting on wire	动画片	animated film
晚间新闻	evening news	侦探片	detective film
电视新闻报道	TV news report	爱情片	love story
新闻公告	press communique	战争片	war film
新闻联播	news hookup	译制片	dubbed film
国际时讯	world express	恐怖电视片	video nasty
实况转播	outside broadcast	黄色录像片	videoporn
国内新闻	home news	反特片	anti-espionage film
国际新闻	international news	科幻片	science fiction
世界新闻	world news	恐怖片	horror film
新闻报道	news report	武打片	acrobatic fighting film
经济新闻	economic news	健康之路	Road to health
新闻提要	news headlines	夕阳红节目	Sunset glow programme
午间新闻	noon news	面对面	Vis-a-vis
午夜新闻	midnight news	法律讲堂	Lecture on law
体育新闻	sports news	实话实说	Calling a spade a spade (or talk it straight)
电视讲座	telecourse		
环球视线	Global watch	今日说法	Legal report /law today
海峡两岸	The both sides across straits	华夏掠影	Glimpse of China
文明之旅	Journey of civilization	万家灯火	Lights of ordinary families / myriad lights of city
综合新闻报道	news roundup		
电视广告	TV advertisement	美术星空	A galaxy of artists
电视小品	a TV sketch	公共频道	Public channel
电视剧	TV play	让世界了解你	Let the world know you
卡通系列片	cartoon series	今日关注	Focus today
电视与观众	TV and viewers	好戏连台	Hits lining up for the stage
电视系列片	TV series	今日亚洲	Asia today
牛仔片	cow-boy film	远方的家	Distant homeland
古装片	costume film	周末文艺	Weekend entertainment

同乐五洲	International student's talent Show
外国文艺	Foreign arts
海峡两岸	Both sides along the strait
中国文艺	Chinese arts
百花园	Flower garden
访谈节目	Interview show
焦点访谈	Interview about focus
世界各地	Around the world
实话实说	Tell the truth
世界体育	World sports
街头巷尾	On the streets and alleys
中国文化	Chinese culture
今日世界	The world today
文化生活	Cultural life
祖国各地	Across the land
军事报道	Military report
大家谈	Questions and opinions
天气预报	Weather broadcast
动物世界	Animal world
经济与法	Economy & law
新闻30'	News 30'
新闻联播	News broadcasting
环球视线	Global watch
城市1对1	One city to another
文明之旅	Journey of civilization
中华情	Chinese emotion
音乐电视	MTV
新闻直播间	Live news

4. 电视制作 (TV Production)

电视摄影棚	TV studio
电视接收机	TV set
电视题词幕	TV-prompter screen
背景音乐	background music
对比度控制	contrast control
音调控制	tone control
频率微调控制	frequency fine turning control
音量控制	volume control
色饱和度控制	color saturation control
亮度控制	brilliant control
高度控制	height control
聚焦控制	focus control
艺术字幕	art title
拍摄方法	photographing ways
远摄镜头	telephoto lens
自由取景	go hunting
变换镜头	flip
摄大角度	loosen up
摄近景	close up
慢镜头	slow motion
慢动作	slow action
旁白者	narrator
录音室	recording room
化妆指导	make-up supervisor
场景灯	set light
泛光灯	floodlight
聚光灯	spotlight
头顶灯	top light
计数灯	tally light
预演灯	preview light
造型光	modeling light
太阳弧光灯	sun-arc
隔音罩	blimp
跟镜头	lens shot

柔光	soft light	配音	dub
主光	keylight	配乐	dub in background music
道具	props	配曲	to set to music
灯光	light	色调	hue / tone
剪接	montage	删剪	cut
客串	guest star	闪动	flicker
配景	entourage	红灯	red light

5. 广播电台节目（Broadcasting Program）

广播新闻节目	radio news program	广播讲话节目	radio talk program
广播经济节目	radio economic program	广播新闻节目	newscast program
		广播评论节目	radio review program
广播农业节目	radio agricultural program	广播社论节目	radio editorial program
广播文艺节目	radio entertainment program	广播猜谜节目	radio quiz show
		广播相声节目	radio comic dialogue program
广播歌剧节目	radio opera program		
广播剧节目	radio drama program	实况广播节目	live broadcast program
广播连续剧节目	radio serial show	地区新闻节目	local news program
广播电话节目	radio phone programme	头号新闻节目	top news program
广播天气预报	radio weather forecast	体育报道节目	sports cast program
广播儿童节目	radio children's program	时事评论节目	current affairs program

6. 其他类（Others）

缓冲摄像机	isolated camera	闭路电视	closed-circuit television
手提摄像机	hand-held camera	有线电视	cable television
电子摄像机	electron camera	直角平面彩色电视机	flat-screen color TV set
电视摄像机	television camera		
彩色摄像机	color camera	电视信号	television signal
电视发射机	television transmitter	电视频道	television channel
彩色电视机	color television set	电视天线	television antenna
开电视机	to turn on TV set	实况录像	tape-delayed
大屏幕电视	large screen television	上电视	be on television
立体电视	stereotelevision	电视媒体	videoland
投影电视	projection television	电视屏幕	telescreen
彩色电视	color television	电视艺术	video art

新词 | 流行词 | 常用词翻译

实况录音　live recording
节目录制　transcription

收听率 / 收视率 rating

16 环境与环保
Environment and Environmental Protection

1. 保护环境 (Protection of Environment)

《联合国气候变化框架公约》	The United Nations Framework Convention on Climate Change
保护地球	to care for the earth
人居环境	a livable environment
绿色环境	green environment
低碳环境	low-carbon environment
环境向量	environmental vector
资源保护	to consere natural resources
环境保护	environmental protection
环境监测	environmental monitoring
环境预警	early warning of environment
环境效应	environmental effect
环境遥感	remote sensing of environment
环境预测	environmental forecasting
环境质量	environmental quality
环境影响	environmental impact
环境资源	environmental resources
环境自净	environmental self-purification
环境绿化	environmental forestation
保护环境	to protect environments
保护天然林	to protect virgin forests
保护性耕作	conservation farming
环境区划	environmental regionalism
红树林保护区	mangrove protection zone
环保专项治理	special projects to address serious environmental problems
加强环境保护	to strengthen environmental protection
环境复杂多变	complex and volatile environment
能源资源节约	energy and resources conservation
保护生态环境	ecological and environmental protection
过度能源消耗	excessive consumption of resources
绿色低碳技术	green and low-carbon technology
长江流域的生态掩体	an ecological shelter along the Yangtze River Valley
节能产品惠民工程	energy-saving products by ordinary households with government subsidies
污水处理	sewage disposal
污水净化	sewage purification
自然环境	natural environment

Translation on New Words, Popular Words and Everyday Expressions

绿色发展	green development
循环发展	circular development
低碳发展	low-carbon development
分布式能源	distribution of energy resources
太阳能	solar power
天然气	natural gas
页岩气	shale gas
煤气层	coal seam gas
生物圈	biosphere
风能	wind power
生物能	biomass energy
水电	hydropower
核电	nuclear power

2. 污染现象及处理（Polluted Phenomenon and Disposal）

环境损害成本	cost of environmental damage
节能减排	energy conservation and pollution reduction
生存排放	survival emissions
人均排放	per capita emissions
消费型排放	emissions attributed to consumption
节能降耗减排	to save energy, to lower energy consumption and to reduce pollutants discharge
污泥浊水	filth and mire
环境恶化	environmental degradation
温室气体排放	greenhouse gas emission
国际转移排放	international transfer emissions
大幅量化减排	deep quantified emission cuts
减缓温室气体排放	to mitigate greenhouse gas emissions
近期和中期减排目标	near-term and mid-term reduction targets
承诺期减排指标	emission reduction targets in the commitment period
友好气候技术	climate-friendly technologies
适应气候变化	to adapt to climate change
污染物	contaminants / pollutant
污染源	pollution source
气候变化	climate changes
二氧化碳排放	release of carbon dioxide
放射性污染	radioactive pollution
污水污染	sewage pollution
空气污染	air pollution
大气层污染	atmosphere pollution
工业粉尘污染	dust pollution / waste gas pollution
噪音污染	noise pollution
污水	foul water
油污染	oil pollution
热污染	thermal pollution
环境污染	environmental pollution
工业污水	industrial sewage
有毒烟雾	toxic smog
工业废水	industrial waste water
生活垃圾	life rubbish
污水处理	sewage treatment
绿化区	green area
二氧化碳排放强度	carbon dioxide

	emissions intensity
二氧化碳排放	carbon dioxide emission
城市污水处理	treatment of municipal sewage
未经处理的污水	untreated sewage
处理城市垃圾	disposal of municipal waste
水污染控制	water pollution control
环境控制	environmental control
环境卫生	environmental sanitation
控制沙漠化	desertification control
废渣物	waste residue
温室效应	green house effect
一次污染物	primary pollutant
二次污染物	secondary pollutant
废物回收	waste recovery
二次能源	secondary energy sources
生活污水	sanitary sewage
工业废液	industrial waste liquid
减少污染	decrease pollution
消除污染	eliminate pollution
煤烟污染	coal-smoke pollution
雾霾污染	foggy pollution
污染膨胀	sludge bulking
石油溢流	oil spill
一氧化碳	carbon monoxide
一氧化物	monoxide
二氧化碳	carbon dioxide
二氧化硫	sulfur dioxide
悬浮物	suspended solids
空气指数	air index
空气质量	air quality
垃圾处理	refuse disposal
净化系统	purification system
防风治沙	to check wind and control sand
防风固沙林	to prevent sand-shifting and control forest
化学防治	chemical control
海洋保护	conservation of ocean
植树造林	afforestation
流域规划	watershed planning
排放标准	to discharge standards
气象监测	climate monitoring
排污收费	pollution charges
园林绿化	landscaping
生态文明	ecological civilization
物理防治	physical control
生物防治	biological control
栽培防治	cultural control
水土保持	water and soil conservation
水土流失	soil erosion
除尘设施	dust removal installations
改造炉窑	to renovate furnaces and kilns
骨干水源	key water sources
引水调水	to divert water
废物利用	to make use of waste materials
燃料循环	fuel recycle
白色垃圾	white rubbish
生态建筑	ecological construction
集体供暖	collective heating
公共供暖系统	public heating system
分户采暖	household-based heating
航空碳排放（航空碳税）	carbon emission tax on airlines
高原反应	altitude sickness
绿色食品	green food
污水处理厂	sewage plant
用化学药品处理	to treat pollution with chemicals

工业废物处理	disposal of industrial wastes
废水生物处理	biological disposal of waste waters
回收有用材料	recovery of useful materials
防止废气污染	to prevent the exhaust gas to pollute air
减少向大气层排放废物	to decrease dirty waste materials into the air
大气污染生物净化	biologically purify atmospheric pollution
环境污染综合防治	integrated control about environmental pollution
控制环境恶化	to control the environmental deterioration
建污水处理场	to build sewage farm / plant
阻止向水域倒垃圾	to stop dumping garbage into the waters
增加森林覆盖面积	to increase forest coverage
大气污染防治工程	atmospheric pollution engineering
食品工业废水处理	to treat waste water of food processing
造纸工业废水处理	to treat waste waters of paper mills
废水臭氧化处理	ozonation treatment of waste water
放射性废水处理	to treat the radioactive waste water
废水活性炭处理	disposal of activated carbon in waste water
废水电解处理	electrolytic disposal of waste water
工业废水处理	disposal of industrial waste water
固态废物焚化	to incinerate solid wastes
废物资回收	waste materials recovery
废水重复利用	to re-use waste water
控制最大排放浓度	to control the maximum emission concentration
自然资源保护	to conserve natural resources
天然林保护	natural forest conservation
建立自然保护区	to set up natural reserve areas
无残留农药	non-persistent pesticide
无污染燃料	pollution-free fuels
使用无污染装置	to use pollution-free installations
野生生物保护	conservation of wildlife
农业环境保护	to protect agricultural environment
天然保护林	natural protection forests
生态保护	ecological preservation
防沙治沙	to prevent and control sandstorms
水土保持	to conserve water and soil
沙漠化治理	to reverse the expansion of stony deserts
湿地恢复	to recover wetlands
清洁生产	clean production
防雾霾	to prevent smog
防尾气排放	to prevent the vehicle

环境与环保
Environment and Environmental Protection

	exhaust emissions
除尘改造	dust removal
淘汰黄标车	to remove old high-emission vehicles
环境绿化管理	to manage the environmental forestation
乡村综合规划	rural integrated planning
淘汰落后产能	to close down outdated production facilities
生态农业系统	ecosystem farming
农业面源污染	non-point agricultural source pollution
生物圈保护区	biosphere reserve areas
生物资源保护	to protect biotic resources
生态补偿机制	ecological compensation mechanism
水污染防治工程	water pollution control engineering
水污染生物净化	biological purification of water pollution
土壤污染生物净化	biological purification of soil pollution
严格控制污染源	to strictly control pollution sources
大气污染防治	to prevent and control air pollution
大气,水,土壤污染	air, water and soil pollution
饮用水源保护	to protect the sources of drinking water
污水处理工程	sewage disposal engineering
农药废水处理	treatment of pesticide waste water
江河湖泊治理	to harness rivers and lakes

169

17 中国法律
China's Laws

1. 法律 (Law)

社会主义法治国家	a socialist country under the rule of law
社会主义法制	socialist legal system
民主与法制	democracy and legal system
普法教育	education in the general knowledge of law
法律援助	legal aid
节约能源法	Energy Conservation Law
公正文明执法	to enforce laws in strict, fair and civilized way
依法治国	to govern the country by law
法律保护	legal protection
法律地位	legal status
法律依据	legal basis
法理依据	basis of legal principle
法律规定	legal provisions
法律程序	legal procedure
法律手续	legal procedure
法律制裁	legal sanction
法律承认	de jure recognition
法律顾问	legal adviser
法人登记	registration of juristic person
法人单位	legal (or juridical) entity
法定法人	legal (or statutory) person
法定代理人	legal representative
法定人数	quorum
法定假期	official holiday
法定货币	legal tender
法定汇率	official rate
法人团体	body corporate
法人资格	legal (or juridical) personality (or qualification)
单独法人	corporation sole
集体法人	corporation aggregate
注册法人	registered juristic person
以言代法	to take one's own words as the law
以权压法	to place one's own authority above the law
徇私枉法	to abuse the law
超越宪法	to overstep the Constitution
法律特权	law's privilege
青少年犯罪	juvenile offenders (or delinquency)
家庭暴力	domestic violence
虐待儿童	to abuse children
学位条例	Regulations on the Academic Degrees
水污染防治法	Law on the Prevention and Control of Water Pollution

大气污染防治法	Law on the Prevention and Control of Atmospheric Pollution
民族区域自治法	Law on the Regional Ethnic Autonomy
合资经营企业法	Law on the Chinese-Foreign Equity Joint Ventures
农业技术推广法	Law on the Popularization and Application of Agricultural Technologies
特别行政区基本法	Basic Law of the Special Administrative Region
科学技术进步法	Law on the Progress of Science and Technology
治安管理处罚条例	Regulations on the Punishments in Public Order and Security Administration
行政处罚条例	Regulations on the Administrative Penalties
居民身份证条例	Law on the Residents' Identification Cards
房地产管理法	Law on the Real Estate Administration
行政复议法	Law of the Administrative Reconsideration
行政诉讼法	Law of the Administrative Procedure
国防教育法	Law on the Education on National Defense
国家赔偿法	Law on National Compensation
刑事诉讼法	Law of the Criminal Procedure
民用航空法	Law on the Civil Aviation
民事诉讼法	Law of the Civil Procedure
侵权责任法	Law of Tort
食品质量法	Food Quality Law
产品质量法	Product Quality Law
食品安全法	Food Safety Law
环境保护法	Environmental Protection Law
环境防治法	Law of the Prevention
权益保护法	Law on the Protection of the Rights and Interests
枪支管控法	Law on the Control of Firearms
就业医师法	Law on the Qualified Doctors in Practice
独资企业法	Law on the Proprietorship Enterprises
外资企业法	Law on the Foreign-funded Enterprises
土地承包法	Law on the land Contract
文物保护法	Law on the Protection of the Cultural Relics
矿产资源法	Law of the Mineral Resources
经济合同法	Law of the Economic Contract
对外贸易法	Law of the Foreign Trade
义务教育法	Compulsory Education Law
职业教育法	Vocational Education Law
现役军官法	Law on the Service of Officers on the Active List
高等教育法	Higher Education Law

民事通则	Administrative Principles of the Civil Law	献血法	Blood Donation Law
依法治国	to govern the country by law	专利法	Patent Law
		劳动法	Labor Law
国防法	Law on the National Defense	仲裁法	Law on Mediation and Arbitration
教育法	Law of Education	赔偿法	Law on Compensation
工会法	Law on Trade Union	调解法	Mediation's Law
电力法	Law on the Electric Power	环境法	Environmental Law
物权法	Property Law	铁路法	Law on Railways
继承法	Succession Law	公路法	Law on Highways
海商法	Maritime law	草原法	Law on Grasslands
投资法	Investment Law	气象法	Law on Meteorology
票据法	Negotiable Intruments Law	防洪法	Flood Cotrol Law
商标法	Trademark Law	森林法	Law on Forest
测绘法	Law on Surveying and Mapping	煤炭法	Law on Coal
标准法	Law on Standardization	审计法	Law on Auditing
采购法	Procurement Law	农业法	Law on Agriculture

2. 民事法（Civil Law）

民事权利和义务	civil rights and obligations	当事人（原告、被告）	parties（plaintiff/defendant）
无效民事行为	null and void civil acts	查封财产	to seal up property / assets
恶意串通行为	acts performed through malicious collusion	查明事实	to ascertain the facts
		被执行人	the person subject to the execution
行使诉讼权利	exercise of one's litigation rights	交叉债务	the cross liability
按撤诉处理	to consider the case withdrawn	变卖财产	to sell off the property / assets
		冻结财产	to freeze the property / assets
按顺序赔偿	to pay off one's debts in order	监督程序	to supervise and urge the procedures
裁判与裁定	judgement and order	法庭调解	judicial conciliation
承担诉讼费用	to bear the litigation costs	一方反悔	one party retracting one's consent
查阅庭审材料	to consult the materials related to the court proceedings of the case	法定继承	statutory succession
		公开审理	to be heard in public

合并审理	to be tried together
合同诉讼	suit for contract
自行回避	to withdraw voluntarily
进行调解	to conduct conciliation
回避制度	system of withdrawal of judicial personnel
再审案件	case for retrial
开庭审理	trial in court
口头上诉	oral complaint
扣押财产	to distrain the property / assets
普通程序	ordinary procedure
执行程序	procedures of execution
上诉期限	time limit for an appeal
申诉理由	cause of complaint
申诉权利	petition rights
诉讼权利	procedural right
诉讼行为	procedural act
诉讼案件	lawsuit
法律诉讼	judicial proceedings
撤销诉讼	to withdraw an accusation / to drop a lawsuit
调解协议	conciliation agreement
调解无效	conciliation efforts being ineffective
民事制裁	civil sanction
民间调解	non-governmental mediation
民事权利	civil right
驳回上诉	reject the appeal
不予执行	disallow the execution
待决诉讼	pending case
仲裁诉讼	arbitration lawsuit (or litigation)
民事上诉	civil appeal
婚姻诉讼	lawsuit in marriage / the marriage lawsuit
民事审判	civil trial
维持原判	to sustain the original judgement
民事管辖	civil jurisdiction
民事罚款	civil penalty
民刑诉讼	civil and criminal lawsuits
债务清偿	performance of debt
就地办案	to conduct the trials on the spot
巡回审理	to make a circuit of trial
有权提审	to have the power to bring the case up for trial itself
评议案件	to deliberate a case
移送管辖	transfer of jurisdiction
制定管辖	designation of jurisdiction
第一审程序	procedure of the first instance
第二审程序	procedure of the second instance
合议庭	collegiate bench / collegial panel
起诉状	bill of complaint / bill of prosecution
上诉人	petitioner
上诉状	petition
申诉人	declarant
申诉书	petition for revision
审判员	judge
审判长	presiding judge
答辩人	respondent
答辩状	defense
调解书	conciliation statement
庭长	presiding judge / president of a law court
受理	to accept a case
和解	to arrange a settlement

回避	to withdraw	案由	cause of action
裁定	orders	反诉	counterclaim

3. 刑事案件 (Criminal Cases)

犯罪嫌疑人	criminal suspect
刑讯逼供案	case of extorting confessions by torture
窝藏罪犯案	case of harboring criminals
首要分子	ringleader
暴力案件	violent cases
罪大恶极	most heinous crime
流窜作案	to go from one place to another committing crimes
流氓活动	hooligan activities
招摇撞骗	to cheat and bluff
寻衅滋事	to stir up fights to cause trouble
窝藏赃物	to conceal booty
敲诈勒索	to extort by blackmail
共同轮奸	to jointly commit rape by turns
故意杀人罪	intentional killing
拐卖人口	to abduct and sell people
过失杀人	to negligently kill sb.
过失犯罪	negligent crime
玩忽职守	to neglect of duty
滥用职权	to abuse one's power
包庇罪犯	to protect criminals
滥用公款	to embezzle public money
挪用公款	to appropriate the public money
泄愤报复	to give vent to spite
徇私舞弊	to do wrong to serve one's friends or relatives
隐匿罪证	to conceal criminal evidence

犯伪证罪	to commit perjury
犯罪行为	criminal act
奸淫幼女	fornication with an underage girl
经济案件	economic cases
贪污公款	corruption involving public funds
重大嫌疑	major suspect
致人伤残	to cause injury or disability to a person
致人重伤	to cause serious injury to a person
杀人案	case of killing a person
陷害案	case of framing a person
假药案	case of selling bogus medicine
谋杀案	case of murdering a person
诈骗案	case of victimization (or fraud)
纵火案	case of arson
强奸案	case of rape
造假币	to make the counterfeit currency
现行犯	active criminal
作案	to commit an offence (or crime)
主犯	prime culprit
从犯	accessory
共犯	accomplice
犯罪	to commit a crime
累犯	recidivist
劫狱	prison raid
教唆	to instigate
在逃	fugitive
走私	smuggling

陷害	to frame sb.	伤害	to injure sb.
诬陷	falsely accuse and frame	诽谤	defamation
诬告	falsely accuse sb.	斗殴	to fight
煽动	to incite sb./ sth.	渎职	dereliction of duty
贪污	corruption	贩毒	to traffic in narcotics
行贿	to give bribes	拐骗	to abduct
受贿	to accept bribes	惯偷	the habitual theft
投毒	to spread poison	盗窃	to steal sth.
偷税	to evade tax	抗税	to resist tax
勾引	to lure sb.	抢劫	robbery
欺骗	deception	伤人	to injure the people

4. 法律术语 (Law Terms)

法律	law	法警	bailiff
法规	laws and regulations	法家	legalists
法定	statutory	法医	legal medical expert
法场	execution ground	法检	inspection by law
法办	to punish by law	法度	law
法案	proposed law	法名	religious name
法治	rule by law	法权	law right
法制	legal system	法事	religious services
法院	court of justice	法纪	law and discipline
法堂	law court	法令	laws and decrees
法庭	court	法理	legal principle
法网	net of justice	法学	science of law
法师	Master of the law	法则	law
法人	juridical person	法统	legally constituted authority
法官	judge		

18 食品蔬菜类
Foods and Vegetables

1. 蔬菜 (Vegetable)

青菜	green vegetables	芸豆	kidney bean
甜菜	beet	苦瓜	balsam pear
香菜	coriander	丝瓜	snake gourd
荠菜	shepherd's purse	黄瓜	cucumber
香椿	toon	南瓜	pumpkin
油菜	rape	冬瓜	wax gourd
菠菜	spinach	辣椒	pepper
芹菜	celery	萝卜	turnip
花菜	cauliflower	山药	Chinese yam
卷心菜	cabbage	番薯	sweet potato
茄子	eggplant	木薯	cassava
番茄	tomato	藕	lotus roots
青椒	green pepper	胡萝卜	carrot
山野菜	wild vegetable	茭白	wild rice stem
榨菜	hot pickled mustard tuber	韭菜	leek
土豆	potato	莴苣	lettuce
黄豆	soya bean	咸菜	salted vegetable
蚕豆	broad bean	蒜苗	garlic bolt
毛豆	young soya bean	洋葱	onion
青豆	green peas	葱	scallion /shallot
绿豆	green bean	蒜	garlic
豌豆	pea	姜	ginger
刀豆	string bean	莴笋	asparagus lettuce
豆荚	legume	芋艿	taro
豇豆	cowpea	苋菜	edible amaranth
扁豆	lentil	水芹	dropwort

Foods and Vegetables

竹笋	bamboo shoots	葫芦	calabash
毛笋	shoots of mao bamboo	慈姑	arrowhead
冬笋	winter bamboo shoots	莼菜	water shield
笋干	dried bamboo shoots	生菜	romaine lettuce
芦笋	asparagus	海米白菜	Chinese cabbage with dried shrimps
蘑菇	mushroom		
草菇	straw mushroom	黄豆芽	soybean sprouts
荸荠/菱角	water chestnut	绿豆芽	mung bean sprouts

2. 豆制品 (Bean Products)

豆腐	soybean curd	豆腐脑儿	jellied bean curd
豆腐皮	thin sheets of soybean curd / skin of soya-bean milk	豆腐乳	fermented bean curd
		豆花儿	bean jelly
腐竹	dried bean milk cream in tight rolls	豆浆	soya-bean milk
豆饼	soya-bean cake	豆豉	fermented soya-beans

3. 肉类 (Meat)

牛肉	beef / veal	火腿	ham
猪肉	pork	肉丸	meat ball
羊肉	mutton / lamb	肉丁	diced meat
鸡肉	chicken meat	肉片	sliced meat
火鸡肉	turkey meat	大排	porkchop
山鸡肉	pheasant meat	蹄髈	pork shank
乌骨肉	black-bone silky fowl meat	猪蹄	trotters
鸭肉	duck	猪油	lard
鹅肉	goose	猪肝	pork liver
冻肉	frozen meat	猪心	pork heart
咸肉	bacon	猪肚	pork tripe
鲜肉	fresh meat	猪头肉	bath chap
肥肉	fat meat	香肠	sausage
瘦肉	lean meat		

4. 鱼类 (Fish)

鲑鱼	salmon	甲鱼	turtle
青鱼	black carp	鲫鱼	crucian carp

刀鱼	ribbonfish	白鲢鱼	silver carp
鳊鱼	bream	泥鳅	loach
黑鱼	snakehead	河蚌	river mussel
章鱼	octopus	黄鳝	finless eel
带鱼	hairtail / cutlass fish	河虾	river shrimp / prawn
鲳鱼	butter fish	河蟹	freshwater / river crab
沙丁鱼	sardine	桂鱼	mandarin fish
大黄鱼	greater croaker	河豚	globefish / balloonfish
凤尾鱼	long-tailed anchovy	河鳗	river eel
鳕鱼	cod	清水虾	freshwater shrimp
黄鱼	yellow croaker	海鳗	conger eel
墨鱼	cuttlefish	条虾	shrimp
鱿鱼	squid	对虾	prawn
白鱼	white fish	虾仁	shelled shrimps
鲤鱼	carp	河鲜	freshwater fish

5. 中餐类菜谱 (Menu in Chinese Food)

1) 猪肉类 (Pork)

米粉肉	steamed pork with rice flour	木须肉	Moo Shu pork
湖南肉	pork of Hunan style	咸鱼烧肉	braised pork with salted fish cutlet
回锅肉	twice-cooked pork	土豆烧肉	braised pork with potato
古老肉	sweet and sour pork	萝卜烧肉	braised pork with turnip
烤排骨	barbecued spare ribs	咸鱼肉饼	steamed minced-pork and salted fish cutlet
东坡肉	Dongpo Pork	什会肉	stewed pork with assorted vegetables
竹笋烧肉	braised pork with bamboo shoots	辣子肉	sauted pork in hot pepper sauce
鲍鱼红烧肉	braised pork with abalone	米粉扣肉	steamed sliced-pork with minced rice
豆腐烧肉	braised pork with bean curd	干豆角回锅肉	sauted spicy pork with dried bean
干菜烧肉	braised pork with dried vegetable	湘味回锅肉	sauted sliced-pork with pepper with Hunan style
地瓜烧肉	stewed diced-pork and sweet potato	芽菜回锅肉	sauted sliced-pork with scallion and preserved
毛家红烧肉	braised pork with Mao's family style		

食品蔬菜类
Foods and Vegetables

	vegetable
蒜香椒盐肉排	deep-fried spare rib with minced garlic and spiced salt
糖醋排骨	braised sweet and sour spare rib
米粉排骨	steamed spare rib with minced rice
椒盐排骨	spare ribs with pepper and salt
炒肉丝	sauted pork slices
鱼香肉丝	Yu-xiang shredded -pork with garlic sauce
雪菜炒肉丝	sauted shredded-pork with preserved vegetable
萝卜炒肉丝	sauted shredded-pork with turnips
腊肉炒香干	sauted preserved pork with sliced dried -bean curd

2）牛肉类（Beef）

五香牛肉	spiced beef
红烧牛肉	braised beef
炖牛肉	stewed beef
鱼香牛肉	yu-xiang beef
萝卜烧牛肉	braised beef with turnip
土豆烧牛肉	braised beef with potatoes
香辣牛肉	braised beef in spicy sauce
罐焖牛肉	stewed beef in casserole
水煮牛肉	poached sliced beef in chili oil
炸牛排	deep fried beef steak
竹笋烧牛肉	braised beef with bamboo shoots
青椒牛肉	sauted beef with green pepper
什菜牛肉	sauted beef with assorted vegetables
辣子牛肉	sauted beef in chili sauce
时菜炒牛肉	sauted beef with seasonal vegetable
鲜菇炒牛肉	sauted beef with fresh mushroom
芝麻牛肉	sauted beef with sesame
中式牛排	beef steek with Chinese style
爆炒牛肋骨	sauted beef rib
麻辣牛肚	braised ox tripe in spicy sauce
青椒牛柳	sauted beef fillet with green pepper
芦笋牛柳	stir-fried beef fillet with green asparagus
豆豉牛柳	braised beef fillet in black bean sauce
洋葱牛肉丝	sauted shredded beef with onion
土豆炒牛柳	sauted beef fillet with potato
红烧牛肉筋	braised beef tendon with home style
咖喱牛肉	curry beef

3）羊肉类（Mutton）

红烧羊肉	braised mutton
炖羊肉	stewed mutton
葱爆羊肉	sauted sliced mutton with scallion
烤羊肉	to roast mutton
萝卜烧羊肉	braised mutton with turnip
风味羊排	deep-fried mutton chop
烤羊腿	to roast lamb leg
卤酥羊腿	stewed lamb leg
炒羊肉丝	stir-fried shredded mutton
羊肉串	mutton skewer

4）鸡、鸭、鹅肉类（chicken, duck and goose）

怪味鸡	multi-flavoured chicken
鸡肉串	chicken string
干锅鸡	sauted chicken with pepper in dry pot
炖鸡	stewed chicken
红烧鸡	braised chicken
鱼香鸡片	yu-xiang chicken slice
白斩鸡	sliced cold chicken in boiled water
咖喱鸡	curry chicken
芦笋鸡片	sauted sliced-chicken with asparagus
芫荽爆鸡片	sauted sliced-chicken with coriander
豆苗鸡片	sauted sliced-chicken with pea sprouts
荠菜鸡片	sauted sliced chicken with pickpurse
时蔬炒鸡片	sauted sliced-chicken with seasonal vegetable
宫爆鸡丁	kung pao chicken
辣子鸡	deep-fried diced-chicken with dried chili
板栗焖仔鸡	braised chicken with chestnuts
脆皮鸡	crispy chicken
枣子花生栗子鸡	stewed chicken with jujube, peanuts and chestnuts
扒鸡	grilled chicken
炸八块鸡	deep-fried chicken with 8 pieces
烧鸡肉串	roasted chicken kebabs
汁烧鸡肉	stewed chicken in sauce
什菜鸡	sauted chicken with assorted vegetables
甜酸鸡	sauted sweet and sour chicken
干烧鸡	braised chicken in chili sauce
贵妃鸡	deep-fried chicken
鲜人参炖土鸡	stewed chicken with ginseng
北京烤鸭	Beijing roasted duck
酱鸭	marinated duck in soy sauce
红烧鸭	braised duck
白切鸡	boiled chicken with sauce
虫草炖老鸭	stewed duck with aweto
黄豆煮水鸭	stewed duck with soybeans
冬菜扣老鸭	braised duck with preserved vegetables
参杞炖老鸭	stewed duck with ginseng and medlar
香辣炒板鸭	sauted salted duck in spicy sauce
双冬鸭	sauted duck with snow peas and mushroom
烩鸭四宝	braised four delicacies of duck
酱爆鸭片	sauted sliced duck in soy sauce
香煮鹅肝	pan-fried goose liver
松茸扒鹅肝	pan-fried goose liver with matsutake
菜头烧板鹅	braised salted goose and lettuce in spicy sauce

5）鱼、蟹、虾等类（Fish, Crab and Shrimp）

红烧鱼	braised fish
红烧草鱼	sauted grass carp
红烧鳝鱼	braised eel
红烧大黄鱼	braised yellow croaker
红烧长江鲥鱼	braised hilsa herring in

食品蔬菜类
Foods and Vegetables

	soy sauce
豆豉鲑鱼	mandarin fish in black bean sauce
清蒸鲑鱼	streamed mandarin fish
清蒸鲈鱼	steamed perch
清蒸鲫鱼	steamed river carp
清蒸多宝鱼	steamed turbot
酸菜鱼	boiled fish with preserved cabbage and chili
油炸鱼	fried fish in oil
剁椒鱼头	steamed fish head braised with chili pepper
生炒鳗鱼	sauted sliced eel
肉烧咸鱼	salted fish braised with pork
糖醋鱼	sauted sweet and sour whole fish
糖醋鱿鱼	sauted sweet and sour squid
香烧鱿鱼	braised squid
宫保鱿鱼	kung pao squid
时蔬鱿鱼	stir-fried squid with seasonal vegetable
西湖醋鱼	steamed grass carp in vinegar gravy
脆皮全鱼	crispy whole fish
冬菜银鳕鱼	steamed codfish with spiced salt
香煎咸鱼	pan-fried salted fish
椒盐鳕鱼	deep-fried codfish with spiced salt
王府酥鱼	deep-fried fish with soy sauce
姜丝鱼片	braised sliced-fish with ginger
葱烧鱼片	braised sliced fish with scallion
鸭汤醋椒鱼	braised mandarin fish with chili pepper in duck bone soup
豆豉鱼片	braised sliced-fish in black bean sauce
时蔬鱼片	stir-fried fish fillet with seasonal vegetable
黄扒鱼片	braised fish maw
白扒鱼片	braised fish maw
蛋花炒鱼肚	sautéd fish maw with scrambled egg
生鱼片	sashimi
菜心扒鱼圆	braised fish meat balls with green vegetable
酥炸蛤卷	deep-fried crispy mussel rolls
黑椒鲜贝	braised scallops in black pepper sauce
豆豉炒蛤	stir-fried mussel with black bean paste
姜葱炒蟹	deep-fried hardshell crab with ginger and scallion
清蒸肉蟹	steamed hardshell crabs
清蒸红花蟹	steamed sea crabs
咸蛋黄炒肉蟹	sauted hardshell crabs with salted egg yolk
豆豉炒肉蟹	sauted hardshell crabs with osmanthus sauce
油醋河毛蟹	braised river crabs in sesame oil and vinegar
炒蟹	sauted crabs
香辣蟹	sauted crabs in hot and spicy sauce
清蒸闸蟹	steamed river crabs
香葱白果虾	sauted shrimps with gingko and chives
炒虾	sauted shrimps
什烩虾	sauted shrimps with assorted vegetables

鱼香虾	yu-xiang shrimps
香辣虾	fried shrimps in hot and spicy sauce
油爆虾	sauted shrimps
鲜果炒津虾	prawns salad with fresh fruit
甜酸虾	sauted sweet and sour shrimps
椒盐基围虾	deep-fried shrimps with spiced salt
白玉虾球	crystal white shrimps balls
干烧大虾	braised prawns in chili sauce
水煮明虾	poached prawnws
干爆大虾	fried prawns with sweet sauce
鲜辣大虾	stir-fried prawns in chili sauce
辣子虾仁	sauted shrimps in chili sauce
清炒虾仁	sauted shrimps
豆苗虾仁	fried shrimps with pea sprouts
宫爆虾仁	kung pao shrimps
金丝虾球	braised shrimps meat balls
百合虾球	sauted prawns meat balls with lily
翡翠虾球	stir-fried prawns meat balls with green vegetables
韭菜炒河虾	sauted shrimps with chives
清蒸龙虾	steamed lobsters
姜葱炒龙虾	sauted lobsters with ginger and scallion
豉椒焗龙虾	gratinated lobster in pepper and black bean
清炒大龙虾	sauted giant lobsters
清蒸虾仁	sauted scallop meat
黄焖大虾	braised pawns in rice wine
海蜇	jelly fish
海带	kelp
海参	sea cucumber
辣子干贝	sauted scallops in chili sauce
鱼香干贝	yu-xiang scallops
宫保鲜贝	kung pao fresh scallops
什烩干贝	sauted scallops with assorted vegetables
清炒贝仁	sauted scallops meat
烧三鲜	braised sliced abalone
汁烩海鲜	sauted assorted seafood
夏果海鲜	sauted assorted seafood with macadamia nuts
龙虎凤大烩	thick soup of snake, cat and chicken
白芍海螺片	scalded sliced conch

6) 素菜类 (Cooked Vegetables)

（1）素菜类(vegetables)

炒菜	sauteed dish
炒鸡蛋	sauted eggs
煎鸡蛋	fried eggs
炒白菜	sauted Chinese cabbage
炒芥菜	sauted Chinese kale
炒生菜	sauted lettuce
炒菠菜	sauted spinach
炒青菜	sauted green vegetable
炒苋菜	sauted amaranth
炒菜心	sauted green vegetable
炒油菜	sauted rape
炒豆苗	sauted pea sprouts
炒土豆丝	sauted shredded potato
炒三鲜	sauted potato, green pepper and eggplant
炒芹菜	sauted celery
炒辣椒	sauted pepper
炒豆芽	sauted pea buds
炒四季豆	sauted green beans
炒韭菜	sauted Chinese chives
炒莴笋	sauted asparagus lettuce

食品蔬菜类
Foods and Vegetables

炒花生	fried peanuts
炒黄瓜	sauted cucumber
烧冬瓜	sauted wax gourd
炒苦瓜	sauted bitter gourd
炒南瓜	sauted pumpkin
西红柿炒鸡蛋	scrambled egg with tomato
炒豆尖	sauted bean sprouts
青椒肉片	sliced pork with green pepper
银杏炒百合	sauted lily bulb with gingko nuts
鱼香茄子	yu-xiang eggplants
芹香木耳	sauted black fungus with celery
炒丝瓜	sauted sponge gourd
黄金玉米	sauted sweet corn with salted egg yolk
红烧茄子	braised eggplants
炒山药	sauted Chinese yam
中式泡菜	Chinese-style pickles
烧香/冬菇	sauted black mushroom
土豆泥	mashed potatoes
蘑菇虾仁	shrimp and fresh mushroom

（2）豆腐（bean curd）

家常豆腐	home-style bean curd
麻婆豆腐	bean curd of sichuan style
脆皮豆腐	crispy bean curd
金菇豆腐	braised bean curd with mushroom
红烧豆腐	braised bean curd
碎肉炖豆腐	stewed bean curd with minced pork
雪菜炒豆腐皮	sauted sliced dried bean curd with preserved vegetable
肉酱豆腐	braised bean curd with minced meat
辣子豆腐	sauted bean curd in hot pepper
麻辣豆腐	spicy bean curd
五味豆腐	braised five-flavored bean curd
虾仁豆腐	sauted bean curd with shrimp
芝麻豆腐	deep-fried bean curd with sesame
砂锅豆腐	bean curd in casserole
香芹豆干	sauted smoked bean curd with celery
海鲜豆腐	braised bean curd with seafood
泥鳅炖豆腐	braised bean curd with loach
火腿炖豆腐	braised ham with bean curd
杏仁豆腐	bean curd with chilled almond
油炸臭豆腐	deep-fried fermented bean curd
面筋	gluten
豆干	dried soybean
硬豆腐	hard soybean curd
粉丝	vermicelli made from bean starch

（3）冷菜（cold dish）

桂花糖藕	sliced lotus roots with sweet osmanthus sauce
姜汁皮蛋	preserved egg in ginger sauce
川北凉粉	bean noodles in chili sauce
拌双耳	black and white fungus
拌豆腐丝	shredded dried bean curd

with sauce
萝卜干毛豆　dried turnip with green soybeans
皮蛋豆腐　bean curd with preserved egg
五香豆干　spiced dried bean curd
五香熏鱼　spiced smoked fish
炝黄瓜　flavoured cucumber
素鸭　dried bean curd
四川泡菜　prickles with Sichuan style
黄瓜条　cucumber strips
酸甜泡菜　sweet and sour prickles
花生米　deep-fried peanuts
水果沙拉　fresh fruit salad

（4）汤羹类（soup）
家常蛋汤　egg soup with home style
菠菜蛋汤　egg soup with spinach
白菜蛋汤　egg soup with Chinese vegetable
番茄蛋汤　egg soup with tomato
萝卜排骨汤　turnip soup with spare ribs
酸辣汤　hot and sour soup
鱼片汤　fish fillet soup
菠菜海鲜汤　spinach soup with seafood
蔬菜海鲜汤　vegetable and seafood soup
龙凤汤　chicken and crucian carp soup
素菜汤　vegetable soup
海鲜酸辣汤　hot and sour seafood soup
豆腐粉丝汤　bean curd and vermicelli soup
豆腐菜汤　bean curd and vegetable soup
榨菜肉丝汤　shredded pork and preserved vegetable soup
冬瓜汤　white gourd soup
冬瓜哈蛎汤　white gourd soup with clam
番茄鸭块汤　tomato and duck meat soup
乌鱼子汤　cuttle fish roe soup
白菜豆腐汤　Chinese cabbage and bean curd soup
紫菜蛋汤　egg soup with laver
芋头排骨汤　spare rib soup with taro
豆腐海带汤　bean curd and kelp soup
鸡汤　chicken soup
萝卜鸡蛋汤　turnip soup with egg
酸辣鱿鱼羹　hot and sour squid soup
鸭汤　duck soup
冰糖莲子银耳汤　lotus seeds and white fungus in rock sugar soup
清蒸鱼肚羹　steamed fish maw soup
凤凰玉米羹/玉米鸡蛋羹　egg soup with sweet corn
牛肉豆腐羹　bean curd soup with minced beef
莲子鸭羹　lotus seed and duck soup
蟹肉粟米羹　crab meat soup with sweet corn
桂花鳕鱼羹　godfish soup with osmanthus flower
龙凤羹　fish soup with minced chicken
干贝银丝羹　bean curd with dried scallop
鱼翅鲍鱼羹　abalone soup with shark's fin
豆腐鸡肉煲　chicken meat with bean curd
南瓜芋头煲　braised taro and pumpkin in casserole
梅菜扣肉煲　braised pork and preserved

食品蔬菜类 / Foods and Vegetables

	vegetable in casserole
海鲜粉丝煲	braised seafood with vermicelli in casserole
海参鹅掌煲	braised goose web and sea cucumber in casserole
白果老鸭煲	duck and ginkgo in casserole
海鲜砂锅	seafood in casserole
鱼香茄子煲	braised yu-xiang eggplant in casserole
砂锅鱼肚	stewed fish maw in casserole
砂锅鱼头	braised fish head in casserole
砂锅鸡肉丸	chicken meat balls in casserole
砂锅滑鸡	stewed chicken and vegetable in casserole

（5）主食小吃类（rice, noodles and local snack）

大米饭	steamed rice / cooked rice
大米稀饭	cooked rice porridge
南瓜粥	pumpkin congee
小米粥	millet congee
牛肉粥	minced beef congee
海鲜粥	seafood congee
腊八粥	congee with nuts and dried fruits
绿豆粥	mung bean congee
麦片粥	porridge
蛋炒饭	fried rice with eggs
炒饭	fried rice / sauted rice
虾仁饭	rice with fried shrimp
红烧牛肉饭	rice with stewed beef
火腿炒饭	fried rice with ham
牛肉盖饭	steamed rice with beef
什锦炒饭	stir-fried rice with meat and vegetable
韭菜炒饭	stir-fried rice with Chinese chives
香菇牛肉饭	rice with beef and black mushroom
辣子鸡饭	rice with chicken and hot peper
虾仁炒饭	stir-fried rice with shrimp
炒面	sauted noodles
汤面	noodles in soup
青菜面	noodles with green vegetable
鸡汤面	noodles with eggs
什锦汤面	noodles soup with meat and assorted vegetables
牛脯汤面	noodles soup with beef brisket
肉丸汤面	noodles soup with meat balls
排骨汤面	noodles soup with spare rib
盖浇面	Chinese style spaghetti
虾球清汤面	noodles soup with shrimp balls
海鲜汤面	noodles soup with seafood
三鲜面	noodle soup with fish maw, abalone and sea cucumber
鸭汤面	noodles soup with duck
牛肉拉面	hand-pulled noodles soup with beef
排骨拉面	hand-pulled noodle soup with spare rib
炸酱面	noodles with soybean paste
雪菜面	noodles soup with preserved vegetable
肉丝面	noodles soup with shredded pork
葱油拌面	noodles in scallion oil and soy sauce

馄饨面	noodles soup with hunton
红烧牛肉面	noodles soup with braised beef
腊肉面	noodles with preserved pork
肉酱手擀面	handmade noodles with minced pork
蘑菇面	noodles with mushroom
凉面	cold noodles with sesame sauce
乌冬面	Japanese noodles soup
阳春面	plain noodles soup
南瓜面	noodles with pumpkin
什锦炒面	mixed and fried noodles
牛肉面	beef noodles
菜肉饺子	Jiaozi stuffed with pork and vegetable
鸡蛋水饺	Jiaozi stuffed with eggs
白菜饺子	Jiaozi stuffed with Chinese cabbage
茴香水饺	Jiaozi stuffed with fennel
韭菜水饺	Jiaozi stuffed with Chinese chives
芹菜水饺	Jiaozi stuffed with celery
香菇油菜水饺	Jiaozi stuffed with mushroom and cole
蒸饺	steamed Jiaozi
鲜虾水饺	Jiaozi stuffed with fresh shrimp
包子	baozi / stuffed bun
鲜肉包	baozi stuffed with fresh meat
酱肉包	baozi stuffed with marinated pork
豆腐包	baozi stuffed with bean curd
韭菜包	baozi stuffed with Chinese chives
咸菜包	baozi stuffed with salted vegetable
雪菜包	baozi stuffed with preserved vegetable
萝卜包	baozi stuffed with turnip
素菜包	baozi stuffed with vegetable
豆沙包	baozi stuffed with red bean paste
蛋黄包	baozi stuffed with egg yolk
鲜虾包	baozi stuffed with fresh shrimp
鸡肉包	baozi stuffed with chicken meat
香菇包	baozi stuffed with black mushroom
小笼汤包	baozi stuffed with juicy pork
家常饼	pancake
咸烧饼	spiced sesame pancake
甜烧饼	sweet sesame pancake
贴饼子	baked corn pancake
南瓜饼	pumpkin pancake
萝卜丝饼	pan-fried turnip pancake
黄桥烧饼	sesame pancake with Huangqiao style
素馅饼	vegetarian pancake
葱油饼	baked scallion pancake
豆沙饼	red-bean paste pancake
卷饼	flat bread
华夫饼	waffle
肉饼	patty
月饼	moon cake
牛肉饼	hamburger patty
烧卖	shaomai
牛肉烧卖	shaomai with beef
猪肉烧卖	shaomai with paok
麦当劳	McDonald
鸡肉汉堡	chicken burger
土豆泥	mashed potato

食品蔬菜类
Foods and Vegetables

盖浇饭	rice served with meat and vegetables
鸡翅	chicken wing
鸡块	chicken nugget
香辣鸡翅膀	spicy chicken
烤鸡	barbecue chicken
蘸料	sauces
甜酸酱	sweet and sour sauces
辣酱	hot sauces
烧烤酱	barbecue sauces
麦当劳大麦克三明治	McDonald Big Mac
鲜虾烧卖	shaomai with fresh shrimp
翡翠烧卖	vegetable shaomai
春菇烧卖	shaomai stuffed with mushroom
煎蛋卷	omelet
蔬菜春卷	spring rolls stuffed with vegetable
香肠卷	sausage rolls
素春卷	vegetarian spring rolls
腐皮卷	bean curd skin rolls
鲜虾春卷	spring rolls stuffed with fresh shrimps
脆皮春卷	crispy spring rolls
海鲜春卷	spring rolls stuffed with seafood
肉卷	meat rolls
鲜蛋春卷	spring rolls stuffed with eggs
糯米卷	glutinous rice rolls
芝麻卷	sesame rolls
银丝卷	steamed rolls
油煎鸡蛋卷	pan-fried egg rolls
炸虾卷	deep-fried shrimp rolls
轧面卷	doughnut / sinker
奶油卷	cream roll
芝麻麻团	deep-fried glutinous rice rolls coated with sesame
锅贴	guotie /pot stickers
猪肉锅贴	guotie stuffed with pork
牛肉锅贴	guotie stuffed with beef
豆腐锅贴	guotie stuffed with bean curd
蔬菜锅贴	guotie stuffed with vegetable
红豆糕	red bean cake
花生糕	peanut cake
萝卜糕	turnip cake
炒年糕	stir-fried rice cake
黄金糕	sponge cake
蒸馒头	steamed mantou /steamed bread
油炸馒头	oil-fried mantou
鲜奶馒头	mantou with milk
烤馒头	baked mantou
黑米馒头	mantou with black rice
白面馒头	mantou with white flour
荞麦馒头	mantou with buck wheat
玉米面馒头	mantou with corn flour
速冻馒头	frozen mantou
羊肉馒头	mantou with lamb meat
羊肉泡馍	pita bread in lamb soup
豆沙粽子	zongzi stuffed with red bean paste
猪肉粽子	zongzi stuffed with pork
汤圆	tangyuan
元宵	yuanxiao
比萨	pizza
咖喱	curry
南瓜酥	pumpkin puff
榴莲酥	crispy durian puff
水果酥	fresh fruit puff
蛋黄酥	egg yolk puff
鸭肉酥	duck meat puff

牛肉串　beef kebabs
鲜虾馄饨　hunton soup with fresh shrimp
炸羊肉串　deep-fried lamb kebabs
鸡肉蘑菇酥　chicken meat and mushroom puff
茶叶蛋　tea flavored boiled eggs
猪肉馄饨　hunton with pork
牛肉馄饨　hunton with beef
鸡汤馄饨　hunton in chicken soup
煮鸡蛋　cooked eggs
菜肉馄饨　hunton soup with pork and vegetable
蒸鸡蛋　steamed eggs
热狗　hot dogs
苹果派　apple pie
莲子红豆沙　sweetened red bean paste with lotus seeds
莲子百合红豆沙　sweetened red bean paste with lotus seeds and lily bulbs
水果拼盘　fresh fruit platter
宫廷点心　small assorted cakes
什锦甜食　traditional assorted sweets

2）酒和饮料（Wine and Drinks）
（1）酒（wine）
茅台　Maotai spirit
五粮液　Wuliangye
陀牌曲酒　Tuopaiqujiu liquor
剑南春　Jiannanchun liquor
汾酒　Fenjiu wine
西凤酒　Xifenjiu wine
竹叶青　Zhuyeqing wine
杜康酒　Dukang wine
双沟酒　shuang gou wine
老白干酒　laobaigan wine

口子窖　Kouzijiao wine
天之蓝酒　Tianzhilan wine
古井贡酒　Gujinggon wine
中国红葡萄酒　Chinese red wine
长城干白葡萄酒　Great Wall dry white wine
黄酒　rice wine
绍兴黄酒　Shaoxing rice wine
虎骨酒　tiger-bone liquor
金陵啤酒　Jinling beer
百威啤酒　Budweiser beer
生力啤酒　San Miguel
轩尼特 X.O　Hennessy X.O
洋河大曲　Yanhedaqu wine
劲酒　Jing wine
马多利蓝带　Martell Cordon Blue
人头马 X.O　Remy Mratin Centaur
人头马路易十三　Remy Martin Centaur Luis XIII
龙舌兰白兰地　Tequila
苏格兰威士忌　Scotch whisky
梅子白兰地　plum brandy
法国白兰地　Cognac
英式杜松子酒　dry gin
戈登英式杜松子酒　Gordon dry gin
朗姆酒　rum
伏特加酒　Vodka
味美思　Vermouth
开味酒　aperitifs
马提尼酒　Martini
鸡尾酒　Cocktail
雪尼酒　Sherry
香槟酒　Champagne
苹果酒　cider
（2）饮料（drinks）

浓茶　　strong tea
淡茶　　weak tea
绿茶　　green tes
红茶　　black tea
茉莉花茶　　jasmine tea
柠檬茶　　lemon tea
龙井茶　　dragon-well tea
菊花茶　　chrysanthemum tea
人参茶　　ginseng tea
3）水果类（Fruit）
国光苹果　　guoguang apple
香蕉苹果　　banana apple
梨子　　pear
砀山梨　　dangshan pear
香梨　　bergamot pear
雪梨　　snow pear
冬梨　　winter pear
柑橘　　orange /tangerine
金橘　　cumquat
桃子　　peach
红橘　　tangerine
橙子　　orange
香蕉　　banana
芭蕉　　plantain
菠萝　　pineapple
李子　　plum
李杏　　plumcot
荔枝　　lichee /litchi
水蜜桃　　honey peach
猕猴桃　　kiwi fruit
芒果　　mango

杏子　　apricot
葡萄　　grape
枇杷　　loquat
柠檬　　lemon
樱桃　　cherry
甘蔗　　sugarcane
草莓　　strawberry
香瓜 / 甜瓜　　muskmelon
西瓜　　watermelon
哈密瓜　　hami melon
白果　　ginkgo
荸荠　　water chestnut
板栗　　Chinese chestnut
柚子　　grape fruit
梅子　　plum
柿子　　persimmon
榧子　　Chinese torreya
枣子　　date
槟榔　　areca nut
山楂　　hawthorn
橄榄　　olive
无花果　　fig
石榴　　pomegranate
杨梅　　red bayberry
杨桃　　carambola
栗子　　chestnut
龙眼　　longan
木瓜　　papaya
坚果　　nut
鲜果　　fresh fruit
干果　　dry fruit

6. 西餐（Western Food）

1）沙拉和派（salad and pie）
豆沙沙拉　　salad with red bean paste

鲜果沙拉　　salad with fresh fruit
尼斯沙拉　　nicoise salad

海鲜沙拉　salad with seafood
金枪鱼沙拉　tuna salad
恺撒沙拉　caesar salad
海鲜派　terrine of seafood
小牛肉派　veal and ham pie
猪肉派　pork pie
鹅肝派　goose liver pie
2）汤类（soup）
牛肉清汤　beef consomm soup
蔬菜干豆汤　hearty lentil soup
意大利蔬菜汤　minestrone soup
西班牙番茄冻汤　gazpacho
奶油蘑菇汤　cream and mushroom soup
奶油胡萝卜汤　cream with carrot soup
番茄汤　tomato soup
法式洋葱汤　French onion soup
匈牙利浓汤　Hungarian gloulash soup
3）主菜类（main course）
扒大虾　grilled king prawn
奶酪汁龙虾　gratinated lobster in mornay sauce
酥炸鱿鱼圈　deep-fried squid rings
煎比目鱼　pan-fried sole
扒金枪鱼　grilled tuna fillet
海鲜串　seafood kebabs
汁清贻贝　gratinated mussel
炸牛排　fried beef ribs
炸鸡腿　fried chicken legs
咖喱鸡　curry chicken
红酒烩鸡　braised chicken with red wine
烤火鸡　roasted turkey
炒鹅肝　sauted goose liver
炸鸡肉串　fried chicken rolls
扒鸡脯　grilled chicken breast

烤牛肉　roasted beef
烧烤鸡腿　barbecured chicken legs
红烩牛肉　stewed beef
扒牛排　grilled beef seak
烤牛肉　roasted beef
火腿煎鸡蛋　fried eggs with ham
烩牛舌　braised ox tongue
青椒汁牛排　beef tenderloin in green pepper and corn sauce
烧烤排骨　barbecured spare ribs
炸猪排　deep-fried pork chops
意大利米兰猪排　pork piccatta
烟熏肋排　smoked spare ribs
扒新西兰羊排　grilled New Zealand lamb chops
扒羊排　grilled lamb chops
巧克力椰饼　chocolate coconut cake
姜饼　ginger cake
意大利奶酪千层饼　cheese lasagna
什菜奶酪比萨饼　vegetarian pizza
海鲜比萨饼　seafood pizza
土豆泥　mashed potato
烤牛肉三明治　roasted beef sandwich
美式热狗　American hot dog
牛肉汉堡包　beef burger
鸡肉汉堡包　chicken burger
红花饭　saffron rice
西班牙海鲜肉　seafood paella
起酥面包　puff bread
硬质面包　hard bread
奶油面包　cream bun
小圆面包　roll / bun
羊角面包　croissant
面包卷　roll
软质面包　soft bread

食品蔬菜类 / Foods and Vegetables

牛角包　croissant
洋葱包　onion loaf
水果丹麦包　fruit Danish
全麦包　whole wheat bread
法式面包　French loaf
粟米面包　sweet corn bread
黑麦面包　rye bread
玉米面包　corn bread
红肠面包　hot dog
短棍面包　baton
奶酪面包卷　cheese roll
棒状面包卷　baton roll
咖啡面包卷　coffee roll
吐司　toast
蛋糕　cake
白蛋糕　angel cake
长蛋糕　oblong cake
长方形大蛋糕　loaf cake
夹层蛋糕　layer cake
草莓奶酪蛋糕　strawberry cheese cake
栗子蛋糕　chestnut cake
咖啡奶酪蛋糕　coffee cheese cake
黄油蛋糕　butter cake
果仁蛋糕　nut cake
水果蛋糕　fruit cake /tart
圣诞蛋糕　Christmas cake

树形蛋糕　tree-shaped cake
马得拉蛋糕　Madeira cake
薄饼 / 烙饼　griddle cake
冰淇淋蛋糕　ice-cream cake
咖啡蛋糕　coffee cake
乳酪蛋糕　cheese cake
杏仁蛋糕　congress tart
薄荷糕　pepper mint patty
山楂糕　haw jelly
热狗　hot dog
姜饼　ginger bread
煎饼　flapjack
姜味小甜饼　ginger biscuit
小馅饼　patty
果馅饼　tart / flan
苹果馅饼　apple pie
巧克力馅饼　chocolate pie
法式甜馅饼　French pastry
生日蛋糕　birthday cake
布丁　pudding
芒果布丁　mango pudding
香草布丁　vanilla pudding
巧克力奶油布丁　chocolate brulee
巧克力酥　chocolate crisp candy
巧克力奶油酥　chocolate butter cake
奶油泡芙　cream puff

7. 中国菜系 (Families of Chinese Cuisine)

北京菜系　Beijing cuisine
四川菜系　Sichuan cuisine
徽菜系　Anhui Huizhou cuisine
上海菜系　Shanghai cuisine
浙江菜系　Zhejiang cuisine
闽菜系　Fujian cuisine
粤菜系　Guangdong cuisine

湘菜系　Hunan cuisine
山东菜系　Shandong cuisine
江苏菜系　Jiangsu cuisine
淮扬菜系　Huaiyang Cuisine
吉林菜系　Jilin cuisine
东北菜系　Northeast cuisine

8. 与菜关联的词语（Words Related to Dishes）

买菜	green grocery shopping	菜瓜	snake melon
做菜	prepare the dishes	菜青	dark greyish green
一道菜	a course	菜色	a sickly pallor of one living on wild herbs / a famished look
种菜	grow vegetable		
菜地	vegetable plot	菜薹	tender flower stalk
菜场	food market	菜圃	vegetable bed
菜园	vegetable farm	菜刀	kitchen knife
菜圃	vegetable garden	菜叶	vegetable leaves
菜窖	vegetable cellar	菜根	vegetable roots
菜摊	vegetable stall	菜梗	vegetable stem
菜单	menu / bill of fare	菜牛	beef cattle
菜市	food market	菜馆	restaurant
菜蔬	vegetable / greens	菜鸟	green hand
菜肴	cooked dishes	菜农	vegetable growers
菜价	dish price / price of vegetables	菜篮子	shopping basket / food basket
菜豆	kidney bean	菜码儿	sliced vegetables to go with noodles
菜籽	vegetable seeds		
菜心	flowering cabbages	菜青虫	cabbage caterpillar
菜油	rapeseeds oil / rape oil	菜籽饼	rapeseed cake
菜花	cauliflower / rape flower		

19 工业与农林牧业
Industry, Agriculture, Forestry and Animal Husbandry

1. 工业（工业，钢铁，化工，煤炭，石油，矿物，机械，纺织，电子和无线电）(Industry—Mine, Steel and Iron, Chemical, Coal, Machinery, Textile, Electronics and Radio)

1）工业，钢铁（Industry, Iron and Steel）
工区　work area
工厂　factory / plant / mill / works
工程　engineering
工地　construction site
工段　a section of a construction
工件　workpiece
工料　labour and materials
工序　working procedure
工艺　craft / technology
工种　type of work in production
工艺设计　technological design
工艺流程　technological process
工业基地　industrial base
工业园　industrial area
工业病　professional disease of industrial workers
工业粉尘　industrial dust
工业企业　industrial enterprise
工业体系　industrial system
工业总产值　output value of industry
钢铁厂　steel works
钢结构　steel structure
钢铁公司　iron and steel company
钢铁联合企业　integrated iron and steel works
钢铁工业　steel & iron industry
钢铁运输线　an unbreakable transportation line
锅炉钢板　boiler plate
无缝钢管　seamless steel tube
焊接钢管　welded steel pipe
钢筋混凝土　reinforced concrete

2）化工（Chemical）
化学工业　chemical industry
化工厂　chemical plant
化工原料　industrial chemicals
化学肥料　chemical fertilizer
化合价　chemical valence
化合物　chemical combination
化学反应　combination reaction
化学作用　chemical action
化学元素　chemical element
化学变化　chemical change

化学试剂	chemical reagent	石油聚集	accumulation of oil
化学成分	chemical composition	石油化学	petrochemistry
化学纤维	chemical fibre	石油产品	the petroleum chemicals
化学性质	chemical property	石油运移	oil migration
化学当量	chemical equivalent	石油脑/轻油	naphtha
化学符号	chemical symbol	石油脑重组	naphtha reforming
化学武器	chemical weapons	石油焦	oil coke
煤炭工业	coal industry	石油气	petroleum gas
煤气厂	gasworks	石油井	petroleum / oil well
煤气机	gas engine	石油开采	oil digging
煤矸石	gangue	开油矿	to exploit an oil mine
煤焦油	coal tar	石油勘探	petroleum prospecting
煤渣	coal cinder	石油美元	petrodollars
煤砖	briquet	石油机械	oil machinery
煤矿	coal mine	残余油	residual oil
煤田	coalfield	残渣油	bottom residue
煤系	coal measures	刹车油	brake fluid
煤窑	coal pit	燃料油	fuel oil
煤气	coal gas	重油	heavy oil
煤灰	coal ash	原油	crude oil
煤化	carbonize	柴油	diesel oil
煤毒	gas poisoning	高级汽油	premium gasoline
煤尘	coal dust	重组汽油	reformed gasoline
煤斗	coal scuttle	裂解汽油	cracked gasoline
石煤	bone coal	喷气机燃油	jet oil
石油工业	oil industry / petroleum industry	轻质原油	light crude oil
石油管道	petroleum pipeline	涂料柏油	cut back asphalt
石油输出国	petroleum exporting countries	车用机油	automotive engine oil
		船用重油	bunker oil
石油化工厂	petrochemical works	防锈油	antirusting oil
石油化工工业	petrochemical industry	分馏油	distillating oil
石油化工产品	petrochemicals	基础油	base oil
液化石油气	liquefied petroleum gas	3）矿业（Mineral Industry）	
液化天然气	liquefied natural gas	矿业	mining industry
易燃气体	inflammable gas	矿山	mine

工业与农林牧业
Industry, Agriculture, Forestry and Animal Husbandry

矿区	mining area	矿山运输	mine haul (haulage)
矿藏	mineral resources	矿山工程图	mine map
矿产	mineral products	矿山机械	mining machinery
矿井	mine pit	矿物燃料	fossil fuel
矿层	ore bed / ore horizon	集块岩	agglomerate
矿田	ore field	碱性岩类	alkali rock
矿体	mineral deposit	酸性岩类	acidic rock
矿床	mineral deposit		

4) 机械 (Machinery)

矿坑	mining pit	机械工业	mechanical industry
矿砂	ore in sand form	机械工程	mechanical engineering
矿石	ore / ore stone	机械化	mechanization
矿尘	mine dust	机械加工	machining
矿泥	sludge / slime	机械制图	mechanical drawing
矿灯	miner's lamp	机械制造	machine building
矿柱	ore pillar	机械动力	mechanical power
矿脉	mineral vein	数控机床	numerical controlled machine tool
矿泉	mineral spring		
矿浆	ore pulp	机械工人	machinist
矿物	minerals	机器油	lubricating oil
矿渣	slag	机具	machines and tools
矿盐	rock salt / halite	机件	machine parts
矿脂（凡士林）	fashilin	机床	machine tools
矿棉	mineral wool	机电	mechanical and electrical
矿苗	outcropping / crop	重工业	heavy industry
矿工	miner	重型机床	heavy-duty machine tool
矿物学	mineralogy	轻混凝土	lightweight concrete
矿物油	mineral oil		

5) 纺织业 (Textile Industry)

矿渣砖	slag brick	轻纺工业	textile and other light industries
矿藏量	ore reserves		
金属矿	metalliferous deposit	轻工业	light industry
层状矿	bedded deposit	纺织工业	textile industry
矿区铁路	mine railway	纺液染色	dobe dyeing
矿山地压	rock pressure	纺液染色纤维	dope dyed fibre
矿渣水泥	slag cement	纺织机	spinning machine
矿山救护	mine rescue	纺织泵	spinning pump

纺织罐	spinning box
纺丝浴	spinning bath
纺织厂	textile mill
纺织机	spinning machine
纺织工人	textile worker
纺织品	textile / fabric
纺织娘	katydid
纺丝	fibre spinning
纺纱	spinning
纺锭	spindle
纺锤	spindle
纺绸	a soft plain-weave silk fabric
纺车	spinning wheel
针梳机	gill box
针织机	knitting machine
织袜机	hosiery machine
针织厂	knitting mill
针织品	knit goods / knitwear
织布厂	knit-cloth mill
织锦厂	brocade mill
织造厂	weaving mill
织锦缎	tapestry satin
织女星	weaving-girl star / Vega
机织物	woven fabric
织针	knitting needle
织女	weaving-maid / the weaving-girl
针织	knitting
织布	weaving cotton cloth
织机	loom
织物	woven fabric
织锦	picture-weaving in silk

6）电子和无线电（Electronics and Radio）

电信公司	telecommunication company
电子工业	electronics industry
电子厂	electronic plant
电子产品	electronic production
电子器件	electronic device
电子显微镜	electron microscope
电子游戏	video game
热电子	thermal electron
电子表	electronic watch
电子管	electron tube
电子钟	electronic clock
电子秤	electronic-weighing system
电子枪	electron gun
电子琴	electronic keyboard / electronic organ
电子束	electron beam
电子云	electron cloud
电子学	electronics
电铸版	electrotype
电珠	light bulb
电子管收音机	valve radio set
传统产业电子化	E-traditional industry
电子商务网站促销	E-website promoting sales
电子邮件系统和标准	E-mail system and standard
中国电子商务网站	E-commerce Website in China
无线电子商务	wireless E-commerce
中国互联网信息中心	China Internet Network Information Centre
电子邮件应用程序接口标准	E-mail application program interface standard
电子回旋加速器	betatron
电子数据交换	electronic data interchange

Industry, Agriculture, Forestry and Animal Husbandry

电子订货系统	electronic ordering system
电子购物中心	electronic mall
电子交易市场	E-marketplace
电子图书	E-book
电子现金	E-cash
电子公告栏	electronic bulletin board system
电子侦察机	electronic reconnaissance
电子伏特	electron-volt
垃圾邮件	useless mail
电子设备	electronic appliance
电子收款机	electronic cash register
电子计算机	electronic computer
电子刻板机	electronic engraving machine
电子游戏机	electronic game player
电子照相术	electrophotography
电子望远镜	electronic telescope
电子显微镜	electron microscope
电子游戏	video game
电子玩具	electronic toys
电子杂志	E-zine
电子刊物	E-journal
电子消费者	E-consumer
电子分销	E-distribution
电子零售	electronic retail
电子钱包	E-wallet
电子商城	virtual electronic commerce city
电子商务	electronic commerce / electronic business
电子港湾	E-bay
电子货币	electronic money
空调机综合测试仪	Air-conditioner multi tester
晶体管特性图示仪	Transistor specificity oscilloscope
光传输用稳定光源	Telecommunication stable optical power source
光回波损耗测试仪	Optical Return Loss Meter
过程仪表认证校准仪	Documenting Process Calibrator
电压跌落模拟器	Voltage Dips Generator
低频电子电压表	LF electronic voltmeter
静电放电发生器	Electronic Discharge Generator
浪涌信号发生器	Surge Signal Generator
彩图信号发生器	Video Signal Generator
函数信号发生器	Function Signal Generator
超高频毫伏表	UHF Electronic Millvoltmeter
测量滤波器	Measuring Filter
脉冲发生器	Pulse Generator
测量接收机	Measuring Receiver
电话分析仪	Telephone Analyzer
谐波测量仪	Harmonic Measuring Instrument
心电监护仪	Electro Cardiac Monitor
音频分析仪	Audio Analyzer
阻抗分析仪	Impedance Analyzer
蓝牙测试仪	Blue-tooth Tester Set
网路分析仪	Network Analyzer

误码测试仪	Error Tester
调度测量仪	Modulation Meter
数字脑电图仪	Digital Electroencephalogram
示波器校准仪	Oscilloscope Calibrator
失真度测量仪	Distortion Meter
射频通信测试仪	RF Communication Test Set
矢量信号分析仪	Vector Signal Analyzer
数字传输分析仪	Digital Transmission Analyzer
通信光谱分析仪	Optical Spectrum Analyzer
无线局域测试仪	WLAN Test Set
IC卡计费装置	Timing and Charging Device for IC card
电话计时计费装置	Equipment
振铃波发生器	Ring Wave Generator
数据采集器	Data Acquisition System
频谱分析器	Spectrum Analyzer
功率传感器	Power Sensor
功率放大器	Power Amplifier
功率吸收钳	Absorbing Clamp
高频Q表	High Frequency Q Meter
电场探头	Electric-field Probe
EMI接收机	EMI Receiver

2. 农林业 (Agriculture & Forestry)

1) 农业 (agriculture)

农产区	agrarian areas
国营农场	state farm
集体农场	collective farm
个体农场	private farm
农村集市	village fair
农贸市场	a market of farm products
农业经济	agricultural economy
农业机械化	agricultural mechanization
农业现代化	agricultural modernization
农业集体化	collectivization of agriculture
农业多种经营	diversified farming
个体经营农业	management of the individual farming
农业产业化经营	industrialized management of agriculture
农副产品加工业	processing industry of farm and sideline products
农工商联合企业	agriculture-industry-commerce complex enterprise
农民承包地使用权	right to use of the farmer-contracted land
农林牧副渔全面发展	all-round development in farming, forestry, animal husbandry, sideline production and fishery
农民家庭经营	business operation of the farmer household
农场经营方式	ways of farm management
优化农业结构	to optimize the agricultural structure
优化产业结构	to optimize the industrial structure
农业生产结构	structure of agricultural production

工业与农林牧业
Industry, Agriculture, Forestry and Animal Husbandry

农业基建投资	investment in agricultural infrastructure
政策性农业补贴	policy-related subsidies for farming
农村社会服务体系	network of the social services in rural area
农村市场信息体系	information system of the rural markets
农业生产效益	efficiency in agricultural production
农业信息网络	agricultural information network
农业计算机网络	agricultural computer network
三农服务原则	principles of serving agriculture, rural community and farmers
农业信息研究	information research in farming
农业技术推广	popularization of the agricultural technology
农业技术站	agrotechnical station
农业结构调整	structural readjustment in agriculture
农业结构改革	to improve the agricultural structure
农产品附加值	added value of agricultural products
加强农业基础地位	to strengthen the agricultural position as the economic foundation
农业增加值	added value of agriculture
高产稳产田	land with high-stable yields
样板田	demonstration fields
试验田	experimental farm-plot
粮食购销体系	grain purchasing and marketing system
粮食流通体系	grain circulation system
农产品流通体系	distribution pattern of agricultural products
农产品市场体系	market system of the agricultural products
农产品质量管理	quality control of the agricultural products
承包专业户	specialized household under contract
减轻农民负担	to lighten the burden on farmers
农产品	agricultural products
农村电气化	electrification of the countryside
"三农"问题	three issues concerning agriculture, countryside, and farmers
农业人口	agrarian population
定点农业	crop-specific farming in selected areas
农业贷款	agricultural loan
扶贫贷款	poverty alleviation loan
扶贫计划	poverty-alleviating program
科技扶贫	to support the poor areas with technology
科技下乡	to take science and technology to the countryside
科技兴农	to invigorate the agriculture by applying science and technology
科学种田	scientific farming

199

农业投入	agricultural inputs	旱地作物	dry crops
效益农业	profitable agriculture	高粱	sorghum
生态农业	eco-agriculture / farm	主要粮食	staple food / grain
立体农业	vertical integration in agriculture	水稻	rice
		油菜	rape
集约农业	intensive farming	大豆	soybean / soyabean
集体承包	collective contract	黍	broom corn millet
价格放开	to relax price control	芝麻	sesame
粮价补贴	grain price subsidies	种子	seed
粮食储备	grain reserve	棉花	cotton
粮食供应	grain supply	玉米	maize / corn
粮食征购	grain purchases	燕麦	oat
农产品关税	duties on the agricultural products	小米	millet
		大麦	barley
订购粮	quota grain	小麦	wheat
农作物	agricultural crops	谷子/粟	foxtail millet
高产农作物	high-yielding crops	荞麦	buckwheat
低产农作物	low-yielding crops	甘蔗	sugar cane
野生纤维作物	wild fibrous crops	粗粮	coarse grain
禾谷类作物	cereal crops	细粮	fine grain
糖料作物	sugar crops	播种	to sow
粮食作物	grain crops	肥料	fertilizer
水田作物	wet crops	耕地	cultivated land
夏收作物	summer crops	可耕地	arable land
晚秋作物	late autumn crops	休耕地	fallow land
早秋作物	early autumn crops	自留地	plot for one's personal needs
早熟作物	early ripening crops	灌溉	to irrigate
越冬作物	over-wintering crops	洪水	flood
热带作物	tropical crops	荒地	waste land
耐水作物	water-tolerant crop	抗旱	drought-resisting
饲料作物	fodder crops	抗洪	flood-resisting
薯类作物	tuber crops	收获	harvest
纤维作物	fiber crops	土壤	soil
油料作物	oil crops	2) 林业 (Forestry)	
抗旱作物	drought-resistant crops	主林带	main forest trees

成材林	standing timber / mature timber	赤杨	alder
常绿林	evergreen forest	赤松	Japanese red pine
针叶林	conifer forest	白桦	Asian white birch
红木林	mangrove forest	水杨	sallow
护堤林	dam-protection forest	水松	Chinese cypress
护岸林	bank-protection forest	枫杨	Chinese wingnut
原始林	primeval forest / virgin forest	桂树	cassia tree
硬木林	hardwood forest	槐树	Chinese scholartree
人工林	artificial forest	银柳	silver willow
落叶林	deciduous forest	杨柳	willow
经济林	economic forest	河柳	flowering-quince willow
季雨林	monsoon forest	红木	redwood
小树林	grove	红松	Korean pine
防风林	windbreak forest	雪松	cedar
防洪林	forest against flood hazard	桦树	birch
防护林	protective forest	橡树	elm
防沙林	sand-break forest	橡木	oak
防霜林	frost-break forest	香榧	Chinese torreya
风景林	aesthetic forest	香椿	Chinese toon
固沙林	to protect the forest for stabilization of sands	黄檀	hupeh rosewood
		黄杨	box tree
海防林	shelter belt for protecting sea coasts	铁杉	hemlock
		冷杉	silver fir
护田林	shelter belts to protect farmland	紫杉	yew
混交林	mingled forest	巨杉	giant redwoods
热带雨林	tropical rain forest	云杉	Chinese spruce
亚热带林	subtropical forest	水杉	dawn redwood
亚热带雨林	subtropical rain forest	柳杉	Chinese cedar
原始热带雨林	primary tropical moist forest	银杉	cathay silver fir
		杉松	Manchurian fir
温带阔叶林	temperate hardwood	杉木	Chinese fir
海岸防护林	coastal protective forest	桑树	mulberry
林木	woods	榕树	smallfruit fig
枫木	maple	梧桐	phoenix tree
垂柳	weeping willow	榨树	Mongolian oak

樟木	camphor
原木	log
榆树	dwarf elm
柚木	teak
油松	Chinese pine
紫檀木	red sandal wood
樟脑树	camphor tree
月桂树	laurel
橡胶树	rubber tree
檀香木	sandalwood
水曲柳	Manchurian ash
山腊梅	shining wintersweet
花梨木	rosewood
华山松	amand pine
黄山松	Huangshan pine
落叶松	larch
木芙蓉	cottonrose hibiscus
白云杉	white spruce
长白松	Changbai pine
冬青树	holly tree
苹果树	apple tree
枣子树	Chinese date tree
柚子树	shaddock tree
白果树	maidenhair tree
板栗树	Chinese chestnut tree
山核桃树	Chinese hickory tree
山楂树	Chinese hawthorn tree
石榴树	pomegranate tree
橙子树	orange tree
荔枝树	litchi tree
柿子树	persimmon tree
桃子树	peach tree
香榧树	Chinese torreya tree
杏子树	apricot tree
杨梅树	Chinese bayberry tree
椰子树	coconut palm tree
樱桃树	cherry tree
槟榔树	betel palm tree
核桃树	walnut tree
金橘树	kumquat tree
栗子树	chestnut tree
李子树	plum tree
龙眼树	longan tree
芒果树	mango tree
柠檬树	lemon tree
梨子树	pear tree
香蕉树	banana tree

3）牧业和家禽（Animal Husbandry & Livestock）

（1）牧业（animal husbandry）

定区牧放	set-stock for grazing
冬季牧场	winter pasture
高山牧场	alpine pasture
人工草场	cultivated pasture
天然牧场	national grazing ground / natural pasture
舍饲肥育	dry-lot fattening
放牧场	pasture
牧草场	pasture grass ground
配种场	mating yard
畜牧场	livestock farm
养猪场	pig farm
养鸡场	chicken farm
种畜场	breeding stock farm
种育场	breeding farm
屠宰场	slaughter house
兽医站	veterinary station
防疫站	epidemic prevention station
授精站	insemination station
交配站	mating station

Industry, Agriculture, Forestry and Animal Husbandry

饲料槽	feed trough	骡子	mule
杂交育种	cross breeding	马鹿	red deer
育成品种	improved breed	马奶	mare's milk
育种目标	breeding objective	公马	stud-horse
杂种优势	hybrid vigor	母马	mare
人工授精	artificial insemination	骏马	fine horse
人工孵化	artificial incubation	小马	pony
双重配种	double mating	种马	stud
人工繁殖	artificial propagation	驴马	domestic ass
品系繁殖	line breeding	阉马	gelding
繁殖能力	reproductive capacity	公驴	donkey
繁殖性能	breeding performance	母驴	female donkey
纯种繁殖	pure breeding	小驴	colt
早期肥育	early fattening	驴骡	hinny
疯牛病	mad cow disease	母骡	mare mule
口蹄疫	foot-and-mouth disease	耕牛	farm cattle
禽霍乱	cholera of fowl	牤牛	bull
禽流感	bird flu.	牦牛	yak
猪流感	swine flu.	奶牛	milk cow
种畜	breeding animal	阉牛	bullock
牲畜	animal	公牛	bull
公畜	sire	母牛	cow
母畜	female animal	黄牛	ox
农畜	farm animal	水牛	buffalo
幼畜	younger stock	小牛	calf
子畜	newborn animal	羊圈	sheep-pen
挤奶	to milk a cow	饲料	fodder
交配	mating	饲养	breeding
鸡瘟	fowl pest	杂种	crossbred
牛瘟	rinderpest	牧人	herdsman
羊痘	sheep pox	牧羊	shepherd
兽医	vet	山羊	goat
游牧	nomadic gazing	公羊	tup
牧区	pastoral zone	母羊	nanny goat
马匹	horses	绵羊	domestic sheep

奶羊	milk goat	（2）家禽（poultry）	
头羊	bell wether	家鸡	chicken / domestic fowl
羔羊	lamb	火鸡	turkey
肉用羊	mutton sheep	母鸡	hen
牧羊人	flockmaster	公鸡	cock
公猪	boar / hog	野鸡 / 山鸡	pheasant
母猪	sow	肉鸡	table poultry /bird
肉猪	hog	鹟鸡	capon /castrated rooster
家猪	domestic pig	石鸡	partridge
野猪	wild pig	松鸡	grouse
小猪	piglet / pigling	竹鸡	bamboo pheasant
仔猪	baby pig / pigling	种鸡	breeding bird / breeder bird
杂交猪	crossbred pig	原鸡	jungle fowl
杂种猪	hybrid pig	小鸡	chicken
脂用猪	lard type pig	童子鸡	broiler
宁乡猪	Ningxiang pig	母珠鸡	guinea-hen
内江猪	Neijiang pig	种雄鸡	breeding cock
陆川猪	Luchuan pig	珍珠鸡	guinea fowl
良种猪	elite pig	杂种鸡	hybrid fowl
垂耳猪	lop-eared pig	雄火鸡	turkey cock
立耳猪	prick-ear pig	小仔鸡	petit poussin
短耳猪	cropped-ear pig	小母鸡	pullet
白毛猪	white pig	小公鸡	cockerel chick
大黑猪	large black pig	乌骨鸡	silky fowl / black-bone chicken
长白猪	landrace pig	泰和鸡	silky fowl
黑毛猪	black pig	寿光鸡	Shouguang fowl
架子猪	feeder pig	生蛋鸡	layer
金华猪	Jinhua pig	狼山鸡	Langshan chicken
太湖猪	Taihu pig	蛋用鸡	egg-laying poultry
肥育猪	fattening pig	木丹鸡	bantam
种公猪	breeding boar	抱窝鸡	brood hen
种母猪	breeding pig	矮脚鸡	dumpy
肉用猪	pork pig	肥育鸡	broiler finisher
小公猪	boar pig	翻毛鸡	frizzle
小母猪	gilt	固始鸡	gushi fowl

工业与农林牧业
Industry, Agriculture, Forestry and Animal Husbandry

交趾鸡	cochin cock	公鹅	gander
柯庆鸡	coching fowl	母鹅	goose
来航鸡	leghorn fowl	小鹅	gosling
北京鸭	Beijing duck	塘鹅	pelican
赤冠鸭	ruddy Sheldrake	天鹅	swan
高邮鸭	Gaoyou duck	填鹅	goose cramming
家番鸭	mule duck	雁鹅	Yan goose
建昌鸭	Jianchang duck	幼鹅	junior goose
金定鸭	Jinding duck	仔鹅	green goose
绿头鸭	mallard	中国鹅	Chinese goose
鸭子	duck	狮头鹅	Shitou goose
仔鸭	green duck	肥育鹅	table goose
野鸭	wild duck	鹅	goose
小鸭	duckling	鸽子	dove
公鸭	drake	雏鸽	squeaker
母鸭	duck	公鸽	cock pigeon
黄鸭	ruddy sheldrake	乳鸽	young pigeon
绍鸭	shao duck	母鸽	hen pigeon
麻鸭	shelduck	幼鸽	dovelet
番鸭	perching duck	林鸽	wood pigeon
雏鹅	gosling	信鸽	carrier-pigeon